New Directions in Regulatory Theory

T0334419

Edited by

Sol Picciotto
and
David Campbell

Blackwell Publishers

First published as a special issue of *Journal of Law and Society*, 2002

Editorial Offices:
108 Cowley Road, Oxford OX4 1JF, UK
  Tel: +44 (0)1865 791100
Osney Mead, Oxford OX2 0EL, UK
  Tel: +44 (0)1865 206206
350 Main Street, Malden, MA 02148-5018, USA
  Tel: +1 781 388 8250
Iowa State University Press, a Blackwell Publishing company, 2121 S. State
  Avenue, Ames, Iowa 50014-8300, USA
  Tel: +1 515 292 0140
Blackwell Munksgaard, Nørre Søgade 35, PO Box 2148, Copenhagen, DK-1016,
  Denmark
  Tel: +45 77 33 33 33
Blackwell Publishing Asia, 54 University Street, Carlton, Victoria 3053, Australia
  Tel: +61 (0)3 347 0300
Blackwell Verlag, Kurfürstendamm 57, 10707 Berlin, Germany
  Tel: +49 (0)30 32 79 060
Blackwell Publishing, 10, rue Casimir Delavigne, 75006 Paris, France
  Tel: +331 5310 3310

First published 2002 by Blackwell Publishers Ltd

Library of Congress Cataloging-in-Publication Data

ISBN 0-631-23565-5

A catalogue record for this title is available from the British Library.

For further information on
Blackwell Publishers visit our website:
www.blackwellpublishers.co.uk

Contents

JOURNAL OF LAW AND SOCIETY
VOLUME 29, NUMBER 1, MARCH 2002
ISSN: 0263-323X, pp. 1–11

Introduction: Reconceptualizing Regulation in the Era of Globalization

SOL PICCIOTTO*

The concept of 'regulation' has become sufficiently ubiquitous in recent years, that it may be helpful to begin this collection of papers with some analysis of the term and its usage. At its most general level it refers to the means by which any activity, person, organism or institution is guided to behave in a regular fashion, or according to rule. In principle, reference may be made to the regulation of any kind of social behaviour, which gives the term a very wide scope indeed. However, it is more particularly used, as in this collection, in relation to economic activity.[1] In the context of socio-legal studies, the concept has two main advantages. First, it leaves a useful ambiguity over the extent to which such regular behaviour is generated internally or entails external intervention. Secondly, it embraces all kinds of rules, not only formal state law.

RETHINKING REGULATION IN THE NETWORK SOCIETY

These two features of the concept of regulation go some way to explain its increased use since the 1970s and in particular the enormous effort spent on rethinking its role and forms. This period has witnessed a prolonged process of social and economic restructuring of the relations between the 'private' sphere of economic activity, and the 'public' realm of politics and the state, interacting with changes in the form and role of these spheres themselves. These changes have been manifested in different ways across the world, including the collapse of centralized, bureaucratic state-socialism in the Soviet Union, eastern Europe, and Africa; the fundamental remodelling of social-democratic welfare-states in Europe, Canada, Australia, and New Zealand; the extensive regulatory reforms in the United States of America;

* Lancaster University Law School, Lancaster University, Lancaster LA1 4YN, England

1 At least as far back as Blackstone's reference to the role of corporations as including 'the advancement and regulation of manufactures and commerce', *Commentaries* (1979, facsimile of original Clarendon Press edition of 1765–69) vol. I, 459.

and the crises of the Asian 'developmental states' including Japan. But this has not simply resulted from a failure of the state. Major transformations have occurred in the forms of organization of so-called private enterprise, that is to say, the business economy dominated by the giant corporation. Large-scale mass manufacturing has been reorganized, and the centralized bureaucratic firm has become the 'lean and mean' corporation, concentrating on its core competences, but operating within a web of strategic alliances, supplier and marketing chains, and financial and governmental networks.[2] In parallel, the public sphere has become much more fragmented, as many activities have been divested from direct state management through privatization, and operational responsibility for an increasing range of public functions has been delegated to bodies with a high degree of autonomy from central government. In this 'network society' it has become harder to distinguish public and private, and their interactions and permutations are more complex.

These historical developments have challenged much of the commonplace thinking about regulation that was the basis of the apparently conflicting political perspectives of many both on the left and the right of politics. Both implicitly accepted the essentially liberal conception that the private sphere, dominated by economic exchange, is powered by the pursuit of individual self-interest ('greed is good'); whereas in the public realm this can be displaced by considerations of the general interest which may justify action or intervention by the state. Thus, the 'left' perspective was that only the discipline of the state based on explicit norms could restrict private greed, whereas the 'right' considered that decentralized decision-making based on private preferences would be most likely to produce outcomes beneficial to all. Implicit in both views is the assumption that normativity must be imposed by the public on the private: they differ only on the extent to which this was justified. Both described the rise of the network society as entailing the triumph of 'the market'. This was hailed from the right as a return to the minimalist state, which should be limited to the protection of private property and the maintenance of order, while many on the left were to be found desperately defending centralized and autocratic forms of state action which not long before they might have criticized as sadly deficient.

Thus, from both these perspectives, the phenomenon of and debates about regulation have been viewed with some suspicion and puzzlement. Much of the commonplace discourse offers no basis for understanding why the 'rolling back' of the state has not simply given free rein to market-mediated social relations, but has involved new forms of regulation and normativity. Although liberalization and privatization initially involved 'deregulation' by undermining existing forms of state action, they were swiftly followed by

2 B. Harrison, *Lean and Mean: The Changing Landscape of Corporate Power in the Age of Flexibility* (1994); M. Castells, *The Information Age: Economy, Society and Culture*, 3 vols. (1998), especially vol. 1, *The Rise of the Network Society*, chs. 3 and 4.

2

'reregulation', by a wide variety of new means, and the rise of a 'regulatory state'.[3] The growth of new forms of regulation was regarded by the right (now referred to as neo-liberals) as evidence of the pressures on politicians and bureaucrats to justify their own existence and to appease special interest groups, while the left criticized them as an abnegation of the attempt to design effective control of private interests through direct state action.

These developments provided potentially rich fields of study for socio-legal research, and an opportunity to rethink old theories in new contexts. Much could be gained by revisiting the classic texts: Marx's account of how the Factory Acts emerged from the struggles reflecting the shift from the old forms of manufacture to 'modern industry'; Durkheim's analysis of the important role of corporatist institutions in establishing 'organic solidarity'; or Weber's discussion of the various forms of law, convention, and usage in the management of economic life. This has been strikingly absent, and the study of regulation quickly became dominated by other (essentially functionalist) perspectives, especially economics.[4] Interestingly, the more fruitful approaches from economics themselves derived fresh inspiration by delving back to and rethinking their own roots, notably with the emergence of the new institutional economics founded on the work of Coase, with its origins in the debates of the first half of the twentieth century.

PRIVATE-PUBLIC SYMBIOSES

It was recognized relatively early in the recent literature that:

> Questions about who participates in and benefits from regulation are certainly important: explaining the complex and shifting relationships between and within organizations at the heart of economic regulation is the key to understanding the nature of the activity. But little can be gained by depicting the relationship in the dichotomous language of public authority versus private interests.[5]

The terms 'responsive' or 'reflexive' regulation were quickly deployed to explore these new private-public interactions. In the influential work of Ayres and Braithwaite,[6] this was a relatively limited concept, referring to the

3 S.K. Vogel, *Freer Markets, More Rules* (1996); M. Loughlin and C. Scott, 'The Regulatory State' in *Developments in British Politics 5*, eds. P. Dunleavy, A. Gamble, I. Holliday, G. Peele (1997) 205; J. Braithwaite, 'The New Regulatory State and the Transformation of Criminology.' (2000) 40 *Brit. J. of Criminology* 222–38.

4 Thus, for example, the selection offered in R. Baldwin et al. (eds.), *A Reader on Regulation* (1998), is largely dominated by perspectives from economics and political science, although it appeared in OUP's short-lived series, Oxford Readings in Socio-Legal Studies. A notable exception has been Gunther Teubner, whose contemporary analyses are often anchored in the classic social and political debates about law.

5 L. Hancher and M. Moran, 'Organizing Regulatory Space' in *Capitalism, Culture and Economic Regulation*, eds. L. Hancher and M. Moran (1989) 271, at 274.

6 I. Ayres and J. Braithwaite, *Responsive Regulation. Transcending the Deregulation Debate* (1992).

3

need to respond to industry structure by limited and conditional delegations of regulatory responsibilities to public interest groups, competitors, and even regulated firms themselves. Responsiveness was to be ensured by the deployment of a 'pyramid' strategy of sanctions by the public bodies monitoring such delegated self-regulation, speaking softly and carrying both big and a variety of smaller sticks.[7]

In our present collection, John Braithwaite follows up that perspective by exploring the reasons for reliance on sanctions rather than rewards in this type of regulatory system. His argument is surprising, since his earlier work started from the perception that voluntary is better than coerced compliance, and he points out that both common sense and behaviouralist social science suggest that rewards would more effectively induce willing acceptance than would punishment. However, economic actors can find ways to adapt to rules without complying with their objectives, to 'play for the gray' as Braithwaite puts it. In this context, highly reliable monitoring mechanisms would be required if extrinsic rewards are not to distort the intrinsic cost-allocation processes. Other kinds of strategic behaviour might result unless the use of rewards is limited to the bottom of the enforcement pyramid. Braithwaite's conclusion, that the most effective type of reward is praise given with finesse, suggests that there is a significant gap between intrinsic and extrinsic normative processes in his regulatory universe. His analysis here may also give surprising support to critics who have argued that the encouragement of voluntary compliance is too often used as an excuse to temper sanctions to the point of ineffectiveness (there is little sign of a big stick in, for example, workplace health and safety regulation), and who reject the 'cooperative' model of regulation, at least as applied to business activities involving risks of serious social harm.[8]

Peter Vincent-Jones's contribution explores a different genealogy of the concept of responsive regulation, stemming from Nonet and Selznick's conceptualization of modern law as a responsive legal order, having evolved from the repressive and autonomous phases of law. He deflects the criticism of Teubner, who proposed a more far-reaching typology of reflexive law, in which the desired purpose is not determined and enforced simply externally but through a reflexive rationality, by proposing a 'subtler conception of purposiveness'. He also builds on Julia Black's suggestion that public decision-making should be open to greater public participation through new forms of deliberative democracy. In his account of the changes in central-local government relations in the United Kingdom he sees a potential for such new forms in the shift towards 'responsibilization', which utilizes the techniques of accounting, audit, and contracting. He analyses what are essentially arrangements for the governance of diffuse activities regarded as

---

7 id., ch. 2.
8 For example, S. Tombs, 'Understanding Regulation? A Review Essay' (2002) 11 *Social & Legal Studies* (forthcoming).

4

in some sense public, or at least requiring public accountability, involving an 'articulation of central and local democratic processes in responsive combinations'.

Colin Scott offers a different perspective on private-public regulatory interactions by analysing the instances of oversight of public regulatory functions by privately-owned bodies, which may have mandates which are permissive or obligatory, statutory or contractual, or may operate extra- or quasi-legally. While such arrangements illustrate the 'interdependence of public and private power in contemporary governance arrangements', they also challenge the adequacy of definitions of the public based on function, and of the private based on ownership (are bodies such as the Consumers' Association and Greenpeace adequately described as private?). Further clarification is important if effective regulation might require, as Scott suggests, enhancement of the powers of such bodies, coupled with increased accountability.

GLOBALIZED REGULATION

Liberalization, privatization, and the emergence of new forms of regulation have also been international processes, and are central to what is described as globalization. National liberalization initially focused on the removal of border barriers (quotas, tariffs, and exchange controls) as the immediate obstacles to the flows of goods and finance. However, the opening up of markets to competition created awareness of the differences between national regulatory requirements, and concerns that such differences constituted 'non-tariff barriers'. This has led to new approaches to international regulatory coordination involving different degrees and combinations of regulatory competition and harmonization.[9]

The new forms of complex interaction between a wide range of normative orders across the globe, described as multi-level governance, have led to a revival of the postcolonial concept of legal pluralism,[10] and have been memorably described by Gunther Teubner (recalling Eugene Ehrlich) as 'Global Bukowina'.[11] From Teubner's perspective, it is private legal orders

---

9 See 'Introduction: Regulatory Competition and Institutional Evolution' in *International Regulatory Competition and Coordination*, eds. W. Bratton, J. McCahery, S. Picciotto, and C. Scott (1996).

10 P. Fitzpatrick, 'Law and Societies' (1984) 22 *Osgoode Hall Law J.* 115–38; B. de Sousa Santos, 'Law, a Map of Misreading: Towards a Postmodern Conception of Law' (1987) 14 *J. of Law and Society* 279–302; F. Snyder, 'Global Economic Networks and Global Legal Pluralism' in *Transatlantic Regulatory Cooperation*, eds. G.A. Bermann, M. Herdegen, and P. Lindseth (2000) 99–115.

11 'Global Bukowina' in *Global Law Without a State*, ed. G. Teubner (1997); see, also, G. Teubner, 'The King's Many Bodies: The Self-Deconstruction of Law's Hierarchy' (1997) 31 *Law and Society Rev.* 763–87; G. Teubner, 'Contracting Worlds: The Many Autonomies of Private Law' (2000) 9 *Social and Legal Studies* 399–417, and comments thereon, especially that by Campbell.

5

that provide the regulatory dynamic in the newly globalized economic system. He argues that they create new forms of decentred or heterarchical lawmaking which are independent of the hierarchical forms of state law, and he paints a seductive picture of 'global law without a state'. Although he considers that private regulation, such as the new '*lex mercatoria*', has an essentially independent dynamic, he nevertheless accepts that it will provoke a repoliticization, although he considers that this will not take place through traditional political institutions but via 'structural coupling' with specialized discourses.

Our central section includes three papers which explore these issues in some depth and empirical detail. First, Perez offers a rich analysis of the conflict between the environmental world-view and major international construction projects, which are governed by a paradigm form of private regulation: complex standard-form contracts. Perez shows how the development of these regulatory norms in the closed world of construction specialists results in institutional blindness to the issues raised by the environmental impact of these projects. This blindness is rooted in the legal tradition of the *lex mercatoria*, which seeks to confine itself strictly to the relationships of the private contracting parties, leaving the mandatory requirements of public law to be dealt with by states (preferably without intruding into the private regulatory realm). This disjuncture is highly problematic as it creates incentives for the private parties to externalize the environmental costs of projects, and precludes the possibility of flexible collaboration between the host community and the construction agents which would be crucial to the success of environmental impact management.

Perez goes further, and offers practical proposals for 'ecologizing' construction contracts by the incorporation of provisions for an environmental management system, combined with a modification of the dispute resolution arrangements to provide a voice for the extra-contractual community. He sees some hope for such a new approach, partly in recent suggestions that the contract should adopt a new managerial model and a 'partnering' ideology, but especially in the awakening of the engineering community to environmental concerns, which might provide a bridge between the environmental and business communities. This perhaps exemplifies Teubner's suggestion of repoliticization of private regulation through new forms of structural coupling. However, it could also be pointed out that, even if the construction contract is a private regulatory form, its power and effectiveness are significantly underpinned by authorizations given by bodies with a public character and functions (although certainly dominated by a private ethos), notably UNCITRAL and the World Bank. If regulation in this important business sphere has been driven by a private logic, it is largely due to the failure of institutions which are supposed to articulate public concerns to do so adequately. Thus, if apparently private bodies may perform public functions, as Scott suggests, it is also true (and perhaps more frequent in recent years) that public institutions may become permeated with a private ethos.

6

The next two papers deal with areas of national public regulation which have come under pressure to harmonize or coordinate due to the globalization of business, which perceives divergent and sometimes conflicting regulatory requirements as imposing costs and distorting competition. Attempts to harmonize regulation through the traditional processes of international law are cumbersome and beset by political considerations, and at best achieve agreement only in very general terms. Consequently, regulators in many fields have developed direct arrangements for cooperation (involving notification, consultation, and information exchange) and sometimes coordination (through procedures such as mutual recognition, simultaneous examination, and elaboration of common standards or codes).[12] These informal and flexible regulatory networks are generally anchored in and legitimated by formal legal provisions at the national and international levels. Hence, it is said that these networks 'herald a new and attractive form of global governance, enhancing the ability of states to work together to address common problems without the centralized bureaucracy of formal international institutions'.[13] More specifically, it has been suggested that technical specialists such as regulators may constitute 'epistemic communities', whose shared understandings might provide a basis for agreement on the detailed nuts and bolts of regulatory arrangements, facilitating the achievement of political consensus on the broader policy principles.[14]

Imelda Maher surveys some of the debates on international policy networks and epistemic communities and offers an account of the various links that formed what she describes as the competition policy network. Following the work of Drake and Nicolaïdis on trade in services, she suggests that early attempts at international agreement on competition policy had little success until the emergence of a global epistemic community of competition regulators in the 1980s, although this overlapped with networks more directly involved with policy, and has more recently intersected with trade policy networks. This account indicates that there is considerable overlap between technical specialists and those with policy responsibilities, and in Maher's judgement discussions of detailed issues among experts can facilitate policy transfer and harmonization.

The contribution by Louise Davies deploys some of the same perspectives as Maher's to examine attempts at the international coordination of patenting. Here there has been greater success in establishing an international legal framework, dating back to reciprocal arrangements in

---

12 For more details, see S. Picciotto, 'The Regulatory Criss-Cross: Interaction between Jurisdictions and the Construction of Global Regulatory Networks' in *International Regulatory Competition and Coordination*, eds. W. Bratton et al. (1996).

13 A.-M. Slaughter, 'The Accountability of Government Networks' (2001) 8 *Indiana J. of Global Legal Studies* 347, at 347.

14 P.M. Haas, 'Introduction: Epistemic Communities and International Policy Coordination' (1992) 46 *International Organization* 1–36.

7

the nineteenth century culminating in the Paris Industrial Property Convention of 1883, now reinforced as part of the establishment of the World Trade Organization (WTO) in 1994 by the agreement on Trade-Related Intellectual Property Rights (TRIPS). However, Davies points out that the key provisions on patentability of Article 27 of the TRIPS are expressed in very general terms leaving considerable scope for interpretation, the implications of which are both important and controversial, especially in the key area of biotechnology. This gives great significance to the work of the informal Trilateral Group of the major patent offices, aiming to develop a common basis and procedures for patent examination through technical studies. Her detailed account shows how the Trilateral's study of the patentability requirements for biotechnological innovations appears to have produced a convergence in the interpretation of the key requirement of industrial utility, although whether this will prove effective in actual examination practice remains to be seen.

The accounts of both Davies and Maher indicate that there is considerable overlap between specialist epistemic communities and broader policy and advocacy networks, and all intersect with more formal national and international state institutions. This suggests that it is perhaps not so easy to dissociate technical issues from their policy implications. To do so may certainly provide a firmer basis for agreement on those aspects which have been isolated for consideration within the specific technocratic frame (for example, criteria to evaluate competition or patentability), but at the expense of externalizing consideration of their broader social implications. Thus, the patent offices have resolutely insisted on excluding from their consideration of patentability of biotechnological innovations not only the ethical issues raised by 'patents on life', but also the social, economic, and scientific impact of gene patenting. No technical analysis can be conclusive, so actors who are able to move between the technical and broader policy forums are in a powerful position to control eventual decisions.

Technical or bureaucratic rationality may certainly be an important defence against the influence which private interests can exercise over regulatory decision-making. However, too often these global regulatory networks seem highly permeable to pro-business viewpoints, often filtered through profess-ional 'hired guns' who also double as experts, while excluding public interest perspectives. It is only since the manifestation of an anti-globalization backlash that there has been some tentative debate about the legitimacy of global regulatory networks. As with the interactions of central and local government analysed by Vincent-Jones, it has been suggested that the global regulatory networks should operate according to principles of deliberative democracy.[15]

15 J.S. Dryzek, 'Transnational Democracy' (1999) 7 *J. of Political Philosophy* 30–51; D. Curtin, 'Civil Society and the European Union: Opening Spaces for Deliberative Democracy?' in *Collected Courses of the Academy of European Law, 1996, vol. VII, Book 1* (1999); S. Picciotto, 'Democratizing Globalism' in *The Market or the Public Domain? Global Governance and the Asymmetry of Power*, ed. D. Drache (2001).

8

This by no means excludes or downplays the importance of specialized technocratic and scientific practices and discourses, but suggests that they should be underpinned by principles of ethical responsibility. In particular, it calls for scientific reflexivity and openness, so that experts should be clear about the limiting assumptions behind their models and data and, rather than claiming a spurious authority and general validity for their conclusions, accept the need to test the robustness of their evaluations against those of others based on different assumptions.[16]

INTERPRETATIVE PRACTICES IN REGULATION

The suggestion that international regulatory coordination might depend far more on the emergence of shared understandings within a community of specialists in the particular regulatory field than on any formal legal texts aiming to harmonize the relevant rules raises the key question of regulation as an interpretative practice. If regulation is understood as a reflexive or responsive process, then it is primarily mediated by the practices of interpretation that are central to the implementation of rules. From this perspective, it is the relative indeterminacy of rules that provides scope for their necessary adaptation in the process of implementation to suit practical circumstances and local contexts. This may be considered to entail creative compliance amounting to avoidance of the intended purpose of the rules;[17] or to help in achieving those purposes;[18] or more broadly to create a social field in which rules and their interpretation help shape but are also shaped by social practices.[19]

Julia Black's work has systematically explored this perspective, and she further extends it in this volume. Her essay here surveys the main themes in

16 Picciotto, id., p. 350.
17 Notably, in the work of Doreen McBarnet and collaborators, see, most recently, D. McBarnet and C. Whelan, *Creative Acounting and the Cross-Eyed Javelin-Thrower* (1999).
18 See, for example, J. Braithwaite and V. Braithwaite, 'The Politics of Legalism: Rules versus Standards in Nursing-Home Regulation' (1995) 4 *Social and Legal Studies* 307–41.
19 For example, N. Reichman, 'Moving Backstage: Uncovering the role of compliance practices in shaping regulatory policy' in *White Collar Crime Reconsidered*, eds. K. Schlegel and D. Weisburd (1992, reprinted in Baldwin et al., op. cit., n. 4 above); J. McCahery and S. Picciotto, 'Creative Lawyering and the Dynamics of Business Regulation' in *Professional Competition and Professional Power. Lawyers, Accountants and the Social Construction of Markets*, eds. Y. Dezalay and D. Sugarman (1995); B. Lange, 'Compliance Construction in the Context of Environmental Regulation' (1999) 8 *Social and Legal Studies* 549–67; J. Black, *Rules and Regulators* (1997); A.C. Pratt, 'Dunking the Doughnut: Discretionary Power, Law and the Administration of the Canadian Immigration Act' (1999) 8 *Social and Legal Studies* 199–226.

9

the wide-ranging debates around discourse analysis, and deftly explores the implications for regulation of five key contentions. This approach provides a more secure foundation for the issue of rule-indeterminacy, setting aside assumptions about administrative discretion or the inherent vagueness of language, and rooting indeterminacy firmly in the basic concept that meaning is socially constructed. Black argues that discursive practices vitally determine regulation by building among the participants shared understandings and definitions of problems and solutions, as well as their identities and relationships. These practices can be used strategically and may therefore be functional in achieving certain ends, and may be coordinative if they produce shared meanings as the basis for action. Equally, however, language encodes certain perspectives and values, and meaning is contested, so that discursive interactions are also sites of conflict over power and ideology. One can add that, even if discursively mediated power is described as 'soft' power, it is nonetheless effective and may have devastating outcomes. Black's chapter casts a powerful light over many familiar issues in regulation, significantly deepening our understanding of them.

Finally, the chapter by Bettina Lange further underlines the social character of regulation by considering its emotional aspects. The usual view, as she begins by pointing out, is to regard emotions as to be excluded, disciplined, or taken account of in what are regarded as the dispassionate and rational processes of the law. However, if regulation is understood to involve debates and conflicts over normative standards and values, the emotional dimension must be seen as integral. Regulatory initiatives and reforms are often the result of highly emotive social episodes or dramas: for example, food scares (BSE, GMOs, and so on), financial crashes (BCCI, Barings), and most recently, the epochal events of September 11th. Indeed, regulatory practices are themselves imbued with emotions, such as fear, shame, and anger which significantly structure their practical operation. Lange goes further and, building on the notion that emotions are not just spontaneous but also guided by unarticulated norms, suggests that 'The specific outcome of various possible interactions between the laws of emotions and formal legal regulation is regulatory law in action.' This perspective challenges the assumption that regulation is simply a cognitive-rational process (legal or bureaucratic), and introduces different considerations which enter into both structure and agency, enabling a much fuller understanding of regulatory systems and institutions. Lange helpfully concludes with some suggestions for integrating the study of emotions into research designs.

TOWARDS A FULLY SOCIAL CONCEPT OF REGULATION

No doubt some will consider the issues raised in many of these papers to add further and unnecessary complications and dimensions to a topic already characterized by its breadth and the range of theoretical perspectives deployed to explore it. But if, as I suggested at the outset, both the phenomenon and the concept of regulation raise some fundamental questions for the nature and future of our forms of social organization, it must be appropriate to try to understand every aspect of the social processes involved. Indeed it could be said that, despite the range and quality of much of the work done in the past twenty or so years on the topic, the dominant approaches have come from a relatively narrow part of the social theory spectrum. Building on this heritage, the papers collected here offer a challenging combination of refinement and extension of the theoretical perspectives, together with richly detailed analyses of a range of key examples.

11

JOURNAL OF LAW AND SOCIETY
VOLUME 29, NUMBER 1, MARCH 2002
ISSN: 0263-323X, pp. 12–26

Rewards and Regulation

JOHN BRAITHWAITE*

Rewards are less useful in regulation than they are in markets. Firms respond to market incentives because most markets are contestable. In markets that are not oligopolies it makes more sense to adopt a competitor mentality than a fixer mentality. Regulatory power in contrast is mostly not contestable. Firms are therefore more likely to adopt a fixer or game-playing mentality. Reactance to regulatory control through rewards is likely to be greater than reactance to market discipline. If a responsive regulatory pyramid is a good strategy for optimizing compliance, then punishment is more useful in regulation than reward. Reward at the middle of a regulatory pyramid brings about a moral hazard problem. Under certain limited conditions reward can be useful at the base of a regulatory pyramid. These conditions are transparent, easy measurement of the performance to be rewarded, an imbalance of power such that the regulatee is weak in comparison to the regulator, and an absence of weapons of the weak for subverting a regulatory system to which the weak are subject. Absent these conditions, and we cannot expect the undoubted efficiency advantages of a market where regulatory outcomes can be traded so that they are secured where the cost of doing so is least. While, in general, punishments are more useful to regulators than monetary rewards, informal rewards (praise, letters of recognition) are rather consistently useful in securing compliance.

Psychologists and economists do not agree on much about how to motivate human behaviour. One major point of convergence, however, is on the view that rewards are more useful than punishments in motivating human behaviour. For the economists, rewards for achieving, say, an environmental outcome have the further advantage that the efficiency of a market for environmental improvement might be accomplished – trading in a market for environmental rewards will secure the greatest reductions in environmental impact where it is cheapest to produce them. But these important efficiency

* *Regulatory Institutions Network, Australian National University, Canberra, ACT 0200, Australia*

advantages will be moot in contexts where rewards fail to motivate behavioural change.

In popular diagnoses of how to get things done as well, the view that carrots are better than sticks is also widespread. This view is regularly articulated with respect to business regulation. In the reaction against the adversarial legalism[1] of command-and-control regulation, the two dominant prescriptions have been a shift from coercive to cooperative regulation, from punishment to persuasion,[2] and from punishment to reward[3] or from command and control to market-based incentives.[4]

Those of us who have been regulatory professionals for a long time have served on endless committees charged with curbing the excesses of command-and-control regulation where one of the issues we were asked to consider was whether carrots could be substituted for some of the sticks used in extant arrangements. And we will have had the experience of coming up empty handed – the committee fails to recommend any reforms it regards as practical ways of substituting rewards for punishments. The reason for this is that in the context of business regulation punishments are in fact more useful tools than rewards. In raising children it is generally better to wait until they manifest a desired behaviour like reading books, then reward it, than it is to punish failure to do so. This is the basis for the psychologist's preference for rewards. In markets, incentive in the form of extra money is what makes the world go round. This is the basis for the economist's preference for rewards. They are both wrong, I will argue, when they translate this preference into the domain of business regulation. Here punishments are more valuable than rewards for securing compliance. This conclusion is not startlingly original; Jeremy Bentham believed that while rewards were powerful in markets and while they had some uses in law, rewards were a less valuable tool for the legislator than punishments.[5] On the former he was in agreement with Adam Smith, but he did not share Smith's enthusiasm for rewards in regulation.[6] 'Punishment is an instrument for the extirpation of noxious weeds: reward is a hot bed for raising fruit, which would not otherwise be produced.'[7] In this essay, I will advance in

1 E. Bardach and R.A. Kagan, *Going By The Book: The Problem of Regulatory Unreasonableness* (1982).
2 F. Haines, *Corporate Regulation: Beyond 'Punish or Persuade'* (1997).
3 P. Grabosky, 'Regulation by Reward: On the Use of Incentives as Regulatory Instruments' (1996) 17 *Law and Policy* 256–81.
4 N.O. Keohane, R.L. Revesz, and R.N. Stavins, 'The Choice of Regulatory Instruments in Environmental Policy' (1998) 22 *Harvard Environmental Law Rev.* 313–67.
5 J. Bentham, *The Rationale of Reward*, eds. J. and H.L. Hunt (1825) 6, 51–2; J. Bentham, *Collected Works of Jeremy Bentham: Principles of Legislation: A Comment on the Commentaries and a Fragment on Government*, eds. J.H. Burns and H.L.A. Hart (1977) 75–7, 79.
6 id. (1825), p. 52.
7 id., p. 51.

13

turn a contestability argument, a reactance argument, and a responsiveness argument for why rewards do not enjoy the superiority over punishment in regulation that they enjoy in markets.

CONTESTABILITY

The rewards provided by markets, as we have said, generally work in motivating productive efficiency. But not always. Most firms respond to the challenge of a market for the product they sell by competing with a customer-service mentality. An alternative path is to seek to fix the market, to rig bids with competitors, to form cartels that fix prices or allocate markets geographically. Most business opts for the competitive mentality rather than the fixer mentality because cartels are hard to hold together. Fixers also find ways to cheat on the other members of the cartel to attract business to themselves, for example, by under-the-table rebates to customers. Markets are always contestable by new entrants which are not members of the cartel when monopoly prices are being charged. This is especially so in contemporary conditions of global markets where foreign competition can enter the market to contest for the business of local cartels.

With business regulation, however, it is not always the case that the competitor mentality dominates the fixer mentality. When a regulator puts in place a system of rewards for achieving an outcome like pollution reduction. firms that already have leading pollution control capabilities will compete aggressively for those rewards. The majority of firms that have poorer capabilities, however, tend to do what they can to put in the fix to prevent the compliance leaders from getting this competitive jump on them.[8] Their pursuit of the fixer mentality takes many forms. They lobby through industry associations to subvert or delay the reforms industry-wide, they make special pleadings for exemptions for themselves, they fudge their compliance data, bribe inspectors who then assert that the compliance data is not as claimed, or complain to their political masters about regulatory unreasonableness, but most commonly of all they indulge in what Doreen McBarnet and Christopher Whelan have called 'creative compliance'.[9] Business regulatory outcomes tend to be complex, not black and white. Hence the dominant fixer mentality is to play for the gray.

Even in comparatively simple domains of regulation the possibility of putting in the fix to subvert the regulatory incentives is there. The Kennedy School of Government at Harvard and the Ford Foundation gave the state of Illinois an innovations in government award in the 1980s for its shift from command-and-control nursing-home regulation to a system of

8 Keohane, Revesz, and Stavins, op. cit., n. 4, pp. 351–3.
9 D. McBarnet and C. Whelan, *Creative Accounting and the Cross-Eyed Javelin Thrower* (1999).

14

rewards (higher Medicaid payments) graduated according to the quality of care delivered (the Illinois Quality Incentives Program). Some other states, including Michigan and Massachusetts, also experimented with this approach. Valerie Braithwaite, Diane Gibson, Toni Makkal and I undertook an ethnographic study of United States nursing-home regulation during this period in all the largest states; this included observing many nursing-home inspections in Illinois.[10] When rewards were put in place for the number of residents participating in activity programmes, we noted sleeping residents in wheelchairs being wheeled in to the room where an activity such as craft or a game was going on so that they could be recorded on the head count as participating. One very important standard at that time related to the existence of a 'homelike' environment. One aspect of this is the capacity of residents to domesticate their little piece of institutional space by putting up pictures of their choosing on the wall. This kind of empowerment could take many forms – rearranging the bed and other furniture, carpets, even bringing a beloved pet in to deinstitutionalize the space. But counting the pictures on the wall was the easiest quantitative way of operationalizing this standard. And, of course, quantitative measures that can be calibrated unambiguously are what inspectorates like when quantitative incentives which could be contested in a court of law hang on their ratings. Sure enough, nursing home staff told us that the large numbers of pictures of movie stars we would notice, often torn from the same magazine, had been slapped up around the nursing home on the instructions of management in anticipation of the arrival of the inspectors. Of course, they were not supposed to know when the inspectors would be arriving; but we found that fixers had a way of knowing these things. Our fieldwork even revealed cases of large numbers of pot-plants on short-term hire that were returned as soon as the inspection was completed. The bigger the incentive, the more complex the phenomenon regulated, the worse creative compliance gets.

One might say that in markets there are fixers who dupe consumers by fudging compliance with product quality or safety standards. The difference is when duped consumers discover they have been duped, they punish the supplier in the market. Inspectors generally do not do this when firms are clever enough to creatively comply with the standards they have written. Regulators figure that if they punish firms in these circumstances the agency will come under political attack for failing to write the rules of reward in a competent fashion and that courts will overturn their decisions to withhold the reward. Instead they admire the ingenuity of the firm; the inspector does not suffer personally for it, the intended beneficiaries of the regulation do. Beneficiaries such as nursing-home residents are not empowered to use

---

10 J. Braithwaite, 'The Nursing Home Industry' in *Beyond the Law: Crime in Complex Organizations*, eds. M. Jorry and A. Reiss (1993).

rewards that are issued by the state to assert their claims to quality and safety.

But the more fundamental fact of this situation is that while a consumer in a market who is duped simply goes to another supplier, an inspector who is duped cannot simply walk away from the transaction. The nursing home will get some level of Medicaid payment; it would be irresponsible to cut off payments that are made to care for the residents unless the situation is life-threatening. The factory inspected by an occupational health and safety official likewise cannot be simply shut down so the inspector can use his time more productively at a factory that is more sincere about compliance. Fraud and creative compliance in market relationships are effectively contested by other suppliers. In the regulatory relationship they are not. This is reciprocally true. In general, the firm faces only one regulator with responsibility for a particular issue. The threat the regulator poses to the profits of the regulated firm is not a threat that is contested by other regulators. This is quite different from the situation with a cartel. The threat to cartel profits is posed by a number of potential entrants to the market. It is harder to put in the fix with all of them than it is with one regulator. There is just one regulator to corrupt, capture or outwit. Hence the competitor mentality dominates the fixer mentality in markets because there is more than one player to fix. The fixer dominates the competitor mentality with regulatory rewards because this contestability is absent: fix one player and you have fixed the whole game.[11] The absence of contestability is therefore a fundamental structural reason why reward has less power in regulation than in markets.

REACTANCE

Experimental research on children and college students demonstrates the counterproductive effect salient rewards and punishments can have: long-term internalization of values like altruism and resistance to temptation are inhibited when people view their action as caused by a reward or punishment.[12]

---

11 We can attenuate this to a degree by making the regulatory game a tripartite one in which the power to pay rewards is contested by the monitoring of non-government organizations (NGOs), see I. Ayres and J. Braithwaite, *Responsive Regulation., Transcending the Deregulation Debate* (1992). But here the NGO is only a proxy regulator of sorts; there is still just one state agency that can pay the rewards. NGOs cannot pay them.

12 M.R. Lepper, 'Dissonance, Self-Perception and Honesty in Children' (1973) 25 *J. of Personality and Social Psychology* 65–74; M.R. Lepper and D. Greene, *The Hidden Costs of Reward* (1978); T. Dix and J.E. Grusec, 'Parental Influence Techniques: An Attributional Analysis' (1983) 54 *Child Development* 645–52; M.L. Hoffman, 'Moral Development' in *Carmichael's Annual of Child Psychology*, ed. P.H. Mussen (1970).

16

Over fifty studies examining the effect of extrinsic incentives on later intrinsic motivation indicate that inducements that are often perceived as controlling (for example, tangible rewards, surveillance, deadlines), depending on the manner in which they are administered, reduce feelings of self-determination and undermine subsequent motivation in a wide variety of achievement-related activities after the reward is removed.[13]

These findings seem to be of fairly general import, being supported in domains including moral behaviour, altruism, personal interaction, aggressive behaviour, and resistance to temptation.[14] Just as strong external incentives retard internalization, using reasoning in preference to power-assertion tends to promote it.[15]

Brehm and Brehm[16] constructed a theory of psychological reactance on the basis of the kinds of studies we have been discussing. Figure 1 shows that the net effect of threats of control is the sum of a control effect and a reactance effect. According to this theory, intentions to control are reacted to as attempts to limit our freedom, which lead us to reassert that freedom by acting contrary to the direction of control. Reactance applies to attempts to control through rewards just as it applies to threats to control through punishment, though reactance effects are not as great with rewards as they are with punishments.[17] Figure 1 also shows that reactance is least when we seek to restrict freedom to do something that is not very important to us, greatest when the freedom subjected to control is something the regulated actor deeply cares about. Tom Tyler might suggest that naked attempts to control us give us some negative information about our identity – that we have a subordinated identity, that we are a slave to the will of another – and this is an identity we do not

13 A.K. Boggiano, M. Barrett, A.N. Weiher, G.H. McLelland and C.M. Lusk, 'Use of the Maximal Operant Principle to Motivate Children's Intrinsic Interest' (1987) 53 *J. of Personality and Social Psychology* 866–79.

14 Boggiano et al., id.; Lepper, op. cit., n. 12; R.A. Dienstbier, D. Hillman. J. Lenhoff, and M.C. Valkenaar, 'An Emotion-Attribution Approach to Moral Behavior: Interfacing Cognitive and Avoidance Theories of Moral Development' (1975) 82 *Psychological Rev.* 229–315; Dix and Grusec, op. cit., n. 12.

15 L.A. Cheyne and R.H. Walters, 'Intensity of Punishment, Timing of Punishment, and Cognitive Structure as Determinants of Response Inhibition' (1969) 7 *J. of Experimental Child Psychology* 231–44; R.D. Parke, 'Effectiveness of Punishment as an Interaction of Intensity, Timing, Agent Nurturance and Cognitive Structuring' (1969) 40 *Child Development* 213–35; Hoffman, op. cit., n. 12; D. Baumrind, 'The Development of Instrumental Competence through Socialization' in *Minnesota Symposium of Motivation,* vol. 7, ed. A.D. Pick (1973); C.Z. Zahn-Waxler, M.R. Radke-Yarrow, and R.A. King, 'Child Rearing and Children's Prosocial Initiations Towards Victims in Distress' (1979) 50 *Child Development* 319–30.

16 S.S. Brehm and L.W. Brehm, *Psychological Reactance: A Theory of Freedom and Control* (1981).

17 id., p. 229.

Figure 1: The Interactive Effects of Force and Importance of Freedom

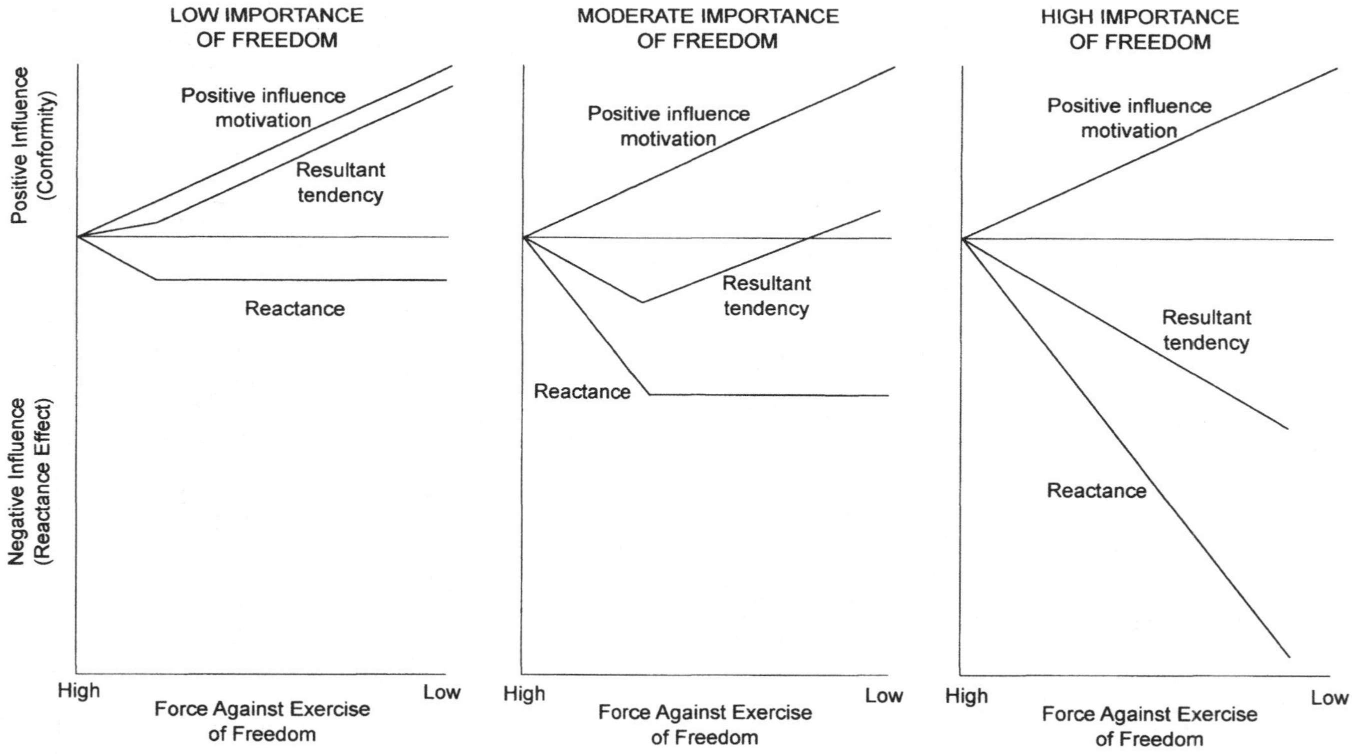

(From Brem and Brehm, op. cit., n. 16, p. 229)

want.[18] We do not get this negative information if it is the rewards of the market that control us; we do if it is a regulator who seeks to control us through rewards. Hence we can expect the invisible hand of the market to generate less reactance than the visible hand of a controlling regulator. The more important the freedom being regulated, the greater this reactance effect will be according to the evidence generated by this theory.

While the theory explains why reactance to regulatory rewards should be greater than reactance to rewards in markets, and therefore why rewards should be less effective than we might expect in making regulation work, reactance theory does not explain why regulatory rewards should be less useful than punishment. For that result we turn to responsive regulatory theory.

RESPONSIVENESS

A more fundamental policy debate about regulatory strategy than that between reward and punishment has been the contest between punishment and persuasion. My own position in that debate, and that of quite a number of others, is that it is best to have a presumption in favour of trying persuasion first, generally reserving punishment for when persuasion fails.[19] Persuasion is cheaper and a more respectful way of treating the regulated actor. However, it is argued that persuasion will normally only be more effective than punishment in securing compliance when the persuasion is backed up by punishment. The idea of responsive regulation grew from dissatisfaction with the business regulation debate – some arguing that business people are rational actors who only understand the bottom line and who therefore must be punished consistently for their law breaking, others that business people are responsible citizens and can be persuaded to come into compliance. In different contexts there is a lot of truth in both positions. This means that both consistent punishment and consistent persuasion are foolish strategies. The hard question is how do we decide when to punish and when to persuade.[20] What makes the question such a difficult one is that attempts to regulate conduct do not simply succeed or fall. Often they backfire, making compliance with the law a lot worse.[21] So the tragedy of

---

18 T. Tyler, *Why People Obey the Law* (1990); T. Tyler and R.M. Dawes, 'Fairness in Groups: Comparing the Self-Interest and Social Identity Perspectives' in *Psychological Perspectives on Justice: Theory and Applications*, eds. B.A. Mellers and J. Baron (1993); T. Tyler and S. Blader, *Cooperation in Groups: Procedural Justice, Social Identity, and Behavioral Engagement* (2000); T. Tyler and Y.J. Huo, *Trust and the Rule of Law: A Law-Abidingness Model of Social Control* (2001).

19 Ayres and Braithwaite, op. cit., n. 11; N. Gunningham and P. Grabosky, *Smart Regulation: Designing Environmental Policy* (1998).

20 J. Braithwaite, *To Punish or Persuade: Enforcement of Coal Mine Safety* (1985).

21 L.W. Sherman, 'Defiance, Deterrence and Irrelevance: A Theory of the Criminal Sanction' (1993) 30 *J. of Research in Crime and Delinquency* 445–73.

Figure 2: An Example of a Regulatory Pyramid

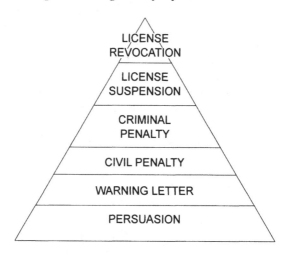

LICENSE REVOCATION

LICENSE SUSPENSION

CRIMINAL PENALTY

CIVIL PENALTY

WARNING LETTER

PERSUASION

consistent punishment of wrongdoers of a certain type is that our consistency will regularly cause us to make things worse for future victims of the wrongdoing. In business regulation circles these days, there is not much contesting of the conclusion that consistent punishment of business non-compliance would be a bad policy, and that persuasion is normally the better way to go when there is reason to suspect that cooperation with attempting to secure compliance will be forthcoming.

The most distinctive part of responsive regulation is the regulatory pyramid. It is an attempt to solve the puzzle of when to punish and when to persuade. At the base of the pyramid is the most restorative dialogue-based approach we can craft for securing compliance with a just law. As we move up the pyramid, more and more demanding and punitive interventions in peoples' lives are involved. The idea of the pyramid is that our presumption should always be to start at the base of the pyramid, then escalate to somewhat punitive approaches only reluctantly and only when dialogue falls, and then escalate to even more punitive approaches only when the more modest forms of punishment fail. Figure 2 is an example of a responsive business regulatory pyramid from Ayres and Braithwaite.[22] The regulator here escalates with the recalcitrant company from persuasion to a warning to civil penalties to criminal penalties and ultimately to corporate capital punishment – permanently revoking the company's licence to operate

If it is right, as responsive regulation claims, that cooperative approaches such as education, persuasicn, and restorative justice are normally better,

22 Ayres and Braithwaite, op. cit., n. 11, p. 35.

Figure 3: Toward an Integration of Restorative, Deterrent, and Incapacitive Justice

ASSUMPTION

Incompetent or Irrational Actor   INCAPACITATION

Rational Actor   DETERRENCE

Virtuous Actor   RESTORATIVE JUSTICE

though not invariably so, as a first strategy, then regulators are best to be presumptively cooperative and only override this presumption when strong reasons to do so appear.[23] When the cooperative approach fails, the regulator escalates up the pyramid. According to the theory, this escalation involves an abandonment of the motivational assumption that the regulated actor is a responsible citizen who is capable of complying (see Figure 3). The next port of call assumes the regulatee to be a rational actor who must be deterred. But of course if the regulatee is a rational firm, it can be motivated by reward just as well as, or better than, by punishment. The problem with a responsive regulatory strategy that would have the regulator escalate from trust and cooperation to reward is moral hazard. The regulatee who really is a rational actor will exploit the opportunity a first preference for trust provides by failing to invest in compliance. Then such a firm will reap the rewards for compliance provided at the next rung up the pyramid. Unpunished free riding followed by rewarded free riding. Escalation to punishment is what is needed to provide incentives for the rational actor to invest in cooperation and risk management.

So why not make reward the first port of call at the base of the pyramid? One reason is that paying rewards is more expensive than asking for voluntary compliance. Second, rewards commonly cause reactance, as we saw in the last section. Third, as we saw in the first section, rewards foster a culture of game playing. Game playing is productive in the context of a

---

23 Responsive regulation moreover argues that this approach is best even with hardened law-breakers. The most irresponsible of us has a socially responsible self. Responsive regulation is a strategy for persuading the worst of us to put our best self forward.

© Blackwell Publishers Ltd 2002

market; in the context of regulation, games of cat and mouse tend to be expensive, inefficient, and result in a win for the corporate cat, defeating the purposes of the regulation.[24] From the theoretical perspective of responsive regulation, putting rewards at the base of the pyramid creates the wrong kind of regulatory culture,[25] the wrong kind of regulatory community.[26] It would give business the message that they are not expected to be responsible corporate citizens. The policy framework would give the message that government only expects corporations to meet their obligations when it pays. The moral content of the law is eroded[27] as nobler motives are eclipsed by baser ones.[28]

Finally, attempts to replace punishment with reward in a regulatory pyramid tend to be illusory. For example, an environmental strategy of rewarding reductions in a certain kind of effluent requires reporting of the fact of such reductions unless the state is going to employ an inspector to be present at the factory measuring effluent every day. The reward strategy thus introduces incentives to cheat on reporting, to say that more effluent has been eliminated than is the case. So a new inspectorate is needed to catch and punish rational effluent cheats. The effect of the reward strategy is to replace environmental inspectors with fraud auditors or tax inspectors. This is a bad outcome because financial auditors are technically incompetent to do the diagnostic trouble-shooting of environmental problems which is among the most effective things environmental inspectors do.[29]

All of that said, there are some conditions where rewards at the base of an enforcement pyramid work well and deliver the economic efficiency advantages of a market for regulatory outcomes contrived by the regulator. One of those conditions is that non-compliance is so transparent that financial auditors are not needed.[30] For example, the policy many governments introduced in the late 1970s and 1980s of reducing taxes on unleaded fuel was part of a package that successfully reduced lead in the environment.[31] While there was some cheating by petroleum suppliers, it

---

24 E. Bardach and R.A. Kagan, *Going by the Book: The Problem of Regulatory Unreasonableness* (1982); R.A. Kagan and L. Axelrad, *Regulatory Encounters: Multinational Corporations and American Adversarial Legalism* (2000).
25 C. Parker, *The Open Corporation* (forthcoming).
26 E. Meidinger, 'Regulatory Culture: A Theoretical Outline'(1986) 9 *Law and Policy* 355–86.
27 J. Braithwaite, 'The Limits of Economism in Controlling Harmful Corporate Conduct' (1981–82) 6 *Law and Society Rev.* 48–504.
28 R. Goodin, 'Making Moral Incentives Pay' (1980) 12 *Policy Sciences* 131, at 139–40.
29 Bardach and Kagan, op. cit., n. 24; K. Hawkins, *Environment and Enforcement: Regulation and the Social Definition of Pollution* (1984); Gunningham and Grabosky, op. cit., n. 19; B.M. Hutter, *A Reader in Environmental Law* (1999).
30 C. Coglianese and D. Lazer, 'Management-Based Regulatory Strategies', Regulatory Policy Program Working Paper RPP-2001-09, Harvard University (2001).
31 Gunningham and Grabosky, op. cit., n. 19, p. 435.

was limited by the fact that putting the wrong kind of fuel in certain kinds of engines would cause problems for consumers. In other words, there was sufficient transparency for the regime to be self-enforcing in the market. A second condition this case meets is of a large imbalance of power between regulator and regulatee in favour of the regulator. Here the regulatee is primarily the motor-vehicle user: they pay the tax, not the motor-vehicle manufacturer. If it were the motor-vehicle manufacturer that was provided with an opportunity to reduce tax on a large scale, we might have seen regulatory cat and mouse in the engineering of motor vehicles in pursuit of that tax benefit. But most of us did not have the economic or technological capability to re-engineer our motor vehicles in pursuit of tax advantages. We were simply too weak (economically and technically) in comparison with the state's power, so we just went along with the regime and took the rewards in the way intended by the policy makers. Another example of successful regulation by reward was the provision in 1999 by the Australian government of a tax rebate for joining a private health insurance fund. This worked in reversing the desertion of Australians from private health insurance, which had been putting a huge burden on the public system. It worked because, like the fuel tax, it was a modest reward to individuals of modest means. In contrast, we know that if we make available a large tax rebate to economically powerful actors, they will hire tax lawyers and accountants to financially engineer the target of the rebate. If research and development expenditure attracts a tax break, companies find ways of interpreting the cleaning of their office floors as R&D on cleaning fluids! If making films is something governments want to reward to assert local culture over the power of Hollywood, then as we have seen in Australia, New Zealand, the United Kingdom, and Canada, film tax shelters proliferate based on films that never illuminate a screen. As Grabosky[32] points out, beyond the risk of inefficacy, there is the risk that tax incentives that are 'back door expenditures' are less subject to scrutiny, blowing out to levels vastly beyond the initial policy justification before anyone notices. This is also one of the reasons, Grabosky argues, that regulation by reward increases distributive inequities. The same dependency mentality as a disincentive to innovation as can be applied to individual welfare dependency can be applied to corporate dependency on state handouts, only with more worrying distributive implications.[33]

Even where these two conditions of transparency and regulatee weakness are met, a third condition needed is an absence of weapons of the weak. In most contexts, for example, piece rates to motive factory workers to produce more, do not work very well. The reason is that workers conspire to self-regulate limits on rates of production that will maximize their income for minimum effort. 'Rate-busters' are punished by ostracism. This

32 Grabosky, op. cit., n. 3, p. 10.
33 id., p. 13.

23

ostracism has proven a most effective weapon of the weak against regulation by reward.

Where these conditions are not met, there is a risk that reward at the base of the pyramid can not only fail, but can make the problem worse. For example, if you pay farmers bounties to plant trees in pursuit of a biodiversity objective,[34] you had better be sure your monitoring of the number of trees on large properties is credible (something more possible with satellite technology). If not, you create incentives to cut down and sell trees in order to gain the bounty from subsequently replanting the area. If you pay for blood instead of relying on voluntary donations to the Red Cross, there is more to worry about than simply eroding altruism and voluntarism.[35] There is also the worry that the unscrupulous will get hold of HIV- or hepatitus-infected blood destined for destruction and divert it to the commercial market in blood. At the more structural level, perverse incentives can be an even more massive problem. If our regulatory policies were to become more inured to regulation by reward, corporate power would be used on a variety of fronts to drive up problems so there can be a bigger pay-off for reducing them. For example, a good strategy for power companies has been to increase their use of dirty coal stocks as they lobby for a regime of rewards to switch to clean coal and non-coal power generation.

SALVAGING REWARD

My conclusion that rewards in markets are effective in shaping behaviour implies that indirect regulatory strategies which have the effect of enhancing market rewards for desired behaviour can be effective. Hence green labelling, mandated disclosure of the fuel efficiency of motor vehicles, and other mandatory disclosure rules can achieve regulatory objectives by enabling consumers to supply rewards in the market for desired behaviour. Of course, the outcomes specified on green labels still have to be easily measured, which they can be with fuel efficiency but not with most environmental impacts.

A form of reward that seems to have unequivocally positive effects on compliance is informal praise – inspectors giving a word of encouragement when they see an improvement. Makkai and Braithwaite[36] found that when nursing homes were monitored by inspection teams that used a lot of praise, subsequent compliance with quality of care standards

34 id., pp. 7–8.
35 R.M. Titmuss, *The Gift Relationship* (1971).
36 T. Makkai and J. Braithwaite, 'Praise, Pride and Corporate Compliance' (1993) 21 *International J. of the Sociology of Law* 73–91.

24

improved, after controlling for other factors. Makkai and Braithwaite therefore went on to commend other slightly more formal forms of praise such as letters from local members of Congress congratulating homes that achieved excellence in quality of care (which we often observed to be framed in nursing home lobbies) and the State of New York Department of Health's practice of putting out a press release on a regular basis announcing the names of nursing homes found to be totally free of deficiencies.

Praise is a gift. It is not required. Like a smile, it is supererogatory. While a smile of approval can motivate us enormously, because it has the character of a gift more than that of a reward, we do not normally interpret it as an attempt to manipulate us. So there is mostly not a reactance problem, not a problem of extrinsic incentive driving out intrinsic satisfaction in doing the right thing. Informal praise is compatible with cooperative problem solving at the base of a regulatory pyramid. The more voluntary compliance is elicited at the base of the pyramid, the more fulsome the praise dispensed. When there has been non-compliance that moved regulation up the pyramid, the return to compliance and movement back down the pyramid can be associated with praise for putting things right. Hence, while punishment is associated with movement up the pyramid, praise is associated with movement down. In practice there does not seem to be much of a problem of regulatees being non-compliant so they can get the benefit of informal praise in a sequence following formal punishment. This is because the power of praise does not reside so much in it being a reward that can be balanced against the cost of punishment. Its power resides in the affirmation of identities – law abiding identities in the case of regulation – communicated by praise.

CONCLUSION

Punishment is not the most important lever of compliance in a responsive regulatory framework. However, we have argued here that it is in most contexts a more useful tool than reward. The form of direct regulatory reward that avoids persistent dangers of counterproductivity is informal praise. And it works because it is not seen as a conscious reward by regulated actors, at least not when it is communicated with finesse. Extrinsic rewards undermine intrinsic motivation, and foster game playing and defiance in response to attempts at control. Punishment as an escalation up a regulatory pyramid combats free riding, reward exacerbates it. Reward not only increases the danger of risks being uncontrolled, but provides reason to increase risk if subsequent reward is calibrated in proportion to the degree to which risks are brought under control. Reward therefore must only be used at the base of a regulatory pyramid and in association with movements down the pyramid. Even then, informal praise of the person oriented to affirming

25

his or her identity as a responsible citizen is more useful than monetary rewards. Praise projects encounters into the rhetoric of obligation, monetary rewards into calculative game playing that strips norms of their moral content.

JOURNAL OF LAW AND SOCIETY
VOLUME 29, NUMBER 1, MARCH 2002
ISSN: 0263-323X, pp. 27–55

Values and Purpose in Government: Central-local Relations in Regulatory Perspective

PETER VINCENT-JONES*

This paper explores the relationship between theories of regulation and governmentality, showing how a synthesis of the two approaches may be used in the analysis of central-local relations. The basis of the current trend towards greater partnership and cooperation in the regulation of local by central government is argued to lie in the linking of increasingly selective imperium *and* dominium *controls with 'responsibilization' strategies involving techniques of accounting, audit, and contracting. Following Nonet and Selznick, the substantive and purposive nature of state action is placed at the centre of the analysis. In this perspective, the ideal of responsive regulation implies not just technical effectiveness, but the harnessing of regulatory forces and 'governmental' resources in endeavours to achieve legitimate regulatory objectives. While New Labour's regulatory style is more likely to prove effective than that of the Conservatives, it may be criticized for a similar failure to implement fundamental values of openness and participation in the determination of regulatory purposes.*

INTRODUCTION

This paper applies theoretical perspectives on regulation and governmentality to the analysis of central-local relations, focusing in particular on the relationship between central and local government. The general failure of these perspectives to engage with the values and purposes informing the state's regulatory endeavours is particularly apparent in this context. While theorists of governmentality appear to be uninterested in such evaluation, regulationists have tended to sidestep the

* Lancashire Law School, University of Central Lancashire Preston PR1 2HE, England

This paper is part of a broader project for which the support of the ESRC is acknowledged (award no. R000271186).

issue, as have advocates of the abandonment of substantive state direction in favour of reflexive strategies[1] or proceduralization.[2] In contrast to these positions, the present paper directly confronts the legitimacy of the state's regulatory objectives and the manner of their determination as part of a broader evaluative task including, but not confined to, the technical assessment of regulatory effectiveness. In so doing, it argues that insights drawn from the literature on governmentality can be incorporated within, and may indeed be regarded logically as part of, a redefined theoretical perspective on responsive law and regulation drawing on the work of Nonet and Selznick.

REGULATION, GOVERNANCE, GOVERNMENTALITY

In its most general sense, regulation may be said to include 'all acts of controlling, directing or governing according to a rule, principle or system'.[3] This broad notion of regulation as systematic control clearly embraces rules restricting behaviour, together with targeted rules or specific sets of commands accompanied by mechanisms for monitoring and promoting compliance.[4] It also includes forms of state intervention such as subsidies and taxation, and policy instruments entailing control by standards, licensing, and inspection. Following Daintith, the state may be viewed as a purposeful actor pursuing economic and social objectives through regulatory strategies involving the linking of state law with power resources, or instruments, of force, wealth, and information and persuasion.[5] As well as extending beyond economic to social behaviour, this definition includes unconscious and non-deliberate processes and mechanisms of social control beyond the formal boundaries of the state.[6]

1 G. Teubner, 'Substantive and Reflexive Elements in Modern Law' (1983) 17 *Law and Society Rev.* 239.
2 For a critique of proceduralization, see J. Black, 'Proceduralizing Regulation: Part I' (2000) 20 *Ox. J. of Legal Studies* 597, at 604–6 and fn. 32.
3 T. Daintith, 'Regulation' in *International Encyclopedia of Comparative Law,* vol. XVII, 'State and Economy', eds. R. Buxbaum and F. Madl 3. See, also, the discussion of definitions of regulation in T. Prosser, *Law and the Regulators* (1997).
4 R. Baldwin, C. Scott, and C. Hood, 'Introduction' in *A Reader on Regulation,* eds. R. Baldwin, C. Scott, and C. Hood (1998) 3; R. Baldwin and M. Cave, *Understanding Regulation* (1999).
5 Daintith, op. cit, n. 3, p. 24. This classification of regulatory resources is a refinement of Daintith's earlier analysis based on the distinction between *imperium* (characterized by commands backed by force, and by duties or rules whose breach is accompanied by negative sanctions) and *dominium* (referring to the employment of wealth, usually in the form of government grants or contracts, as incentives to comply with central policy). This analysis allows that compliance with rules may be rewarded through their relaxation, and that withdrawal of wealth benefits may serve a sanctioning purpose: T. Daintith, 'The Techniques of Government' in *The Changing Constitution,* eds. J. Jowell and D. Oliver (1994) 212.
6 Baldwin and Cave, op. cit., n. 4, p. 2.

The attempted exercise of systematic control for the attainment of public policy objectives is likely to impact upon a variety of state and non-state actors and institutions in unforeseeable ways. All such repercussions need to be taken into account in the analysis and evaluation of the success or failure of regulation in any particular regulatory context.

This definition of regulation also embraces the phenomenon of regulation within government (or 'bureaucratic regulation'), which has begun to receive academic attention only relatively recently. Christopher Hood and collaborators have conceived of such regulation as the range of ways in which activities of public bureaucracies are subject to influence from other public agencies, beyond direct 'chain-of-command controls' and orthodox constitutional checking mechanisms such as the legislature and the courts.[7] In this conception, regulation is argued to take place against a backdrop of various types of control over bureaucracy, with traditional oversight (involving command-and-control techniques supported by arm's length inspectorates, audit bodies, and ombudsmen) being supplemented by competition (control through rivalry and choice), mutuality (control through professional, collegial, and group influences), and contrived randomness (control through unpredictable processes).[8] While the main focus is on how the behaviour of public organizations is shaped by other public bodies, private actors (accountants, auditors, private sector inspectors) also figure in the regulatory process. The importance of bureaucratic regulation is set to increase as traditional hierarchical controls are replaced by private management techniques, and as the public sector becomes more fragmented through the creation of semi-independent government agencies, client-contractor splits, and the separation of responsibilities for policy making and service provision.

In parallel, critics of traditional notions of 'government' maintain that while the language of political philosophy (state and civil society, freedom and constraint, sovereignty and democracy, public and private) plays a key role in the organization of modern political power, 'it cannot provide the intellectual tools for analysing the problematics of government in the present'.[9] Addressing this deficiency, currently one of the most productive variants of the governance approach in political science and socio-legal studies draws on Foucault's famous definition of government as 'the conduct of conduct'. In this perspective, 'government entails any attempt to shape with some degree of deliberation aspects of our behaviour according to particular sets of norms and for a variety of ends'.[10] Again, 'government refers to all endeavours to shape, guide, direct the conduct of others, whether

---

7 C. Hood, O. James, G. Jones, C. Scott, and T. Travers, *Regulation Inside Government* (1999).

8 id., pp. 13–17.

9 N. Rose and P. Miller, 'Political Power Beyond the State: Problematics of Government' (1992) 43 *Brit. J. of Sociology* 173, at 201.

10 M. Dean, *Governmentality: Power and Rule in Modern Society* (1999) 10.

these be the crew of a ship, the members of a household, the employees of a boss, the children of a family or the inhabitants of a territory'.[11] Linked with this conception of government, Dean distinguishes two senses of the term 'governmentality.' First, in contrast to the traditional focus on institutions, organizations, and structures, governmentality indicates the relationship between government and thought – specifically the forms of knowledge, expertise, techniques, and means of calculation involved in governmental processes.[12] In a second sense, governmentality is linked with the historical emergence of new forms of governing in certain societies – at the time when the exercise of power on the basis of sovereignty, rules, and constitutions came to be supplemented by the exercise of disciplinary power over individuals in schools, hospitals, workhouses, armies, and other modern institutions.[13] According to Rose:

> Governmentality is a way of problematizing life and seeking to act upon it. It both extends the concerns of rule to the ordering of the multitudinous affairs of a territory and its population in order to ensure its well being, and simultaneously establishes divisions between the proper spheres of action of different types of authority.[14]

The overlap between the concepts of regulation and government, evident in the common emphasis on endeavours or attempts at 'controlling', 'directing', 'influencing', or 'shaping' behaviour, is further illustrated in the related notions of self-regulation and self-governance. In contrast with the essentially pragmatic acknowledgement of the advantages of self-regulation in the business regulation literature,[15] the ideas of self-direction, self-guidance, and self-conduct lie at the heart of the governmentality approach.[16] Beyond a concern with the state and politics, government here embraces the practices and processes through which individuals and bodies come to govern themselves.[17] This view of government as self-governance has implications for the way in which the freedom of the subjects of governance is conceived. For Miller and Rose:

> Modern political power does not take the form of the domination of subjectivity . . . Rather, political power has come to depend upon a web of technologies for fabricating and maintaining self-government.[18]

---

11 N. Rose, *Powers of Freedom: Reframing Political Thought* (1999) 3.
12 Dean, op. cit., n. 10, p. 16.
13 id., p. 19.
14 N. Rose, 'Government, Authority and Expertise in Advanced Liberalism' (1993) 22 *Economy and Society* 283, at 288.
15 See, for example, I. Ayres and J. Braithwaite, *Responsive Regulation: Transcending the Regulation Debate* (1992); N. Gunningham and P. Grabosky, *Smart Regulation* (1998).
16 Dean, op. cit., n. 10, pp. 10–11.
17 Rose, op. cit., n. 11, p. 3.
18 P. Miller and N. Rose, 'Governing Economic Life' (1990) 19 *Economy and Society* 1, at 28.

In this conception, power is exercised through the active (rather than passive or submissive) subject. The development of new technologies and rationalities of power stimulates agency while reconfiguring (rather than removing) constraints on the freedom of choice of agents, resulting in 'governing through freedom' and 'responsibilized autonomy'.[19] Government as 'the conduct of conduct' opens up for examination self-government, whether the actor be a human individual, or a collective or corporation in which there are multiple actors, or entities such as states and populations.

Thus, there is sufficient common ground in regulation and governance theories to suggest that a synthesis is possible and may be useful in the analysis of central-local relations.[20] However, while the approaches share a concern with processes of social control, direction and influence, there are fundamental differences in the form of inquiry and scope of explanation. In the regulation approach, the motivating force is the state as a 'purposeful actor'.[21] Governance theorists studying the exercise of political power through governmentality, on the other hand, address the narrower issue of what authorities of various sorts want to happen, in relation to problems defined how, in pursuit of what objectives, and through what strategies and techniques.[22] Here, the state is not the main focus of analysis. The concern is not with deliberate policy making or with the institutions and organizations involved the implementation of regulatory strategies, but with what Dean describes as 'an analytics of government.' The method of inquiry here involves examination of the intermeshing of 'regimes of practices', defined as 'more or less organized ways ... we think about, reform and practice such things as caring, administering, counselling, curing, punishing, educating and so on.'[23] While regimes of practices are associated with and become the objects of explicit *programmes* directed at transforming those practices, they have their own logic, and cannot be reduced to, or simply read off from, particular programmes or policies for reform. A further and related difference is the refusal of theorists of governance and governmentality to engage in policy evaluation. Miller and Rose are explicit on this point:

19 J. Morison, 'Democracy, Governance and Governmentality: Civic Public Space and Constitutional Renewal in Northern Ireland' (2001) 21 *Ox. J. of Legal Studies* 287.
20 For an exploration of the relationship between regulation and governmentality specifically in the field of housing, see D. Cowan and A. Marsh, 'Making Connections' in *Two Steps Forward: Housing Policy into the New Millennium*, eds. D. Cowan and A. Marsh (2001).
21 Accordingly, self-regulation may be defined as an internal regulatory process induced by government or public authority (compare M. Aalders and T. Wilthagen, 'Moving Beyond Command and Control: Reflexivity in the Regulation of Occupational Safety and Health and the Environment' (1997) 19 *Law and Policy* 415, at 427). Despite an apparent relaxation of control, 'the standards to be achieved, the limits to be observed are still set from above, or outside' – A. Dunsire, 'Holistic Governance' (1990) 5 *Public Policy and Administration* 4, at 6.
22 Rose, op. cit., n. 11, p. 20.
23 Dean, op. cit., n. 10, p. 22.

31

Policy studies tend to be concerned with evaluating policies, uncovering the factors that led to their success in achieving their objectives or, more usually ... their failure. We, on the other hand, are not concerned with evaluations of this type, with making judgements as to whether and why this or that policy succeeded or failed ...[24]

Since the present paper is concerned precisely with such evaluation, the perspective and analysis are basically regulatory, incorporating insights from theories of governance. The issue is not whether a regulatory approach is appropriate in the analysis of central-local relations, but what kind of regulatory approach. Even within regulatory theory, comparatively little attention has been accorded to policy objectives and the processes involved in their determination. In many fields, the fundamental regulatory purposes and underlying values may be relatively self-evident or uncontentious, as in the control of recognized 'harms' involving accidents and ill-health at work, cataclysmic damage to the environment, or high prices caused by producers' inefficiencies and excessive profits and wages. Problems of evaluation are multiplied in other regulatory contexts in which regulatory goals are not so obvious, where the harms are not so clear-cut, or there are choices to be made between conflicting public goods.[25]

VALUES AND PURPOSE: RESPONSIVE REGULATION

This section argues that responsiveness in regulation is closely bound up with values and purpose in government, particularly with issues concerning the design and implementation of policy. It also demonstrates how insights drawn from theories of governmentality may be incorporated within a refined regulation perspective drawing mainly on Nonet and Selznick's theory responsive law.

In Nonet and Selznick's account, responsive regulation is just one facet of a more general quest for the development of responsive law and a responsive

24 Miller and Rose, op. cit, n. 18, p. 4.
25 In environmental regulation, the sub-goals involved in the attainment of sustainable development are many and varied. The development of United Kingdom environmental law has been analysed in terms of the movement from a series of disparate controls 'towards a more co-ordinated system or systems of control, with perhaps a number of incipient guiding goals or (as appropriate) "principles"' (J. Steele and T. Jewell, *Law in Environmental Decision-Making* (1998) 11). Generally, 'optimality' is harder to assess when objectives of equity and political acceptability have to be considered alongside those of efficiency and effectiveness (Gunningham and Grabosky, op. cit., n. 15, p. 26). In the United Kingdom privatized utilities sector, economic policy objectives are overlain with social and distributive goals, based on the desire to counter the effects of unequal distribution of wealth and opportunity (Prosser, op. cit., n. 3, p. 10). Hidden economic objectives, garnered from the behaviour of regulators rather than policy statements, include the development of competitive markets (id., pp. 13–14). The more complex or politically sensitive the regulatory arena, the more problematic becomes the task of evaluation.

legal order. Following prior evolutionary stages of repressive law and autonomous law, responsiveness describes that stage in legal development where law is no longer the servant of repressive power, nor just a differentiated institution capable of taming repression and protecting its own integrity, but becomes rather a 'facilitator of response to social needs and aspirations'.[26] Responsive law is a problem-solving enterprise, bringing to bear a variety of powers and mobilizing an array of intellectual and organizational resources in dealing with change, and implying the 'capacity for responsible, and hence discriminate and selective, adaptation'.[27] The resolution of the tension between such openness to the external environment and legal integrity requires the 'guidance of purpose':

> Only when an institution is truly purposive can there be a combination of integrity and openness, rule and discretion ... hence, responsive law presumes that purpose can be made objective enough and authoritative enough to control adaptive rule making.[28]

The existence of a public interest or 'common good' that can be advanced through policy is fundamental to responsive law. With the growth in purposiveness, the distinction between legal analysis and policy analysis becomes blurred.[29] What is meant by policy is 'not detailed prescriptions but basic perspectives that determine how public purposes are defined and how practical alternatives are perceived'.[30] Nevertheless, a critical phase of responsive law is 'the definition of mission, that is, the translation of general purpose into specific objectives'.[31] The hallmark of the responsive legal order is *competence* in the exercise of public powers and functions by the legislature, executive, and administration generally. The notion of responsive regulation emerges against this background:

> If there is a paradigmatic function of responsive law, it is regulation, not adjudication. Broadly understood, regulation is the process of elaborating and correcting the policies required for the realization of a legal purpose. Regulation thus conceived is a mechanism for clarifying the public interest. It involves testing alternative strategies for the implementation of mandates and reconstructing those mandates in the light of what is learned.[32]

The centrality of policy and purpose in this account has been lost in subsequent adaptations of 'responsiveness' in the regulation literature. In their seminal work on responsive regulation, Ayres and Braithwaite comment only

26 P. Nonet and P. Selznick, *Law and Society in Transition: Toward Responsive Law* (1978; 2001, 2nd edn.) 14. This notion, which involves a commitment to the achievement of substantive as well as procedural justice, is rooted in the legal realist tradition of Jerome Frank and the sociological jurisprudence of Roscoe Pound (id., p. 73).
27 id., p. 110.
28 id., p. 77.
29 id., pp. 82–3.
30 id., p. 3.
31 id., p. 83.
32 id., pp. 108–9.

in passing on the similarity of their usage of this term with that of Nonet and Selznick, voicing scepticism of the evolutionary model of legal development and concerns about the risks of jettisoning the safeguards against repression provided by autonomous law.[33] A tradition of responsive regulation studies has grown up in which the fundamental purposes of regulation and the values underlying policy-making processes have not (for the reasons already indicated) been central issues. The result has been a tendency to reduce the assessment of regulation to the technical evaluation of efficiency and effectiveness in the attainment of given ends. In Nonet and Selznick's perspective, on the other hand, much tougher questions about governmental purposes and the implications for the integrity of law are to the fore.

1. Some difficulties with purposiveness

Three distinct but inter-linked problems may be said to arise from this attempt to elevate purpose and substance to a central position in regulatory analysis. These concern the past record of failure of welfarist interventions; the question of how state policies and regulatory objectives are determined; and the tension between substantive interventions and traditional rule of law values. These will be considered in turn.

First, with regard to the poor performance of welfarist regulation and the accompanying legitimation crisis of the state, it might be argued that Nonet and Selznick's thesis sits uneasily with the general acknowledgement of the failure of state direction and control, and with the still more fundamental loss of confidence in the state characteristic of post-modernity. Such factors informed Teubner's disenchantment (in 1983) with the goals and structures of the regulatory state, and his argument that Nonet and Selznick's typology of evolution of legal *orders* (from repressive, to autonomous, to responsive) should be substituted with an evolutionary typology of modern legal *rationalities* (from formal, to substantive, to reflexive). In particular, Teubner argued that Nonet and Selznick's account of the development of responsive from autonomous law had failed to distinguish adequately between two separate forms of rationality – on the one hand, the substantive rationality of results, and on the other hand, 'the "reflexive" rationality of the process-oriented structuring of institutions and the organizing of participation'.[34] The notion of responsive law, while containing elements of reflexivity,[35] was contaminated with substantive rationality – the ultimate cause of the state's regulatory failures. In Teubner's interpretation, 'purposiveness' in the state's actions is associated with *purposive programmes* implemented through regulations, standards, and principles;[36]

33 Ayres and Braithwaite, op. cit., n. 15, p. 53.
34 Teubner, op. cit., n. 1, p. 251.
35 id., p. 256.
36 id., p. 254.

34

with the authoritative prescription of 'ways and means of social integration';[37] and with the attempt generally 'to regulate social structures by legal norms, even though these structures do not always or easily bend to legal regulation'.[38] In contrast, reflexive law (founded on reflexive rationality) is not purposive in this sense; it 'retreats from taking full responsibility for substantive outcomes',[39] seeking instead 'to design self-regulating social systems through norms of organization and procedure'.[40] Teubner's thesis is open to numerous criticisms that will not be rehearsed here.[41] In the present context, the main point is that the 'sovereignty of purpose' in Nonet and Selznick's conception of responsive law does not necessarily imply a commitment to substantive state interventions involving either particularistic regulatory goals, or detailed prescriptions as to the means by which such goals should be achieved.[42] The solution to problems associated with the failures of state interventionism and welfarist regulation may be found in a more subtle conception of purposiveness than Teubner allows, either in the original concept of responsive law, or in its further refinement and development.

Secondly, there remains the question of what exactly might constitute responsiveness in state purposes, policies, and regulatory activities. Nonet and Selznick's original analysis addresses this issue only indirectly, arguing in general terms for the broadening of legal and political participation and the increased involvement of groups and organizations in the making of public policy through legal action and social advocacy.[43] As Black has pointed out, the argument for greater participation or deliberation in debates on regulation or policy-making offers not a solution but a new set of problems.[44] In this regard, Selznick's later work on institutional morality explores 'self-regarding or reflexive responsibility' as a dimension of responsiveness.[45] Decision making within institutions should be informed by

37 id., p. 255.
38 id., p. 274.
39 id., p. 254.
40 id., p. 255.
41 See Black, op. cit., n. 2.
42 Teubner's analysis does appear to allow for purposeful state activity in an analogous sense. Reflexive rationality 'shares with substantive law the notion that focused intervention in social processes is within the domain of law . . .' (op. cit., n. 1, p. 254). This begs the question of the nature of the 'focus', and how it is produced. See, also, Black's critique, op. cit., n. 2, pp. 604–5.
43 Nonet and Selznick, op. cit., n. 26, p. 96.
44 J. Black, 'Proceduralizing Regulation: Part II (2001) 21 *Ox. J. of Legal Studies* 33, at 37.
45 P. Selznick, *The Moral Commonwealth: Social Theory and the Promise of Community* (1992), at 338: 'Responsibility runs to an institutional self or identity; to those upon whom the institution depends; and the community whose well-being it affects. Thus responsiveness entails reconstruction of the self as well as outreach to others. Established structures, rules, methods, and policies are all open to revision, but revision takes place in a principled way, that is, while holding fast to values and purposes. This we might call self-regarding or reflexive responsibility.'

35

'process values' (eliminating bias, providing opportunities for reasoned argument, assuring accurate and reliable determination of facts, upholding legal stability, and so forth) underlying formal administrative and legal procedures.

> The idea of process is richer than that of procedure. It contains the whole matrix of values, purposes, and sensibilities that should inform a course of conduct. The integrity of process, thus understood, cannot be protected unless we appreciate those values, purposes and sensibilities. Therefore process requires the integration of means and ends.[46]

Similarly rejecting the purely procedural approach to legitimacy associated with Habermas, Black argues that issues of public decision-making need to be addressed through a conception of 'thick proceduralization' based on deliberative democracy. Allowing that 'public reason' has the potential to lead to shared understanding and consensus, Black points to the practical obstacles preventing the attainment of this ideal, and explores how differences between participants render problematic the notion that proceduralization can provide a model for regulation. These practical and theoretical problems are argued to require the *mediation* of deliberative democracy. Such mediation might provide the conditions of effective communication and public reason in various ways, by mapping differences and conflicts between deliberants, 'translating' otherwise incommensurate languages, making deliberants aware of the inclusionary and exclusionary effects of problem definition and modes of discourse, and facilitating strategies of dispute resolution.[47] This raises questions as to the precise role of the state in policy-formation, in particular regarding the locus of decision-making and whether regulators can act as mediators:

> A proceduralist model of regulation in which the deliberants themselves decide is indeed a qualitative shift in the nature of regulation. For no longer is the question how best to ensure that the ends that the state has determined are achieved within society, but how to arrange matters such that participants themselves can make the decisions as to what those ends should be.[48]

This implies that the proper role of the state might be to structure deliberations among decision-making fora beyond its boundaries, rather than just to guarantee the conditions of communication necessary for effective debate and public reason within the legislature. Habermas's conception of procedural law is ultimately limited 'in not providing for sufficient pluralism in norm formation or in the loci of regulation'.[49] As Black concedes, this analysis raises further questions, concerning the precise stages in the regulatory process deliberation might be expected to occur effectively, and the likelihood that thick proceduralization might

46 id., p. 331.
47 Black, op. cit., n. 44, p. 57.
48 id., p. 54.
49 id., p. 57.

36

need ultimately to abandon the search for full normative consensus and integration in favour of developing policies of tolerance to deal with irreconcilable difference.

Finally, with regard to the rule of law, Nonet and Selznick acknowledge the resemblance of responsive law to repressive law in certain respects (the loss of firm institutional boundaries between law and politics, the weakening of authority of rules, the enlargement of discretion, and the merging of legal and policy analysis) and the risk of regression from responsiveness to repression. Nevertheless, a 'moral gulf' is argued to separate the two legal orders:

> In repression, the integration of law and politics abridges the civilizing values of the rule of law, that is, legality conceived as fairness and restraint in the use of power. In a responsive legal order, the reintegration of law and government is a way of enlarging the meaning and reach of legal values from a set of minimal restrictions to a source of affirmative responsibilities.[50]

This argument is in line with modern interpretations of the rule of law, which are less concerned with particularism, administrative discretion and the absence of formal legality than with the rationality and justification of regulation, judged in terms of moral purpose and underlying values.[51]

2. Responsive regulation – a restatement

The threads of the foregoing analysis may now be drawn together in a restatement of the key characteristics of responsive regulation. In essence, regulation may be defined as the systematic exercise of control for the pursuit of public purposes (social as well as economic) through the linking of law to policy instruments of force, wealth, and information and persuasion.[52] While systematic control is likely to have been initiated by the state, a wide range of state and non-state actors may have regulatory inputs. The determination of regulatory objectives occurs in a 'public sphere', not confined to formal state institutions, involving more or less democratic political processes and more or less adequate public debate and deliberation. The designation 'responsive' implies that regulatory goals are

50 Nonet and Selznick, op. cit, n. 26, p. 117. At the heart of the protection of legal integrity, the commitment to participation ensures that the legal arena becomes a kind of political forum and that the scope of legal inquiry is enlarged, so contributing to the competence of legal institutions. Also underpinning the responsive legal order are legal pluralism and respect, not just for ordinary people and their legitimate expectations but for the 'living law' of private institutions (Selznick, op. cit., n. 45, p. 472).

51 See, for example, R. Cotterrell, 'The Rule of Law in Transition: Revisiting Franz Neumann's Sociology of Legality' (1996) 5 *Social and Legal Studies* 451.

52 Compare Selznick's definition of regulation as 'sustained and focused control by a public agency over activities that are valued by a community': P. Selznick, 'Focusing Organizational Research on Regulation' in *Regulatory Policy and the Social Sciences*, ed. R.G. Noll (1985) 363.

37

legitimate, this assessment being made with reference either to the quality of deliberative processes leading to policy formulation ('thick proceduralization'), or to the inner morality and 'process values' at work in public institutions ('thick institutionalization'), or to their combination. This position accords with Black's central argument that 'the technical aspect of a regulatory strategy cannot be considered in isolation from the normative or moral aspect',[53] and with the view that such a divorce of means and ends, and the primacy of the former, are precisely what the new orthodoxy in regulation studies appears to have achieved.[54] Nevertheless, responsiveness as a quality of regulation also implies efficiency and effectiveness in the use of regulatory means to the attainment of given ends.[55] The mechanisms and processes constituting 'smart' or 'optimal' regulation will be an essential part of any adequate analysis of regulation, or indeed of governance.

CENTRAL-LOCAL RELATIONS: REGULATION AND RESPONSIBILIZATION

While many of New Labour's policies appear indistinguishable from those of the Conservatives, current regulatory developments cannot be analysed adequately through perspectives rooted in the political conditions of the previous decade. It will be argued that the distinctive feature of central-local relations in the new millennium is *responsibilization* – a novel phenomenon that is not captured in the conceptual opposition of command and control/ oversight on the one hand, and partnership/collaboration/mutuality on the other.[56] This section considers in turn the purposes informing New Labour's programme for the reform of local government, the regulatory mechanisms being deployed in efforts to achieve them, and the role of techniques of responsibilization in regulatory processes.

53 Black, op. cit., n. 44, p. 57.
54 There is, however, a significant difference of emphasis and methodology in the two approaches. Whereas Black develops an analysis of proceduralization based on a critique of Habermas, the present paper returns to Nonet and Selznick's original notion of responsive law and to its later refinement in Selznick's work on institutional morality
55 On the theoretical difficulties of maintaining a distinction between means and ends, see Selznick, op. cit., n. 45, pp. 328–30.
56 It would not be enough, for example, simply to suggest that the present relationship between central and local government is characterized by greater mutuality, or a reduction in juridification. This would not explain the basis of the less adversarial and confrontational nature of that relationship.

1. Regulatory purposes under New Labour

In their current incarnation, government policies are underpinned by a general regulatory objective of replacing the confrontational and adversarial climate of the Conservative years with a new commitment to cooperation and partnership in the relationship between central and local government. While regulatory rationales cannot simply be deduced or read off from political statements or policy documents, and may have to be found in other sources and in the practical operation of regulatory schemes,[57] three fundamental purposes may be discerned in the present government's reform agenda.

First, central government policy continues to be directed at allocating new local functions, and redistributing functions hitherto performed by local government, among a wider range of public, private, and voluntary sector bodies. The growth in quangos or non-department public bodies (NDPBs) has long been a feature of local governance.[58] Under Conservative administrations, the ostensible aim of cutting down local authority bureaucracy hid the thinly-disguised purpose of bypassing elected local government.[59] The continued channelling of funding for public service provision through local public bodies such as housing associations, urban development corporations, grant-maintained schools, and training and enterprise councils may be regarded as part of a strategy aimed at fragmenting local powers and loyalties. At the political level, regional government in the form of regional development agencies or regional chambers, while scarcely a threat to local government at present, has the potential to become so in future.[60]

A second policy objective is to promote substitutes for markets (where these cannot be directly involved in provision of public goods) through quasi-markets combining increased consumer choice with competition between suppliers of services. While such arrangements have the capacity to increase economy, efficiency, and value for money in comparison with direct provision, the accompanying shift from political to consumer accountability also involves a weakening of traditional local government. Leigh has commented in this regard that 'experience suggests that local responsibility and accountability for services can be undermined not only by frontal attack but also by the creation or government sponsorship of parallel providers'.[61] The main rationale of a range of policies inherited from the Conservatives and continued in some form under New Labour is to create the conditions that will allow a mixture of public, private, and voluntary sector

57 Prosser, op. cit., n. 3, p. 10.
58 See I. Leigh, *Law, Politics and Local Democracy* (2000) 331–5.
59 id., p. 333.
60 id., p. 305.
61 id., p. 31.

provision to be locally determined by competitive forces. In housing, initiatives have been designed to expand the role of the non-profit sector and to encourage local authority landlords to compete with registered social landlords (RSLs). In education, while there have been some reversals of previous policy, the effect of league tables and other published information about schools is to create competition within the state sector. The corollary of competition between suppliers in these sectors is increased choice by consumers. In both housing and education, the position of local authorities as exclusive service providers has been undermined by the granting of individual and collective 'exit' rights to enable consumers to opt out of state provision.

Thirdly, current government policy is aimed at transforming the role of local authorities from one of direct service provision to that of community leadership and coordination. For example, in the housing field, the government wants to see a change in the local authority housing role from owning and managing stock ('housing management' as traditionally conceived), to 'managing housing' in the sense of overseeing provision by a variety of social landlords and different tenures.[62] In the communitarian version of the 'enabling' local authority, the function of councils is to identify local needs and problems, and to respond flexibly to these by facilitating initiatives involving partnerships between a wide range of actors in the local private and voluntary sectors. This new role entails a broadening of the responsibilities of local authorities, illustrated in the statutory duty under Best Value to make arrangements to secure continuous improvement in the way in which their functions are exercised, having regard to a combination of economy, efficiency, and effectiveness.[63] It also requires an expansion of legal competence, evident in the new power of councils to do anything, having regard to the effect on the achievement of sustainable development in the United Kingdom, which they consider is likely to promote or improve the economic, social, or environmental well-being of their area.[64]

2. Regulatory mechanisms

While the full range of regulatory resources has been used in various combinations in the recent history of the regulation of local by central government, in the period of Conservative political domination compulsion assumed a particularly prominent role. Under New Labour, there has been a distinct shift towards greater reliance on other regulatory mechanisms. Since the 1997 general election, increasingly varied *dominium* incentives and

---

62 P. Vincent-Jones, 'From Housing Management to the Management of Housing: The Challenge of Best Value' in Cowan and Marsh, op. cit., n. 20.

63 Local Government Act 1999, s. 3(1).

64 Local Government Act 2000, s. 2(1).

40

competitive pressures have been combined with more subtle forms of *imperium*. The major difference between Labour and Conservative policy, following widespread acknowledgement of the failures of crude 'command and control', lies not in policy ends but in the regulatory means being deployed for their attainment.

First, legislative commands backed by monitoring and sanctioning machinery remain a fundamental feature of current regulation. The recent change in regulatory style implies neither decentralization nor the disappearance of force. Although it is for local authorities themselves to devise how Best Value is to be achieved, this is to be done in the context of a centrally-determined framework based on performance indicators and standards. While sanctions are nowhere exactly specified, there are widely drafted default powers leaving considerable central discretion in their exercise. A feature of the Best Value framework is the ease with which rules and commands may be fine-tuned to particular local authority circumstances.[65] Less obviously, regulatory fine-tuning occurs through the selective relaxation of prohibitive rules, for example, governing local authority finances. 'Beacon' authorities that meet central government's criteria of excellent performance may be exempted from financial controls and restrictions that would otherwise apply, reflecting the philosophy that central interference should vary inversely with the demonstrable ability of authorities to manage their own affairs. The relaxation of financial prohibitions has also been used, in conjunction with the granting of new powers for specific purposes, as a means of inducing local authorities to explore new forms of service provision in partnership with the private sector.[66]

Secondly, the deployment of wealth instruments in the control of local authority activities is based on the increasing dependence of councils on

---

65 Authorities must have regard to any guidance issued by the Secretary of State concerning the conduct of Best Value reviews and the making of performance plans. Additional duties may be individually imposed on different authorities, applying at different times. Authorities may be required to consider or assess their objectives, performance, and progress in relation to any particular function, or whether they should be exercising the function at all.

66 Where councils have decided to retain housing stock, they are being encouraged to separate this ownership function from that of housing management through the Private Finance Initiative (PFI). Such schemes allow access to private finance unencumbered by public expenditure controls, without having to transfer ownership. In this type of PFI arrangement, the winning bidder is responsible for raising the funds to do the work (for example, refurbishment works, continuing management, repairs and maintenance services) with payment by the authority on a performance basis and in the form of annual service fees under a long-term contract rather than initial capital expenditure. In a separate initiative, new regulations will permit the setting up of arms-length companies, *controlled* or *influenced* by the local authority, to perform the specific function of housing management, so bypassing the normal rule that capital expenditure restrictions apply to local authority companies unless ownership is completely transferred to the voluntary sector.

central government funding following decades of erosion of their financial autonomy.[67] Such dependence enables local public functions to be finely controlled through the conditions attaching to specific grant schemes, as for example under the housing investment programme (HIP). Financial allocations by government offices for the regions (GOs) are based not just on indices of relative need, but on assessments of the quality of authorities' housing strategies, programme delivery, housing management, and tenant participation. These assessments are used in the allocation of half the housing capital resources, with higher shares going to better performers. Authorities that fall to meet targets may be penalized by the reduction of allocations by as much as one-fifth. Lack of financial independence also explains the increasing attractiveness to local authorities of 'voluntary transfer' of council housing stock as a means of 'generating' income through the release of otherwise frozen capital receipts, and off-loading housing responsibilities and liabilities to other social landlords (who enjoy relative freedom from public borrowing constraints).

Thirdly, the role of competition as a means of modifying the behaviour of local authorities has increased in recent years,[68] most clearly expressed in the policy of compulsory competitive tendering (CCT). Local authorities are under continuing pressure to outsource ancillary services to the private or voluntary sectors rather than provide them directly. The key difference between CCT and its successor, Best Value, is that competition is now being encouraged in a more subtle and less coercive manner. Rather than being prescribed for any particular function, the spirit of competition pervades the entire regulatory framework. While on the face of it a local authority has the freedom to provide services using traditional or innovative methods, it is unlikely in practice to be able to demonstrate Best Value to the satisfaction of auditors and the Secretary of State by following just the 'traditional' route. In another sense, local authorities are competing among themselves – for the achievement of performance targets and for position in league tables, for the rewards attaching to Beacon status, for the financial benefits associated with qualification for PFI and arms-length company schemes, and for the right to transfer housing stock to the private sector. Local authorities are competing also with other providers in the private and voluntary sectors for the right to provide core services such as housing and education, and for recognition as

67 In the 1980s the introduction of the 'block grant' mechanism enabled central government to withhold grants from local authorities that overspent centrally imposed targets. From 1984 'rate capping' restricted the ability of councils to raise funds through local taxation. The financial autonomy of local authorities was further curtailed after 1992 by stringent controls on spending based on Standard Spending Assessments (SSAs). While 'crude and universal' capping was abolished under the Local Government Act 1999, it was replaced with more 'discriminating and flexible' reserve powers to limit council tax increases deemed excessive by central government.

68 Hood et al., op. cit., n. 7, p. 94.

42

primary vehicles for the promotion of innovation and partnership in the performance of public functions.[69] In a further sense, as has been seen, the rationale for encouraging private-public sector partnerships and joint ventures is to improve performance of public functions through the involvement of private management skills honed in organizations that have been operating under competitive market conditions.

Fourthly, the availability and circulation of information is playing an increasingly important part in regulatory processes. The relative performance of providers in the same and different sectors is being made increasingly transparent through information published in performance tables, which may inform future choices made by public purchasers or enable pressure to be brought to bear by consumers. The Service First (successor to the Citizens Charter) programme, which applies to local government as well as to the central state, quangos, privatized and public sector utilities, requires the setting and publication of standards, and the publication of performance against these. This information can be used as a method for calling officials and councillors to account, requiring them to justify their priorities in comparison with those of other councils. Such information may also reveal disparities between providers that are not the product of conscious choice, may provide politicians with clear evidence of how officers are performing, and may enable any improvement or deterioration of performance within given authorities to be plotted over time.[70] Performance indicators and targets are thus drivers of improvement, providing a measure against which authorities, service users, external auditors, the Housing Inspectorate, and government offices can judge how well a service is performing. Under Best Value, local authorities are required to provide information to local people in conducting reviews as part of the consultation process. Local people will be informed of progress on targets set in previous years in published performance plans. The reports of auditors and the Audit Commission will similarly be published. The general publication of information is intended to encourage authorities to learn from one another and to spread good practice.

Finally, with regard to the form of law, it has been suggested that there has been a general shift in the mode of regulation away from reliance solely on legislation imposing powers and duties towards legal devices, most obviously contracts, associated with the private sector.[71] Clearly the changing role of local authorities implies the need for general reform of contractual powers if they are to fulfil new responsibilities. One of the main tasks confronting central government is how to provide institutional mechanisms for the 're-assembly' of the fragmented local state through contracts, partnerships, and joint ventures linking the various private and

69 M. Loughlin, *Legality and Locality: The Role of Law in Central-Local Government Relations* (1996)
70 Leigh, op. cit., n. 58, p. 146.
71 id., p. 305.

public agencies performing public functions.[72] However, the unqualified view that private legal institutions are becoming more important may underplay the public character of many of the new contracting arrangements, and the extent to which they are the specific creations of government policies. Rather than just regulating pre-existing contracts, state intervention in such instances is giving rise to novel contractual forms that are the specific product of policies implementing them. Research is investigating the proposition that at the heart of these developments lies a distinctive mode of governance characterized by the delegation and devolution of contracting powers to local authorities (and to other public agencies such as education bodies, school head-teachers, public-private partnership organizations, the Legal Services Commission, youth offender panels) in regulatory frameworks preserving central government controls and powers of intervention.[73]

3. Techniques of responsibilization

From the perspective of governmentality, these regulatory developments may be said to be expressed in (and synonymous with) the responsibilization of local government, reflecting the alignment of the organizational thinking and strategies of local authorities with central policy objectives through the common acceptance and application of 'neutral' criteria of proper administration. The focus here is on how power relations are constituted through forms of knowledge, calculation, and evaluation, rather than through regulatory institutions and mechanisms. Augmenting the regulatory analysis provided in the previous sections, this approach addresses the key question of how a situation has been created in which the 'game' between central and local government has ceased to be adversarial and conflictual in nature, and to have become governed instead by common objectives supported by a renewed commitment to partnership and cooperation. It helps explain the apparent paradox of continuing centralization involving erosion of the traditional powers and autonomy of local government on the one hand, combined with less prescriptive regulation and even increased powers in certain fields on the other. The fundamental shift in the role of local government is being achieved, not by commands backed by force, but through 'responsibilized autonomy'. Three responsibilization techniques are of particular significance in the present context: accounting, audit, and contracting.

As regards accounting, the gradual imposition of new modes of financial calculation has been crucial to the transformation of the public sector. Financial management regimes have played a major part in reforming public bureaucracies and in displacing governance by traditional hierarchical norms.

---

72 See id., ch. 10.
73 P. Vincent-Jones, 'Regulation and Responsibilization: The New Public Contracting in Socio-Legal Perspective', ESRC Research Fellowship award no. R000271186.

Developments in accounting technology have resulted in the incursion of financial rationality, with its vocabulary of costs, incomes, savings, and profits, into all aspects of the operation of local authorities. Like other public sector organizations, local authorities have become increasingly accountable in these financial, rather than bureaucratic or professional terms. Under CCT, direct service organizations (DSOs) became cost centres with trading accounts, subject to 'accounting logic'.[74] Where NPM reforms have devolved decision-making power to individuals or business units within organizations, the activities have been rendered governable in new ways, through the neutrality and objectivity of accounting. Within the complex of financial techniques for the government of bureaucratic and professional expertise, audit is playing a key role.[75] Audit is part of a more general process that renders modern government possible and judgeable through quantitative information in the form of rates, tables, graphs, trends, and numerical comparisons that enable the scrutiny of authority in contemporary society.[76] Through enumeration and quantification, governance is organized through objective principles and neutral 'facticity'. The formal autonomy of local authorities or of departments or business units within them may increase at the same time as they become more governable through the use of techniques that render activities and decisions more visible and amenable to external scrutiny.

In essence audit involves the use of routines that 'purport to enable judgements to be made about the activities of professionals, managers, businesspeople, politicians, and many others'.[77] Government by audit 'transforms that which is to be governed' in a similar manner to accounting, in this instance through the emphasis on defined and measurable goals and targets, the setting of objectives, the standardization of forms of assessment, and new systems of record-keeping and accountability. In local government, the function of audit has shifted from ensuring that public money is spent lawfully and without fraud, to checking the reasonableness of discretionary expenditure and value for money in the delivery of services. Since 1982 the Audit Commission has been an enthusiastic promoter of NPM reforms, assuming an increasingly proactive role in disseminating private management practice, undertaking studies into specific areas of public services, and overseeing and coordinating audit processes.[78] What is significant in the present context is not the statutory duties of the Commission or its oversight functions, but the methods and techniques on

---

74 R. Laughlin, 'Accounting Control and Controlling Accounting: The Battle for the Public Sector' (1991) Sheffield University Management School discussion paper no. 92–29.
75 Rose, op. cit., n. 11, p. 153.
76 id., p. 198.
77 id., p. 154.
78 Leigh, op. cit., n. 58, p. 128. The Commission's role is expanding through increased powers under recent legislation to undertake comparative reviews of local authority functions as well as services – LGA 1999, s. 19.

45

which its judgements are based. Under both Best Value and the Service First initiatives, audit takes the form of comparative evaluation of the relative performance of local authorities with reference to centrally determined performance indicators and standards, involving a combination of flat-rate and flexible (self-imposed) targets. The impact of audit (rendering transparent the decisions of councillors and officials over their priorities, revealing disparities that are not the product of conscious choice, providing politicians and consumers with evidence on how authorities are performing, and enabling comparison of performance over time within particular authorities[79]) is magnified through the increasingly detailed and sophisticated presentation of comparative information.

Finally, the growth in contracting is not just an institutional response to the need for links between more fragmented agencies (public, private, and voluntary) performing local public functions; rather, it entails a distinctive way of thinking about public organization, with its own rationality and logic. The penetration of contracting as a technique of governance is evident in the increasingly varied use of contractual terminology and discourse in social contexts far removed from the lawyer's traditional concerns.[80] The selective granting by central government of increased contractual powers (to certain authorities for certain purposes and subject to certain conditions) is illustrative of responsibilization. In narrow economic terms, the argument for contracting as a mode of organization in preference to direct public provision is that it offers benefits of increased efficiency associated with competition and exposure to market forces.[81] More broadly, public contracting enables the public purchasing or client agency to control the provision of services in a way that would not be possible under bureaucratic organization. Just as important, however, the new public contracting also implies a governance relationship between the state and public agencies, through the regulatory conditions attaching to powers granted and the subjection of these bodies to on-going monitoring and supervision by central government.

The very relationship between central and local government is being cast as a social contract in which councils may earn increased freedoms in return for undertakings to pursue courses of action in conformity with central government policy. Local authorities in England are currently being encouraged to sign 'local public service agreement' (PSAs), in which administrative freedoms are granted and extra funds made available

---

79 id., p. 146.
80 P. Vincent-Jones, 'Contractual Governance: Institutional and Organizational Analysis' (2000) 20 *Ox. J. of Legal Studies* 317.
81 J. Le Grand and W. Bartlett (eds.), *Quasi-Markets and Social Policy* (1993); W. Bartlett, C. Propper, D. Wilson., and J. Le Grand. (eds.), *Quasi-Markets in the Welfare State: The Emerging Findings* (1994); W. Bartlett, J. Roberts, and J. Le Grand (eds.), *Quasi-market Reforms in the 1990s: A Revolution in Social Policy* (1998).

to councils making commitments to ambitious targets for improving services. The combination of increased funding and the easing of the burdens of the intensive local government and auditing regime are intended to operate as an additional incentive for local authorities to develop strategic plans to tackle identified problems in the fields of crime control, transport, social work, and education and training. The underlying principle of 'earned autonomy' is openly acknowledged in policy documents, and is likely to inform a similar scheme soon to be introduced in the health sector to reward the best NHS Trusts. The transparent agenda of 'micro-management' of local government, in effect 'bribing councils to make the government's priorities their own', is also recognized in criticisms of the new contracts.[82] Nevertheless, the government maintains that it was local authorities themselves (through the Local Government Association) that provided the impetus for the current pilot scheme. Furthermore, while councils were given an indication of the areas in which ministers wanted to see improvements through PSAs, they made their own choices and developed their own proposals. This specific responsibilization policy operates in addition to more general Best Value and related schemes that are already underpinned by the philosophy of responsibilized autonomy. The apparent popularity and success of the initiative can only be understood in the context of the operation of a whole range of regulatory mechanisms and particular responsibilization techniques whose combined effect has been not just to make local authorities willing participants, but proactive instigators of their self-regulation.

RESPONSIVENESS IN CENTRAL-LOCAL REGULATION

This section suggests how these recent trends in central-local regulation might be assessed with reference to criteria of responsiveness. Rather than attempt a detailed evaluation, the more limited aim here is to provide an overview of the major issues that need to be addressed in further studies in particular sectors. Before going on to consider regulatory effectiveness and the policy-making and implementation processes, the principle and practice of central interference with local autonomy will be briefly considered.

1. Central control versus local autonomy?

Under United Kingdom constitutional law there is no protected core of local government functions safe from central interference. Local authorities as organizations are the subject of regulatory intervention in a much more

---

82 S. Parker,'It's A Deal' *Guardian*, 4 July 2001.

fundamental sense than businesses.[83] Whereas the objectives and powers of the private corporation may be covered by wide objects clauses in standard memorandum and objects of incorporation, in local government the legal parameters are imposed by tightly drawn statutory powers and duties that cannot be changed by the authority itself.[84] The interests, objectives, and structures of the regulated bodies are also very different.[85] What is being regulated in the local government sector is the performance of a whole range of 'public' functions by a large number of heterogeneous individual local authorities that differ in nature, size, and geographical location. Rather than being directed at the prevention of harms, the object of regulation is the improvement of the performance of public functions or delivery of public goods. Consideration of the legitimacy of central interference with local autonomy is complicated by the status of local councils as elected representatives, with their own democratic mandate and claims to legitimacy.[86] Nevertheless, the case for the central state having ultimate authority and control subject to proper democratic accountability is compelling. Central government has superior resources and better access to information in determining local issues, and is also in a position to coordinate reform on the basis of best local management practice among all authorities. Central controls over local taxation and expenditure are necessary in order to maintain international competitiveness and to pursue national economic and social policy goals. For these and other reasons it is difficult to define a minimum core of local government functions that should be constitutionally guaranteed. Such a guarantee might also carry the danger of preventing or impeding forms of centrally imposed reorganization necessary to deal with local authorities that had become unresponsive.[87]

The discussion of governmentality has already indicated the limitations of the notion of state interference with individual autonomy as an organizing theoretical perspective in modern political analysis. In the present context, what is of interest is not so much the scope of local government powers and freedoms, as the potential for the articulation of central and local democratic processes in responsive combinations. This implies a need for forms of

---

83 While in company law 'the legal regime is concerned with procedural matters only, leaving the raison d'être of the enterprise to those who control and own it, in local government the law governs both' (Leigh, op. cit., n. 58, p. 36).

84 id., p. 38.

85 In their comparative analysis of environmental and occupational health and safety regulation, Aalders and Wilthagen begin by contrasting the regulated 'target' groups in terms of the interests, objectives, and structures of the actors (op. cit., n. 21, p. 417).

86 The European Charter of Local Self-Government 1985, ratified by the United Kingdom in 1998, commits parties to the Treaty to basic rules guaranteeing the political, administrative, and financial independence of local authorities, and elections based on universal suffrage.

87 'We must not be starry-eyed about local government': Loughlin, op. cit., n. 69, p. 380.

representation and participation that give adequate expression to local preferences, but within a deliberative 'public sphere' in which fundamental regulatory purposes are determined ultimately at the national level through a variety of democratic processes and fora, underpinned by core democratic values. The key issue in the assessment of changes brought about by central government interventions concerns whether the performance of, and accountability for, local 'public' functions have thereby been improved or diminished. Where local authorities as opposed to other bodies are involved in such functions, the question is similarly whether their ability to operate as responsive institutions has been increased or impaired. But local government, either in its present or any future form, appears to have no ontologically privileged claim over other public agencies exclusively to perform local public functions.

2. Regulatory effectiveness

The quality of a regulatory regime may be assessed most directly in principle through scrutiny of its effectiveness. The issue here concerns the efficiency of the regulatory means deployed for the attainment of given ends, and in particular, whether policy goals are being achieved at the least possible level of inputs or costs.[88] This way of posing the problem assumes that technical evaluation can be isolated from distributional considerations, and that regulatory objectives can be deduced from policy documents or other sources. The implication is that regulation cannot be responsive if policy goals either are not achieved, or are incapable of achievement. Neither can regulation be responsive if the costs associated with the mechanisms implementing the policy are disproportionate to the ends being sought. These conditions of responsiveness raise difficult questions, for example, about how and when success or failure are judged, especially in the case of general or nebulous goals; about whether any policy can ever be said to be finally and completely successful; about the level at which costs become regarded as excessive and therefore indicative of regulatory ineffectiveness; and about what kinds of costs (economic, social) are taken into account in the evaluation process.[89]

Assuming the theoretical validity of the questions posed, various aspects of implementation of policy might be assessed through empirical research. With regard to *imperium* regulation, the issue is whether the powers and duties of local authorities are appropriate or sufficient to enable them to achieve central policy objectives. Regulation cannot be

---

88 See Baldwin and Cave, op. cit., n. 4, pp. 81–2.
89 Even in narrow economic terms, the evidence suggests a relative lack of awareness of the cost of regulation in local government, and a tradition of 'overlapping and cost-unconscious' regulation in the growth of inspectorates, overseers, ombudsmen, and auditors: see Hood et al., op. cit., n. 7, pp. 98–101.

49

responsive where the agencies charged with the performance of public functions are so hobbled by legal restrictions and constraints that they are incapable of achieving the targets they have agreed or been set. Leigh argues generally that central government interference and controls are undermining local responsiveness in just this sense. The same point may be made differently by asking whether the combination of legal powers, duties, and constraints under which local authorities are having to make choices about how public services are provided enables them to make 'optimal' selections of the best institutional arrangement in the given conditions.[90] With regard to *dominium* regulation, the analogous issue is whether tasks are capable of performance with the level of resources provided, given the financial dependence of local authorities on central government and the extent of public borrowing restrictions and spending controls. With regard to information and competition, the question in particular geographical locations or regulatory fields is how well these mechanisms are working, and how to identify and remove obstacles impairing their operation.

In addition to such assessment of the effectiveness of individual regulatory mechanisms, the overall effect of the interplay between them needs to be considered. The term 'collibration' has been used to describe the attainment of a desired balance of conflicting forces in a regulated field, resulting from some form of intervention or interference involving the selective introduction of bias or compensatory pressures.[91] While this concept suggests a positive outcome of the mixing of regulatory mechanisms, a negative outcome would be one where the mechanisms cancelled one another out, or operated to the detriment of other values or desired goals.[92] The outcome would also be negative where the mechanisms did not conflict, but where there was duplication of effort, or inefficiencies resulting from poor communication between agencies performing complementary tasks.

90 P. Vincent-Jones, 'Hybrid Organization, Contractual Governance, and Compulsory Competitive Tendering in the Provision of Local Authority Services' in *Contracts, Co-operation, and Competition: Studies in Economics, Management and Law*, eds. S. Deakin and J. Michie (1997).

91 A. Dunsire, 'Tipping the Balance: Autopoiesis and Governance' (1996) 28 *Public Administration* 299. Whereas Dunsire considers collibration to be a third mode of control distinct from both regulation and self-regulation (Dunsire, op. cit., n. 21, p. 6), the notion may be incorporated within a regulatory perspective. For a theoretical development and application in this vein, see C. Scott, 'Accountability in the Regulatory State' (2000) 27 *J. of Law and Society* 38.

92 For example, there may be a tension between the free availability of information necessary for consumers to make choices about public services and for providers to be held to account, and the need for commercial confidentiality to prevent the substance of contracts and negotiations leading up to their award becoming public and so undermining competition.

50

The assessment of regulatory effectiveness requires consideration not just of whether policy objectives are achieved and at what cost, but of unintended consequences and side effects. For example, where PSA schemes succeed in improving council performance in targeted service areas, this might result in other services being relatively neglected and starved of resources. Where the policy of increasing diversity of social housing provision is successful in reducing the landlord role of local authorities, new problems may be being created by excessively large and unresponsive housing associations, and by the escalating costs to the taxpayer of the housing benefit system that subsidizes the private rented sector.[93] Present housing policies might also be judged severely deficient if their effect is to perpetuate social disadvantage by further marginalizing an 'underclass' of citizens in poor quality council housing.[94]

While such questions remain to be addressed, it is likely that the change in the style of regulation under New Labour has led to increased regulatory effectiveness by comparison with preceding Conservative administrations. Policy-makers appear to have learned the lesson of the failures of prescriptive and formalistic regimes such as CCT, which merely encouraged local authorities in the 1990s to divert their energies from the improvement of services into undermining regulatory processes.[95] The form of regulation adopted by New Labour is more likely to succeed in achieving the government's immediate policy objectives. Best Value and associated policies are also likely to be relatively successful in the sense of reducing the economic costs of stipulating rules in detail and monitoring and adjudicating disputes, and avoiding numerous cultural costs associated with the command-and-control style of regulation.[96]

3. Deliberation and participation in policy making

It has been suggested that there are no convincing arguments in principle against the regulation of local by central government by whatever means, including compulsion and the use of force. The manner in which the reform of local government has been brought about, however, is more open to

93 F. Field, 'How to beat the new slum landlords' *Guardian*, 7 August 2001.
94 Generally, see Cotterrell, op. cit., n. 51, p. 460.
95 The attempt to close loopholes by tightening the rules through secondary legislation led to further avoidance, confusion, and the constant revision of implementation timetables. As McBarnet and Whelan commented in a different but analogous context, 'How do you control those playing by the rules? New rules simply mean new games' (D. McBarnet and C. Whelan, 'The Elusive Spirit of the Law; Formalism and the Struggle for Legal Control' (1991) 54 *Modern Law Rev.* 848, at 873).
96 The lack of precision in Best Value rules undermines the basis of strategies of avoidance by local authorities (even assuming they had the will to oppose regulation) since there is little that is concrete with which they can 'creatively comply.'

question. In the period of Conservative government from 1979, there was a general decline in public consultation and debate in the legislative process, with a trend away from Royal Commissions, official inquiries, and Green Papers, and fewer White Papers.[97] As regards structural reorganization, there was little consultation or debate prior to the abolition of the GLC and metropolitan county councils in 1986, in contrast to earlier reforms that had been preceded by years of deliberation. Where there were procedures for independent review, as by the Local Government Commission examining proposals for reform of the two-tier system in non-metropolitan areas, there was constant interference by ministers promoting their preferred option of unitary authorities.[98] At the same time, changes in parliamentary procedure further restricted the opportunity for debate through 'guillotine' motions, and there was a marked increase in provisions enabling primary legislation to be amended by ministers in secondary legislation without full parliamentary scrutiny.

Given this lack of debate and consultation over the principles and purposes of legislation both in Parliament and in the public arena more generally, it is unsurprising that law-making in this period is widely considered to have lacked legitimacy. In terms of the present analysis, it failed thereby to meet an essential criterion of responsiveness. The 'hidden agendas' of Conservative policy (destroying the public-sector unions, undermining Labour-controlled local authorities, weakening local government generally) may hardly have been secret, but neither were they expressly articulated or adequately debated. It is not that such ends might not have been legitimate, but that there was a significant democratic deficit in the absence of public debate on the purposes and values underlying the government's reforms. Since the 1997 general election there has been greater consultation over the agenda for modernizing local government, and the present legislative programme appears to have a more popular mandate.[99] The adversarial relationship between central and local government has given way to one of greater partnership and cooperation. Even assuming that these

97 The general experience was of 'fewer consultative documents being issued, containing less information and analysis, and often being produced on a timetable which seems to defeat the ostensible objective of the exercise' (Loughlin, op. cit., n. 69, p. 387). Consultation documents assumed an increasingly promotional rather than exploratory form.
98 Leigh, op. cit., n. 58, pp. 16–22.
99 There was a two-year period of consultation on Best Value, including the publication of principles and consultation papers, the commissioning and monitoring of pilot projects, and Select Committee hearings at which ministers were required to explain policy and clarify details. The government has taken account of academic research on the experiences of Best Value pilot authorities, and made concessions during the legislative process. Representative organizations such as the Local Government Association and the Improvement and Development Agency have been consulted and involved in policy development, for example, in relation to Best Value performance indicators and inspections.

52

developments are indicative of increased legitimacy, however, further aspects of responsiveness remain to be considered. From a liberal theoretical standpoint, the change in regulatory style might be regarded as having done little to reverse the trends in previous law making, and may even be a retrograde step. Adopting Fuller's criterion of the 'internal morality' of law, which requires a rule-system that is general, accessible, prospective, and predictable enough to serve as a guide to action, then the present regime may be found wanting.[100] The Best Value framework may be criticized for its particularistic mode of regulation, broad administrative discretion, and lack of consistency and predictability in application.[101] A range of widely drafted default powers may be exercised by the Secretary of State in response to Best Value failures, including the power to direct that specified functions be subject to 'emergency intervention.' Generally, outcome regulation of the type embodied in Best Value may be regarded as inherently uncertain and unpredictable.[102] The concern has been voiced that under Best Value, 'freedom will be given only to those councils where the straitjacket is a snug fit'.[103] In this perspective, strategies of responsibilization and the effectiveness of regulation acquire sinister connotations of manipulation and control.

While such dangers are real and should not be underestimated, the argument of the present paper is that the new forms of regulation are potentially fully consistent with increased responsiveness. As has been seen, the use of force backed by central authority may be justified in principle in order to deal with unaccountable and unresponsive corporate bodies, including local authorities, wielding excessive power.[104] The most important condition of responsiveness is adequate public participation and deliberation over the purposes being pursued in policies on central-local relations, as a source not just of legitimacy but of more effective policy-making leading to better regulatory outcomes.[105] In this light, the involvement of responsibilization in regulatory processes becomes more ambiguous in its implications. The inherent 'neutrality' of the technologies of audit,

---

100 Loughlin's assessment of local government reforms in the 1980s uses this benchmark (op. cit., n. 69, p. 398).
101 See P. Vincent-Jones, 'Central-Local Relations under the Local Government Act 1999: A New Consensus?' (2000) 63 *Modern Law Rev.* 84, at 89–92.
102 By comparison, the CCT rules were prospective and enabled authorities to calculate the likely consequences of their compliance with or infraction of formal rules (although the rules became increasingly unclear and difficult to implement as the white-collar programme progressed).
103 *Local Government Chronicle*, 6 November 1998.
104 The fact that power relations are embedded in relational structures does not mean that those relations should never be broken up; see P. Vincent-Jones, 'The Reception of Ian Macneil's Work on Contract in the UK' in *The Relational Theory of Contract: Selected Works of Ian Macneil,* ed. D. Campbell (2001).
105 J. Steele, 'Participation and Deliberation in Environmental Law: Exploring a Problem-solving Approach' (2001) 21 *Ox. J. of Legal Studies* 415.

53

enumeration, and quantification implies autonomization and a capacity for increasing freedom. The responsive potential here may lie in challenging policy prescriptions of central government and the actions of regulators in these same languages, which may thereby operate both as constraints and pressures for improvement in the performance of regulatory institutions. In a similar manner, the growing use of contracting systems provides parties to contractual arrangements with grounds to challenge central authority and the actions of regulators for breach of terms of the agreement.

The core values of democracy, participation, and citizenship are at the heart of responsiveness in the regulatory process. Participation as a constitutional value needs to apply to both policy formation and implementation, and to occur on a continuous and ongoing rather than original and once-and-for-all basis. The proper ground for criticism of both the Conservative and New Labour regulatory styles is failure to observe these values. The issue of whether values informing regulatory policy are, in ideological terms, individualistic or collectivist should be irrelevant in the evaluation of regulatory responsiveness.[106]

CONCLUSION

This paper has provided an account of contemporary developments in central-local relations, focusing on local government not just as a regulated entity, but on the technologies and practices through which it is governed and participates in its own governance. The most important factor in securing the alignment of local authority strategy with central policies, and the pre-requisite for successful *dominium* regulation, has been the imposition of public borrowing regulations and expenditure controls that have restricted the financial autonomy of councils. This has prepared the ground for the assimilation within the operations of local authorities – as necessary means to their survival as organizations – of common vocabularies of financial calculation and techniques of measurement, evaluation, and monitoring, without the need for central direction. An environment has been created for councils in which outcomes desired by central government are being produced by self-regulation, rather than being specifically required or dictated. Under such conditions, particularistic interventions become both unnecessary and counter-productive, being replaced by mechanisms of the 'government of government'.

The focus on central-local relations has raised issues of general relevance and significance for the theory and practice of regulation, in particular concerning the need for a broad framework for the evaluation and assessment of regulation in its multiple technical, purposive, and procedural

---

106 This is not to deny that the absolutist character often assumed by rights discourse tends to marginalize collective values – see Loughlin, op. cit., n. 69, pp. 415–16.

dimensions. The ideal of responsive regulation implies not just effectiveness, but the harnessing of all regulatory forces and 'governmental' resources in endeavours to achieve legitimate regulatory purposes. Questions of legitimacy have been pushed to the forefront of the present discussion due to the essentially political character of local government, and the inevitable contentiousness of attempts by central government to restructure, reform or otherwise circumscribe the sphere of operations of councils. But such issues are likely to be of similar (if less obvious) importance in other regulatory arenas.

The question of whether the conditions of public reason and deliberation are adequately met in current policy on central-local relations raises further issues concerning the proper nature, extent, and locus of debate. There needs to be greater local choice and involvement in matters affecting local people, for example, in decisions about how local public services are provided and how public infrastructure projects such as hospitals are financed and managed. But in what ways should local interests and preferences be included in the determination of central policy? To what extent should decision-making be devolved to local government, or to other public agencies, or to regional assemblies? The 'participation' that central government is currently keen for local citizens to enjoy may not be the type of participation they either need or want. Generally, the precondition of adequate public participation and involvement would appear to be greater openness, better and more complete information, and a much higher standard of public debate over central-local policy than has recently been the case.

JOURNAL OF LAW AND SOCIETY
VOLUME 29, NUMBER 1, MARCH 2002
ISSN: 0263-323X, pp. 56–76

Private Regulation of the Public Sector: A Neglected Facet of Contemporary Governance

Colin Scott*

The centrality of regulation among the tools deployed by governments is well established in the social science literature. Regulation of public sector bodies by non-state organizations is an important but neglected aspect of contemporary governance arrangements. Some private regulators derive both authority and power from a legal mandate for their activities. Statutory powers are exercised by private regulators where they are delegated or contracted out. Contractual powers take collective (for example, self-regulatory) and individuated forms. But a further important group of private regulators, operating both nationally and internationally, lack a legal mandate and yet have the capacity to exercise considerable power in constraining governments and public agencies. In a number of cases private regulators operate more complete regulatory regimes (in the sense of controlling standard setting, monitoring, and enforcement elements) than is true of public regulators. While private regulators may enhance the scrutiny given to public bodies (and thus enhance regimes of control and accountability), their existence suggests a need to identify the conditions under which such private power is legitimately held and used. One such condition is the existence of appropriate mechanisms for controlling or checking power. Such controls may take the classic form of public oversight, but may equally be identified in the checks exercised by participation in communities or markets.

* Centre for the Analysis of Risk and Regulation, London School of Economics and Political Science and Law Program, Research School of Social Sciences, Australian National University, Canberra, ACT 0200 Australia

I am grateful to participants at the joint Law and Society Association and Research Committee for the Sociology of Law annual meeting, Budapest, July 2001 and to Peter Cane, Sacha Courville, Christopher Hood, Peter Grabosky, Robert Kaye, Martin Lodge, Janet McLean, and Imelda Maher for comments on an earlier draft.

INTRODUCTION

Regulation has become the modality of choice for state activity in recent years, prompting claims that we live in the age of the 'regulatory state'.[1] These claims are based largely on the observation of the centrality of government regulation of business to modern governance arrangements and the displacement of governance modes associated with the welfare state such as public ownership, direct provision, and integrated bureaucracies for policy making and operational tasks. More recently the growth industry in the regulation of public sector bodies by other parts of government has been identified, mapped, and analysed.[2] This article provides an analytical framework for understanding a further, related trend, towards systematic oversight of government (akin to regulation) carried out by *private* (that is, non-state or non-governmental) actors. The role of private organizations – and in particular firms and NGOs – in modern governance has long been recognized, in particular in the public policy literature on networks.[3] However this literature has largely focused on policy making rather than implementation.[4] The literature on regulatory enforcement has analysed the interdependence of the private and public sectors in the implementation process.[5] However, systematic oversight by the private sector of public sector policy implementation has been substantially neglected both by public policy analysts and regulatory scholars and represents a significant lacuna in the literature.[6]

Private regulation of the public sector is far from new. A variety of private families and companies have exercised controls over particular states at various times since the inception of the nation state.[7] More recently both firms and interest groups have exercised something akin to systematic

1 J. Braithwaite, 'The New Regulatory State and the Transformation of Criminology' (2000) 40 *Brit J. of Crim.* 222 and references cited therein.
2 C. Hood et al., *Regulation Inside Government: Waste-Watchers, Quality Police, and Sleaze-Busters* (1999).
3 D. Marsh and R.A.W. Rhodes, *Policy Networks in British Politics* (1992).
4 An exception is provided by P. Grabosky, 'Using Non-Governmental Resources to Foster Regulatory Compliance' (1995) 8 *Governance* 527.
5 For example, B. Hutter, *Compliance* (1997); P. Grabosky and J. Braithwaite, *Of Manners Gentle* (1986); J. Freeman, 'The private role in public governance' (2000) 75 *New York – University Law Rev.* 543.; C. Hall et al., *Telecommunications Regulation. Culture, Chaos and Interdependence Inside the Regulatory Process* (2000).
6 For example there is no discussion of private regulation over government in H. Aquina and H. Bekke, 'Governance in Interaction: Public Tasks and Private Organizations' in *Modern Governance: New Government-Society Interactions*, ed. J. Kooiman (1992) or in other essays in that influential collection. Private regulation over government is also neglected in K. Ronit and V. Schneider, 'Global Governance Through Private Organizations' (1999) 12 *Governance* 243. The potential for private oversight of government illegality is discussed by P. Grabosky, 'Concluding Observations on Public Sector Illegality and Its Control' in *Government Illegality*, ed. P. Grabosky (1987).
7 J. Braithwaite and P. Drahos, *Global Business Regulation* (2000) 27.

oversight in respect of state activities ranging from the operation of economic policy through to policing.[8] In common with public regulation some of this private oversight is exercised over both public and private sector (by 'mixed economy' regulators – for example, advertising and animal welfare), and some applies to the public sector alone (for example, contracted-out public sector audit). Not all private oversight is intended to form a regulatory regime, but where it has regulatory effects it properly belongs within the set. An example of a regime which has the effect but not the object of regulating is the activities of credit rating agencies in assessing the appropriate rating for sovereign credit. Private regulators, though they may be lacking in formal power, are more likely than public regulators to operate 'complete' regimes (in the sense that they may set standards, monitor for compliance, and carry out enforcement without the need for intervention from others such as government departments and courts). Put simply, there is a tendency for some private regulators to be able to act more autonomously than would be true of public regulators.

This article sets out the case for the identification of a set of private regulators of the public sector and offers a means for classifying them based on the concept of legal mandates. Thus it offers an analysis and description of the range of forms which such private regulation takes in the United Kingdom. The concluding section examines the implications of the analysis both for the way we understand governance and regulation and for normative theories concerned with the control and accountability of governance institutions.

THE PUBLIC AND THE PRIVATE

The key distinction underlying the analysis in this paper is that between the public and private sectors. This paper makes this distinction on a simple ownership basis (in common with much analysis in political science). Legal scholarship and judicial analyses have recently shifted towards a functional analysis as the test for what is public and private. Although legal analyses show a tendency towards using such a functional distinction,[9] the very invisibility of many of the private regulators of the public sector suggests that the logic of the functional approach is not fully applied. In particular, it appears to be reserved for questions about amenability to judicial review and not to wider questions of institutional design within which private actors fulfil significant public roles. Examination of statutory enactments under

8 S. Schwarcz, 'Private Ordering of Public Markets: The Rating Agency Paradox' (2002) 22 *University of Illinois Law Rev.* (forthcoming), P. Grabosky, 'Law Enforcement and the Citizen: Non Governmental Participants in Crime Prevention and Control' (1992) 2 *Policing and Society* 249.
9 Freeman, op. cit., n. 5.

which the trigger for application is the 'publicness' of an organization reveals no clear approach. Thus the functional approach is reflected in the provisions of the Human Rights Act 1998, which are to apply to acts of 'public authorities', defined as 'any person certain of whose functions are functions of a public nature'.[10] Conversely the Freedom of Information Act 2000, which applies openness rules to public bodies, operates by means of an exhaustive list of organizations to which the Act applies and generally uses an ownership approach.[11] If the functional analysis were followed through, we might expect private regulators exercising public functions to be treated as public for all purposes (rather than the more limited purposes of judicial review and human rights).

Private regulation of the public sector is distinctive in a number of ways. First, in contrast with private-sector participation in policy making, there is a tendency towards the exercise of private regulatory functions within discrete, free-standing regulatory organizations. Second, and in contrast with public regulatory activity, the capacity to exercise regulatory power is not necessarily linked to the holding of a legal mandate. A further contrast with public regulatory activity is that there is a tendency for private regulators to take responsibility for all three elements of a regulatory regime: standard setting, monitoring, and application of sanctions, where it is more common (at least in European regulatory regimes) to find standard setting reserved to government departments and application of sanctions to courts.[12] This feature is important because it tends to reduce the capacity for other organizations to check the power of private regulators through the existence of interdependent powers.[13] We might expect the courts to

10 Human Rights Act 1998 s. 6(3)(b). It is clear that the Human Rights Act has indirect horizontal effects on private actors in any case through the duty of the courts to apply convention rights. This is said to give the courts at least a discretion, if not a duty, to apply interpret private law and private law relations consistently with the convention: G. Phillipson, 'The Human Rights Act, "Horizontal Effect" and the Common Law: a Bang or a Whimper?' (1999) 62 *Modern Law Rev.* 824, 843.
11 Freedom of Information Act 2000, sched. 1. The functional approach is reflected in the inclusion of persons providing medical and dental services under the National Health Service Act 1977 and equivalent Northern Ireland measures (paras. 44, 45, 51) and of educational institutions receiving funding under s. 65 of the Higher Education Act 1992 and equivalent Northern Ireland measures (paras. 53, 55).
12 There has been a trend towards giving public regulators fuller powers in recent United Kingdom legislation. Thus the Financial Services Authority has been empowered both to make rules and apply administrative penalties: Financial Services and Markets Act 2000, s. 138 (general rule-making powers); s. 123 (penalties for market abuse); and the Office of Fair Trading has been empowered for the first time to issue administrative penalties without recourse to the courts: Competition Act 1998 s. 36 (power to impose penalties for breach of chapter 1 and chapter 2 prohibitions): see I. Maher, 'Juridification, Codification and Sanctions in UK Competition Law' (2000) 63 *Modern Law Rev.* 544, 558.
13 C. Scott 'Analysing Regulatory Space: Fragmented Resources and Institutional Design' [2001] *Public Law* 329.

59

respond to such concentration of power within private regulatory regimes with more stringent scrutiny under judicial review. In fact the tendency has been in the opposite direction, with the Administrative Court (as it is now called) indicating that because contract-based private regulatory regimes are themselves the source of their own powers (rather than a legislature) then the doctrine of *ultra vires* will be less strictly applied than it is to public authorities.[14] Private oversight of the public sector has in common with public regulation a tendency towards internationalization and globalization.[15] Private overseers of national governments include among their ranks international NGOs such as Amnesty International, Transparency International, and Greenpeace International. Transparency International also seeks to curb corruption in international organizations. These international overseers raise rather different issues from those operating purely nationally, since they are less likely be socially or economically embedded within society and the quality of their relations with democratic governments are likely to be different from that between governments and national groups.

OVERSIGHT

Earlier research on public oversight of the public sectors has defined 'regulation inside government' as systematic arms-length control of one public sector organization by another with some element of official mandate.[16] To have an effective regulatory regime there must be a standard-setting element, and monitoring and enforcement. These three elements need not be located in a single organization and are not necessarily all located privately. Thus a regime may consist of publicly set standards monitored and enforced by private overseers. Private oversight of the public sector is different from this in at least two ways. First the external regulator is not a public sector organization and, second, there may not be an legal mandate. Where there is an legal mandate, an organization which is privately owned may be classified as public for juridical purposes (on the basis of a functional analysis).[17]

---

14 *R* v. *Panel on Takeovers and Mergers ex p. Guinness* [1990] 1 Q.B. 146, 149; C. Scott, 'Juridification of Regulatory Relations in the UK Utilities Sectors' in *Commercial Regulation and Judicial Review*, eds. J. Black, P. Muchlinski, and P. Walker (1998) 39–41.

15 A full account is provided by Braithwaite and Drahos, op. cit., n. 7, p. 41.

16 Hood et al., op. cit., n. 2.

17 *R* v. *Panel on Take-overs and Mergers Ex p. Datafin Plc* [1987] Q.B. 815 [1987] 2 W.L.R. 699 [1987] 1 All E.R. 564 (exercise of public functions by a private body rendered it amenable to judicial review); *Foster* v. *British Gas Plc* [1991] 2 A.C. 306 [1991] 2 W.L.R. 1075 [1991] 2 All E.R. 705 (special and exclusive rights may render a privatised utility public for purposes of public procurement rules).

It has been suggested that the bases of control for public regulation of the public sector extend beyond hierarchical oversight to include competition, mutuality, and contrived randomness.[18] One explanation for the mixture of forms of control was that public regulators of the public sector tend to be deficient in formal powers, particularly in respect of rule-making and the application of sanctions. A regulator with no formal power to apply sanctions can nevertheless invoke competitive pressures and community disapproval, for example, by publishing information, and can manipulate uncertainty, for example, by carrying out random inspection. The weakness of formal authority is perhaps more common for private regulators of the public sector, many of whom lack any legal mandate for their work. In some instances pure competition between private and public sector emerges.[19] What we are likely to find is a wide range of mixes of control forms with greater capacity for hierarchical control among those regulators with formal authority, derived either from statute or contract, as discussed below.

AUTHORITY AND MANDATES

It is immediately apparent that private overseers are not all of one type. They are all privately owned. They all exercise some form of systematic arms-length oversight over some part of the public sector. The chief purpose of seeking to classify the army of private regulators is to define the whole set so as to prove a reasonably exhaustive analysis of the issues raised by the different forms which private regulation takes. The central dimension in which there is variety is in the nature of the mandate (Table 1). The concept of mandate is concerned with the source and nature of the authority to act. It has at least two dimensions: powers and duties. Public regulators typically have powers and duties derived from statute (though many public regulators of the public sector have strictly limited powers). Private overseers are more likely to have a permissive mandate (the power

18 Hood et al., op. cit., n. 2.
19 It has been argued that the success of organized crime in some parts of Japanese society arises from the capacity of criminals to deliver institutions of property rights enforcement and protection services which the state fails to provide effectively: C. Milhaupt and M. West. 'The Dark Side of Private Ordering: An Institutional and Empirical Analysis of Organized Crime' (2000) 67 *University of Chicago Law Rev.* 41. An appropriate response in these circumstances is for the state to improve the quality of the civil and criminal justice systems and attempt to control the problem of organized crime through competition rather than the exercise of hierarchical authority. In a different context, the Protection and Indemnity Clubs which provide mutually based marine insurance are said to be in competition with EC competition authorities over the environmental regulation of shipping firms which is based on principles of mutuality antithetical to EC competition law rules: P. Bennett, 'Anti-Trust? European Competition Law and Mutual Environmental Insurance' (2000) 76 *Economic Geography* 50.

61

Table 1: Classification of Private Regulators

Mandate	Modality	Key Examples
Statutory	Quasi-public monitoring and/or enforcement Coercive	(i) Contracted-out public audit (ii) Private enforcement of criminal laws (for example, RSPCA) (iii) Enforcement of civil laws with statutory mandate (for example, Consumers' Association)
Contractual	(i) Collective (ii) Individuated Voluntary	(i) Advertising self-regulation (ii) Service providers (for example, insurance, certification of compliance with standards) (iii) Major service takers
None	(i) Litigation (for example civil proceedings, judicial review) (ii) Dissemination of Information (iii) Deployment of organizational capacities for example, direct action, boycotts	(i) Financial institutions (for example, credit ratings agencies) (ii) Interest groups (for example, prison reform groups, Federation Against Software Theft) (iii) Investigative journalism

but not the duty to act). It is sometimes suggested that contractual mandates originate in voluntary agreement whereas statutory mandates establish relationships coercively. This may be correct up to a point, though we should note that many regulatory regimes originating in contract are effectively imposed participants in the regime. Private governance may be as coercive as its public counterpart.[20]

Some private overseers, like their public counterparts, have a clear and official mandate based in statute. A typical case occurs within systems where a public regulatory function is delegated or contracted out to a private organization. Examples of the delegated regulatory power include controls over the care of animals, delegated to the Royal Society for the Prevention of Cruelty to Animals (RSPCA) (which operates in the manner of a specialized

20 N. Duxbury 'Robert Hale and the Economy of Legal Force' (1990) 53 *Modern Law Rev.* 421, 434–7.

62

police service over public and private sectors – its functions include monitoring the welfare of police dogs[21]), self-regulation of medical practitioners employed by the National Health Service under a statutory regime,[22] and enforcement of consumer laws which derive from EC directives by the Consumers' Association.[23] Examples of contracting-out of public regulatory power over the public sector are found in the regimes of local authority audit assigned to the Audit Commission[24] and schools inspection organized by the Office for Standards in Education (OFSTED).[25] On one measure this class of overseer is private, in the sense that the state has no element of ownership. But a functional analysis of the type used in public law litigation might suggest that these organizations are exercising public functions and should be subject to the full range of control applying to public bodies, not limited to judicial review but also including full parliamentary oversight.

Another class of private regulators is those who lack any form of statutory mandate but nevertheless have formalized powers of control derived from contracts (which may thus be characterized as voluntary in origin). There is a substantial literature on the role of contracts in state regulation of the private sector.[26] Such contracts are said to pose significant problems of transparency, accountability, and efficiency.[27] The exercise of regulatory control over the public sector by contracts is an even more hidden phenomenon. This group of contractual relationships can be

---

21 Protection of Animals Act 1911; see H. Carter, 'Cruel Police Dog Officers Jailed for Four Mouths' *Guardian*, 11 June 1998; A. Gilligan, 'RAF Under Fire for "Breaking" Dog Welfare Law' *Daily Telegraph*, 21 June 1998. In the first of these incidents the RSPCA initially used a resource-based sanction – suspension of the supply of dogs to police forces pending an investigation (*Times*, 4 December 1997) – and then followed up with the exercise of its statutory power to prosecute.

22 The main body which monitors and enforces standards for clinical conduct of the medical profession is the General Medical Council: Medical Act 1983.

23 Unfair Terms in Consumer Contracts Regulations S.I. no. 2083/1999 r. 11 and sched. 1; The Stop Now Orders (EC Directive) Regulations S.I. no. 1422/2001.

24 Audit Commission Act 1998, s. 3; About 30 per cent of local audits are carried out by private auditors drawn from a panel of six major accounting firms: Audit Commission, *How Your External Auditors are Appointed and How You Can Influence the Choice* (no date).

25 Education (Schools) Act 1992, ss. 3, 9, 10. A comparison between inspections carried out by local education authority (LEA) inspectors working in their own authority, LEA inspectors inspecting schools in a different authority, and private teams of inspectors revealed that private inspectors failed a significantly larger proportion of the schools which they inspected. Whether this is because OFSTED allocated to private inspectors the more problematic cases or because private inspectors applied higher standards is not clear. But either way it suggests that private inspectors play a distinctive role in the regime: Hood et al., op. cit., n. 2, pp. 150–1.

26 For the United Kingdom, see H. Collins, *Regulating Contracts* (1999) ch. 13; P. Vincent-Jones, 'The Regulation of Contractualisation in Quasi-Markets for Public Services' [1999] *Public Law* 304.

27 J. Freeman, 'The Contracting State' (2000) 28 *Florida State University Law Rev.* 155.

63

subdivided between collective and individuated relationships. Key examples of the collective form are self-regulatory schemes which may govern public and private bodies in some aspect of their operations. The Advertising Standards Authority, notionally a self-regulatory organization, has a jurisdiction which appears to extend beyond those who are members of the Advertising Association, and thus its mandate cannot truly derive from contract.[28] Its decisions are given force by the fact of their recognition by media organizations generally and their capacity to withhold space in their publications from particular advertisers. In New Zealand, the Court of Appeal has excluded one public authority, the Electoral Commission, from the jurisdiction of the private Advertising Standards Complaints Board on the basis both of a narrow construction of the Board's own codes (as excluding public advertisements not intended 'to promote the interests of any person, product or service') and on the broader ground that the scheme of the relevant Electoral Act gave rise to a presumption that Parliament had decided that it was for the statutory organization and not some private body to determine how the Commission should carry out its functions in providing publicity on elections.[29] This latter basis for the decision could have very wide application in restricting private regulation over public bodies exercising statutory functions, and appears to contradict the finding that the Advertising Standards Complaints Board was judicially reviewable precisely because it was exercising a public function. In some jurisdictions the development of self-regulation has outpaced privatization leaving publicly owned utilities suppliers to be regulated by private self-regulatory organizations. An example is provided by the dominant incumbent Australian telecommunications operator, Telstra, which remains publicly owned but which is overseen by, among others, the self-regulatory Telecommunications Industry Ombudsman.[30]

An example of the individuated contractual controls is that of organizations providing various forms of professional services to public sector bodies. These service providers are exemplified by, though not limited to, insurance companies and certification bodies. Private accreditation and certification arguably plays a larger role in United States public policy than in the United Kingdom, though this is most commonly in the accreditation of private companies offering public services such as health care and education. Thus, accreditation supports

---

28 C. Munro, 'Self Regulation in the Media' [1997] *Public Law* 6. A considerable amount of information about the self-regulatory regime is provided by the ASA at <www.asa.org.uk> (visited 17 October 2001).

29 *Electoral Commission* v. *Cameron* [1997] 2 N.Z.L.R. 421.

30 K. MacNeill, 'Self-Regulation: Rights and Remedies – The Telecommunications Experience' in *Sunrise or Sunset: Administrative Law in the New Millennium*, ed. C. Finn (2000).

public regulation of the private sector rather than acting as private regulation of the public sector.[31]

Insurers have the capacity to set standards for the conduct of public sector bodies in respect of risk through contractual terms and monitor and enforce compliance via decisions on payment and premium levels. While a certain amount is known about how insurers manage their relations with private clients, and the control systems which are created,[32] there is very little evidence available as to how widely public bodies take out insurance policies (as opposed to self-insuring) and even less relating to the extent to which insurers use their contractual power to 'regulate' the conduct of public bodies. However, we may hypothesize that changes in the way private insurers 'control' their clients are also affecting the public sector. Recent research suggests a tendency among insurers following neo-liberal logic to create greater segmentation of risk, attempting to target high-risk clients more accurately so as to charge higher premiums or refuse insurance, while benefiting lower-risk clients who no longer have to share the coverage of the high-risk groups.[33] This trend is already undermining certain public policies, such as compulsory third-party motor insurance (increasingly difficult for high-risk individuals to obtain) and private health care (where government policies in support of private health insurance, for example, in Australia and the United States of America, have been premised upon a substantial cross-subsidy between healthy and unhealthy insureds). The effects of this trend on insurers' control over the public sector may be positive, encouraging public sector organizations to so manage their activities as to be within lower-risk groups. But equally it creates the possibility of an acceleration of the trend among higher-risk organizations to self-insure, denying the public sector as a whole the virtuous effects of oversight by insurers of risks in those sectors. Alternatively, public sector organizations may be encouraged to withdraw from certain high-risk activities (even though public sector participation may provide social or economic benefits which markets would not provide).

Certification of public sector bodies' compliance with standards such as ISO 9000 (quality management) and ISO 14000 (environmental management) gives third-party certification organizations considerable power to steer the management of those bodies by reference to standards set by private standards organizations such as the national British Standards Institute and the International Standards Organization. As with insurance, these

---

31 *Private Accrediation in the Regulatory State*, special issue (1994) 57:4 *Law and Contemporary Problems*. See, especially, C. Havighurst 'The Place of Private Accrediting Among the Instruments of Government' 1, at 5–10.
32 The classic socio-legal study is C. Heimer, *Reactive Risk and Rational Action: Managing Moral Hazard in Insurance Contracts* (1985). See, also, N. Reichman 'Managing Crime Risks: Towards an Insurance Based Model of Social Control' in *Research in Law, Deviance and Social Control*, eds. S. Spitzer and A. Scull (1986).
33 R. Ericson, D. Barry and A. Doyle, 'The Moral Hazards of Neoliberalism: Lessons from the Private Insurance Industry' (2000) 29 *Economy and Society* 532.

relationships and their management are not much documented. A further form of individuated contractual power arises where private organizations take services from public sector providers in sufficient quantity that the contract for services effectively becomes an instrument of regulation.[34]

The third class of private overseer is the organization which has no legally binding mandate derived from statute or contract. Though there is no legal mandate conventionally understood, this group may nevertheless have power to seek behavioural modifications from public sector bodies. This power is neither voluntary nor coercive. The main resources relevant to the holding of governance power generally are authority, information, organization, and wealth.[35] For those who lack formal authority, power is derived from having the wealth to bring public interest litigation, either in public or private law, the possession of information and the resources to disseminate it, and the capacity to deploy organizational resources, for example, in the form of direct action (such as boycotts and physical blockades).

Public interest litigation and the threat of litigation are widely deployed by pressure groups as a means to enforce or develop standards on public sector bodies. Examples of such judicial rule making abound in connection with prisons, social security, and housing.[36] The capacity of pressure groups to use litigation as *part* of their overall strategies, for example, to raise prison standards, is dependent upon judicial interpretation of rules relating to standing to sue and rights of intervention in actions commenced by others. With prison rules, pressure groups are able to cite standards of humanity which command widespread support (though they may vary in interpretation). In other domains, such as social security, where there is less consensus over appropriate standards, litigation is more problematic since victory at law can be reversed by legislation. Accordingly, Prosser

---

34 Collins. op. cit., n. 26, discusses the reverse issue, of government using contract as a regulatory instrument over the private sector (pp. 311–15). An instance of the phenomenon I am discussing might theoretically arise in one of the sectors where public bodies remain important suppliers of services as with the postal sector and possibly the reconstituted rail infrastructure company which will emerge from the collapse of Railtrack plc.

35 C. Hood, *The Tools of Government* (1983) 4-6 refers to these four basic resources of government as 'nodality' ('the property of being in the middle of an information or social network'), 'treasure', 'authority', and 'organization'. I have not only adopted his terms but also suggest that they are the resources of governance more generally (that is, applying beyond governmental actors).

36 For prisons, see M. Loughlin and P. Quinn, 'Prisons, Rules and Courts: A Study in Administrative Law' (1993) 56 *Modern Law Rev.* 497. A major United States study is M. Feeley and E. Rubin, *Judicial Policy Making and the Modern State* (1998), especially on the role of the Public Interest Law Firm in opening to scrutiny the standards of the Santa Clara jail system in California at 111–28. The seminal study of litigation over social security rights is T. Prosser, *Test Cases for the Poor* (1983). On housing, see I. Loveland, *Housing Homeless Persons: Administrative Law and the Administrative Process* (1995) ch. 10.

concluded that in the social security domain a valuable role for the courts was for setting process standards for decision making. In other instances though a legal action might be unsuccessful it could be a prelude to political campaigning.[37]

We may speculate that the modest liberalization of these rules engineered by the Administrative Court will give to pressure groups greater capacity to use litigation in support of their overall objectives. Loosening of the rules on standing appears to displace restrictive rules under which only those affected by administrative decisions could apply for judicial review and creates a greater possibility that the Administrative Court be used for a 'generic enforcement function'.[38] There has also been a greater willingness of the courts to permit interest groups to intervene as third parties to actions. In light of these developments we might expect judicial review to be used more widely in support of interest groups' objectives in controlling public sector actors. It has been argued that if English law is to develop a principle of 'citizen standing' then its application should be reserved to cases involving 'the most important of the public's interests'.[39]

An example of information-based regulation is the systematic oversight of the finances of public and private organizations by credit ratings agencies. Here the main instrument of control is the publication of information. This process has been most important, in the terms of this article, in the development by the four main international ratings agencies of ratings for 'sovereign credit'. Factors affecting the assessment are liable to include the stability of government arrangements and the independence of the judiciary, in addition to perceptions of the prudence or otherwise of fiscal policies. Agencies aim to provide a gradation between highly speculative to extremely safe credit.[40] Ratings agencies derive their power from trust in the information which they produce. They have been characterized as 'global mediating organizations'.[41] The south-east Asian economic crisis of 1997 has been partly attributed to excessive trust in those ratings agencies which were too sanguine about the economic stability of nations such as Thailand.[42]

37 Prosser, op. cit., n. 36, pp. 83–4.
38 C. Harlow,'Public Law and Popular Justice' (2002) 65 *Modern Law Rev.* 1. The seminal case is probably *R* v. *Secretary of State for Foreign Affairs ex p. World Development Movement* [1995] 1 W.L.R. 386, in which a pressure group successfully challenged the grant of funds by the government for the construction of the Pergau Dam in Malaysia.
39 P. Cane, 'Standing, Representation and the Environment' in *A Special Relationship? American Influences on Law in the United Kingdom*, ed. I. Loveland (1995) 150.
40 A. Rhodes, 'The Role of the SEC in the Regulation of the Ratings Agencies: Well-Placed Reliance or Free-Market Interference' (1996) 20 *Seton Hall Legislative J.* 293.
41 J. Pixley, 'Impersonal Trust in Global Mediating Organizations' (1999) 41 *Sociological Perspectives* 647.
42 L. Jacque, 'The Asian Financial Crisis: Lessons from Thailand' (1999) 23 *Fletcher Forum of World Affairs* 87.

Where the media maintains effective systematic oversight (as with some investigative journalism – for example, systematic scrutiny of local corruption by local journalists) then it may come within this third class of mandateless regulators. Certainly the media exerts considerable information power in contemporary society.[43] However the capacity of newspapers to carry out such systematic investigation is limited. The kind of long-term research required of investigative journalism is both very costly and somewhat at odds with the general day-to-day cycle of media activity.[44] A contemporaraneous account of the Watergate Affair suggests that only a handful of newspapers would have had the resources to carry out the investigation necessary to make a significant impact on the story and, of those, only one, the *Washington Post*, chose to devote only the time of two relatively junior journalists to the task.[45] A further reason that news and other media editors might not pursue investigative journalism is the risk associated with liability for defamation – either that the chilling effect of a threat of a defamation action may prevent a story being run, or the actual costs of defending an action subsequently.[46] A United Kingdom empirical study found that these considerations were likely to inhibit local and regional press more than national news media, and in turn those national media which employed their own in-house lawyers were likely to show less caution than those who relied on outside advice.[47]

Examples of the deployment of organizational resources are provided by the efforts of NGOs in organizing direct action to inhibit states from activities which breach the NGO's standards. Greenpeace is a world leader in such direct action[48] but it is far from the only example. A leading case study for the application of private organizational capacities in controlling government arose in the anti-apartheid movement in the 1980s. International governmental support for sanctions against South Africa had largely been

43 J. Curran and J. Seaton, *Power Without Responsibility: The Press and Broadcasting in Britain* (1997, 5th edn.).
44 J. Waterford, 'Investigative Journalism and Government Illegality' in *Government Illegality*, ed. P. Grabosky (1987).
45 L. Chester, C. McCrystal, S. Aris, and W. Shawcross, *Watergate: The Full Inside Story* (1973). The journalists' own account is C. Bernstein and B. Woodward, *All the President's Men* (1974).
46 S. Renas, C. Hartmann, and J. Walker, 'An Empirical Analysis of the Chilling Effect: Are Newspapers Affected by Liability Standards in Defamation Actions?' in *The Cost of Libel: Economic and Policy Implications*, eds. E. Dennis and E. Noam (1989).
47 E. Barendt, L. Lustgarten, K. Norrie, and H. Stephenson, *Libel and the Media: The Chilling Effect* (1997).
48 Tsoukas describes the methods used by Greenpeace in its efforts to stop Shell abandoning a defunct oil rig at sea – an action targeted both at the multinational oil producers and governments which allowed them to do this: 'David and Goliath in the Risk Society: Making Sense of the Conflict between Shell and Greenpeace in the North Sea' (1999) 6 *Organization* 499. See, also, P. Wapner, 'Politics Beyond the State – Environmental Activism and World Civic Politics (1995) 47 *World Politics* 311.

restricted to arms embargoes. The international anti-apartheid movement provided leadership in encouraging its supporters to boycott firms which invested in South Africa leading to the initiation of financial sanctions against South Africa, not by governments, but by the Chase Manhattan Bank in 1985. These private financial sanctions snowballed, causing businesses within South Africa to actively lobby government for reform of the apartheid system.[49] One analysis suggests that the greatest success of the anti-apartheid movement came.

> not from lobbying the federal [US] government to legislate restrictions, but rather from directly confronting the corporation with boycotts, stock divestments, shareholder activism, and through persuading state and local governments to link municipal contracts to withdrawal from South Africa.[50]

Thus the banks were pressured to act as regulators of the South African government.

Many of the mandateless private regulators deploy more than one set of resources. Thus pressure groups such as the prisons reform groups are likely to deploy both the information strategies and interest litigation. Similarly international NGOs such as Greenpeace use litigation, information dissemination, and direct action in concert.

SETTING STANDARDS

The values which private regulation of the public sector promotes are diverse and include efficiency, greenness, security, and humanity. The public-private interface in the making of the applicable standards takes at least three forms: publicly-set standards; privately-set standards; public and private standards in competition. In some regimes the applicable standards are set publicly but monitoring and perhaps enforcement are the responsibility of private regulators. For efficiency, an example of such a public/private mix is provided by contracted-out public audit. For humanity, the private monitoring and enforcement of public rules against cruelty to animals provides an example. Such publicly-set standards tend to be monopolistic in character, although that tendency may be mitigated to some extent by diffuse monitoring and enforcement practices as with public audit. The negotiation of the meaning of standards in regulatory settings makes it impossible to fully separate the monitoring and enforcement processes from standard setting.[51]

49 K. Schwartzman, 'Can International Boycotts Transform Political Systems? The Cases of Cuba and South Africa' (2001) 43 *Latin American Politics and Society* 115.
50 K. Rodman, 'Public and Private Sanctions against South-Africa' (1994) 109 *Political Science Q.* 313.
51 N. Reichman, 'Moving Backstage: Uncovering the Role of Compliance Practices in Shaping Regulatory Policy' in *White-Collar Crime Reconsidered*, eds. K. Schlegel and D. Weisburd (1992).

Privately-set standards are a characteristic of the more complete private regulatory regimes, as with those established for self-regulation of advertising and by credit ratings agencies. In these domains either there are no public standards, or public standards provide only a floor (as with rules against misleading advertising). Such standards may be monopolistic, as with advertising self-regulation in the United Kingdom, or competitive, as with credit rating agencies. Credit rating agencies participate in markets where the maintenance of their reputations is very important. In some regulatory domains, publicly-set standards are in competition with privately-set standards. An example is the prison humanity regimes where standards set by the Home Office are challenged by implicit or explicit standards set by the prison reform groups. By definition, these groups see their role as seeking to raise prison humanity standards and they do this not only by lobbying but also by monitoring prison standards and seeking to develop higher standards (for example, in respect of rights to legal representation of prisoners) through litigation. Litigation thus provides an example of how the monitoring and enforcement process may result in the standards being reset. The private regulator is using litigation to initiate a judicial standard setting process and to put forward its preferred model.

There is considerable variety in the sources of standards deployed by private regulators who lack any formal authority or mandate. Many such organizations develop their own conception of appropriate standards (for example, for humanity regimes in prisons or protection of the environment) and will monitor public sector organizations for compliance with those standards. These standards can be used as the basis for 'enforcement' which uses informational and/or organizational resources (such as publication of information or boycotts). However, when it comes to any attempt to enforce the standards formally through the courts, such organizations are restricted either to the enforcement of official standards (whether established by legislation or by judges) or to pressing the case for new, judge-made standards to be developed and applied (as has commonly occurred with much litigation over prison standards).

Some private regulators have no particular interest in developing their own standards and rely almost exclusively on legislative standards (although they may lobby to have legislative standards revised from time to time). Such an approach to standards is exemplified by the British groups which seek to privately police intellectual property laws – the Federation Against Software Theft (FAST) and the Federation Against Copyright Theft (FACT). Both organizations are mixed-economy regulators, in the sense that they oversee compliance, primarily with copyright legislation, by both public and private sectors. Their activities are akin to private policing of these laws.

Those private regulators who never use litigation as a mechanism of formal enforcement are clearly not restricted to the application of official standards. An example is provided by the activities of credit rating agencies in providing ratings for sovereign debt. The ratings agencies are free to set

70

their own standards and criteria by which to assess the credit-worthiness of national governments and to decide whether or not to make these standards public. Equally, international NGOs such as Transparency International and Greenpeace International are free to set their own standards and criteria by which to assess the conduct of national governments.

MONITORING AND ENFORCEMENT

Research on public regulators of the public and private sectors reveals a wide variety of mechanisms for asserting control. In many cases formal enforcement actions – the application of civil or criminal penalties and revocations of authorizations – sit towards the apex of a pyramid in which lower-level strategies of education, advice, and warnings are routinely deployed to secure compliance.[52] Some regulators of the public sector, such as prisons and schools inspectorates, lack the power to apply formal sanctions and are dependent on public or private censure or on informing others who do have formal powers to act.[53] A similar picture of variability in powers to enforce emerges with private regulation of the public sector.

As with regulation generally, we should not assume that hierarchical control is the only mechanism by which controls over public sector activities can be exercised. A central element of recent public sector reform activity has been to subject public sector actors to the private controls of the market. In a significant proportion of its market, the publicly owned Post Office is in competition with private postal and parcel companies. However, the extent of control through the market should not be overstated as in many sectors where there appears to be public/private competition (such as health and education) it is frequently the case that the private sector is providing a different product. This product differentiation occurs in the postal sector too.[54] Arguably competition between state schools, fostered by the publication of league tables of performance, provides a more significant (if controversial) competition-based control.

Some private overseers resemble public regulators of business in that they possess strong formal powers (for example, of prosecution or removal of authorizations) which can be deployed sparingly in support of more routine educational and advisory strategies. This group is rather rare. The RSPCA and the General Medical Council are examples. Since the GMC acts chiefly through formal hearings it is less likely to use its power to apply sanctions in the pyramidal manner of an inspection-based regulator and more likely to select what it deems to be the appropriate arrow from its quiver of sanctions

52 I. Ayres and J. Braithwaite, *Responsive Regulation: Transcensing the Deregulation Debate* (1992).
53 Hood et al., op. cit., n. 2.
54 Case C 320/91 *Corbeau* [1993] ECR 1-2533.

in any particular case coming before it. Others among the statutory private regulators do not possess such formal powers. Thus, private auditors and schools inspectors, operating within statutory regimes have only the power to report on what they find.

A rather larger group is constituted by those private overseers who possess contractual power as the basis for enforcement. In cases of collectivized contractual power (as with self-regulation), quite elaborate regimes for the monitoring and application of sanctions may be devised which resemble public regulatory regimes. Whereas in public regulatory regimes some penalties are only capable of being applied by courts (notably criminal penalties and injunctions), in private regimes the penalties are applied by the regulator itself These range from censure through fines and expulsion.[55] The Advertising Standards Authority, a private regulator of both public and private sector, used it position of 'nodality' at the junction of media and advertising industries to develop a new sanction for serious breach of its rules when it required the Commission for Racial Equality, a public agency, to submit all poster advertisements to the Committee on Advertising Practice for pre-vetting prior to publication.[56]

The mandateless private overseer has no legal power and is dependent on the deployment of other resources. Some private overseers deploy wealth in litigation. For some organizations such litigation involves the identification of appropriate test cases which are used as a means not only to enforce in the particular case but also to establish or develop standards of wider application. This involves the distillation of issues, calculation of the risks of the test case strategy (for example, that an unfavourable interpretation of the legal position may be endorsed by the courts) and, where an action by an individual is being supported, the identification of an appropriate individual. There is a substantial body of research on test-case strategies.[57] An effective test-case strategy may be deployed at the apex of a pyramid of informal enforcement strategies. It is clearly dependent upon there being some arguable legal case. However, because of the uncertainty, cost, and delay of bringing test cases, this strategy may not lend much credible threat to this lower-level activity as far as the regulatee is concerned.

Some mandateless regulators use legal processes not merely in the form of test cases but as part of routine enforcement. Thus the Federation Against Software Theft (FAST) acts in a policing role on behalf of its members in raiding premises, applying for cease-and-desist orders, and pursuing civil litigation where it finds breach of intellectual property laws. FAST's Digital Crime Unit, established in 1989, investigates breaches of criminal law and

55 C. Scott and J. Black, *Cranston's Consumers and the Law* (2000, 3rd edn.) ch. 2.
56 Advertising Standards Authority, *Annual Report* (1998) 28. The sanction was lifted from the CRE after a two-year period without further infringement: Advertising Standards Authority, *Annual Report* (2000).
57 Prosser, op. cit., n. 36; C. Harlow and R. Rawlings, *Pressure Through Law* (1992).

72

collects technical evidence for use by customs officers, trading standards departments, and the police in support of prosecutions.[58] Thus, in the criminal sphere, FAST operates a central monitoring role but requires cooperation from state agencies for enforcement.

A key example of information as the basis for control is the regular publication by Transparency International (TI) of its Corruption Perceptions Index, which uses a league table format to criticize countries with a reputation for being corrupt.[59] TI combines this publication with a strategy of working with civil society organizations in particular countries to build the societal 'pillars' which aim to squeeze corruption out of government systems. Where the private overseer has good information and that information has salience in the media, we might expect the threat of publication to be capable of grounding lower-level strategies of education and advice. However, not all private overseers will see this as part of their function. Credit-rating agencies do not seek compliance with any particular set of norms, but rather seek to describe the risks associated with any particular borrower. Thus for such agencies publication of information is the only strategy – and a very powerful one. The significance of the ratings offered by the agencies is that the better the rating (that is the lower the risk identified), the easier it is for borrowers to borrow and the more favourable are the interest rates.[60] Thus the effect is to public bodies incentives to minimize the general risks associated with their operations that are relevant to their capacity to repay debt.

CONCLUSIONS

The concept of private regulation of the public sector set out in this article encompasses a wide range of processes governing diffuse public organizations and activities. Common to each is the identification of the systematic deployment of private power in controlling what are regarded as public activities. The emergence of private regulatory power in these forms is not surprising and its identification represents an elaboration of well-established understandings of the interdependence of public and private power in contemporary governance arrangements.

The exercise of statutory regulatory power by private bodies generally forms part of well established and fairly well understood regimes. Among the more intriguing questions raised by such power is what is the appropriate mix of the public and the private in different aspects of the regime. How

58 Information provided at FAST's website <http://www.fast.org.uk/> (visited 17 October 2001).
59 <http://www.transparency.org/documents/cpi/2000/cpi2000.html> (visited 17 May 2001).
60 Schwarcz, op. cit., n. 8.

much of a role should private bodies have in standard setting? What advantages are to be gained from mixing public and private monitoring as occurs with schools inspection and local audit? Collectivized contractual power, in the form of self-regulatory regimes, is perhaps the best documented of the different private regulation phenomena discussed in this article. The subjection of public bodies to private self-regulation raises few novel issues that have not been well canvassed in the context of arrangements for the independence and accountability of self-regulatory bodies generally.[61]

The two forms of private regulation of the public sector which have the greater novelty (at least in exposition) are those involving individuated contractual power and those which do not derive from a legal mandate. Clothed in the form of commercial contracts, contractual regulation of the public sector is remarkably hidden, to the extent that there is virtually no literature on the phenomenon. This group of private regulators together with some members of the group with no formal mandate are striking for the extent to which they wield regulatory power over the public sector outside normal modes of control and accountability. A central hypothesis emerging from the analysis is that regulatory power does not need the backing of statutory authority to be effective and important. This hypothesis could be tested both in the domain of private regulation and more generally.

These observations raise a number of normative questions. Any dependence on private regulation within the wider architecture of contemporary governance must recognize important limits to private regulatory capacities. Many private regulators lack the clout they would have if they were public agencies and if that leads to weakness in fulfilling public mandates, then they may need to be enhanced (for example, by changing rules which inhibit investigative journalism or the capacity of NGOs to pursue litigation). Conversely, some non-statutory private regulators operate complete regimes in the sense of having the capacity to set standards, to monitor, and enforce without the intervention of other organizations. Where this is the case, they wield more power than those public regulators which are constrained by the need to follow standards set by legislatures or government departments and to pursue litigation in order to apply legal sanctions. There is thus a remarkable concentration of private power over public organizations. This is perhaps most striking with those private regulators operating internationally whose judgements on such matters as financial or fiscal credibility, probity or greenness significantly affect decisions of notionally democratic governments. This question is particularly pertinent when applied to international private overseers which have the capacity to provide a counter-balance both to democratic and undemocratic government. Credit agencies and NGOs exemplify the

61 J. Black, 'Constitutionalising Self-Regulation' (1996) 59 *Modern Law Rev.* 24.

'private, oligarchic forms' which are said to dominate contemporary, globalized governance structures.[62]

To identify substantial power is not to argue that private regulators should necessarily be subject to similar control and accountability mechanisms as those which apply to public regulators. It is both a strength and a weakness of private organizations that they are subject to different forms of control from the public sector. On one account, the effective delegation of public functions to private bodies magnifies a problem of accountability which already existed with agencies.[63] But arguably the relative independence which private regulators have from government could insulate them to a greater degree from the political intervention which has tended to bedevil notionally independent public agencies. An alternative response is to undertake more detailed analysis of particular regimes than has been attempted here with a view to identifying the range of mechanisms through which particular private regulators are held in check or made to answer for their activities. Some regulators, such as those carrying out contracted out audits and inspections, are subject to direct oversight by public bodies. Private regulators can be more tightly embedded within public regimes, as happened in 1988 with the Advertising Standards Authority whose enforcement powers were linked to the new injunctive powers of the Office of Fair Trading.[64]

Others, such as professional associations[65] and non-governmental organizations, may be strongly embedded within a wider community which offers a legitimate alternative to control through democratic government channels. Such experience could be developed to build communities of private overseers to share best practice and act as mutual checks on one another (as happens within the mixed public/private British and Irish Ombudsmens' Association).[66]

A third group, such as financial and accreditation institutions, may effectively operate within a market within which the quality of their

62 P. Cerny, 'Globalization and the erosion of democracy' (1999) 36 *European J. of Political Research* 1.
63 J. Freeman, 'Private parties., public functions and the new administrative law' (2000) 52 *Admnistrative Law Rev.* 813.
64 Control of Misleading Advertisements Regulations S.I. 1988/915 (as amended by S.I. 2000/914). The relationship created by the Regulations between the ASA and the Office of Fair Trading is examined in *Director General of Fair Trading* v. *Tobyward* [1989] 2 All E.R. 266. The OFT's injunctive power has, never been used against a public body.
65 For example, the statute-backed self-regulator of the medical profession, the General Medical Council, has a council of 104 members, 75 per cent of whom are doctors. The constitution of the GMC is currently under review: General Medical Council, *Effective, Inclusive and Accountable: Reform of the GMC's Structure, Constitution and Governance* (2001) 6.
66 Brief details of the association are provided at <http://www.bioa.org.uk> (visited 17 October 2001).

judgements is assessed and may lead to diminished loyalty where they prove defective.[67] However the viability or appropriateness of competition may depend on the sophistication of the 'consumers' of the information.[68] Accordingly we might be most concerned about those private regulators which operate monopolistically within their domains and in a fashion which is detached from wider communities. Where private regulators are setting standards at odds with democratic values (for example, insurers more risk averse than public sector bodies, prisons reformers more humane than Parliament) a possible response is to build democratic representation into private regimes. This is a reverse take on the classic proceduralization prescription which seeks to build civil society into public decision making.[69] An alternative possibility is to think of a reverse form of 'co-regulation' within which the regime of private regulation stimulates public involvement in such matters as setting standards or enforcement priorities

An important counter to international private power generally is the formation of networks of governments and regulatory authorities, often organized around particular scientific and technical areas.[70] Arguably this tendency represents an application of the law of requisite variety, seeking to meet the challenges of private networks of power through the development of equivalent or interdependent governmental communities. But in the delicate equilibria which arise from such arrangements it is often none too clear who is in charge. Incentives may lie in opposite directions. For example, a few months after Ireland was censured by the European Council for breach of European guidelines relating to fiscal policy in a national budget,[71] the private rating agency, Standard and Poor's, raised Ireland's long-term sovereign credit rating to AAA.[72]

Private regulation of the public sector deserves to be recognized as a significant and growing constraint on governmental activities both nationally and internationally. The phenomenon presents both new possibilities for reviewing and checking the exercise of public power and old problems of controlling and accounting for the exercise of power in new forms. It requires further analysis to understand the conditions under which private regulators are most potent and effective and to examine whether the constraints which apply to private regulators within particular domains are adequate or need reconfiguration.

---

67 Pixley, op. cit., n. 41.
68 Havighurst, op. cit., n. 31, p. 10.
69 J. Black 'Proceduralizing Regulation: Part 1' (2000) 20 *Ox. J. of Legal Studies* 597.
70 A.-M. Slaughter, 'The Accountability of Government Networks' (2001) 8 *Indiana J. of Global Legal Studies* 347; Braithwaite and Drahos, op. cit., n. 7.
71 D. Hodson and I. Maher 'The Open Method as New Form of Governance: The Case of Soft Economic Policy Co-ordination' (2001) 39 *J. of Common Market Studies* 719, 736.
72 Standard and Poor's, 'Ireland's Rating Raised to "AAA"', press release, 3 October 2001.

76

JOURNAL OF LAW AND SOCIETY
VOLUME 29, NUMBER 1, MARCH 2002
ISSN: 0263-323X, pp. 77–110

Using Private-Public Linkages to Regulate Environmental Conflicts: The Case of International Construction Contracts

 OREN PEREZ*

The article takes a pluralistic view of the 'trade-environment' conflict by exploring one of the settings of this conflict: the lex constructionis *– international construction law. It seeks to unravel the way in which the unique structural-cultural attributes of this legal domain have affected its environmental (in)sensitivity. The article's main argument in that context is that the contractual tradition of the* lex constructionis *(as manifested in the standard contracts that dominate this field) and its unique institutional structure, have created a culture of ecological indifference. This culture has important practical consequences because of the deep ecological problematic of international construction projects. The article develops an alternative contractual model, which depicts the construction contract as a semi-political mechanism, rather than a private tool. This conceptual change seeks to break the public/private separation that characterizes the contractual discourse in the international construction market. The article explores, further, whether this alternative contractual vision could be realized in practice, and proposes several implementing modules which could further this goal. While the article explores a particular international regime, its methodology and conclusions – in particular, the political-constitutional interpretation of the contract and the critique of the public/private dichotomy (see sections III.3 and III.4) – should be relevant to the regulation of many other (national or international) environmental dilemmas.*

The tension between environmental concerns and the global economic system has been a recurrent theme in the recent wave of anti-globalization protests – from Seattle 1998 to Quebec and Genoa 2001. The environmental 'cause' was invoked again and again in numerous street protests, pamphlets,

* *Faculty of Law, Bar-Ilan University, Ramat-Gan, Israel 52900*

The article draws on the research I did for my PhD thesis during 1997–2000 at the London School of Economics and Political Science. It has benefited from the comments of my two supervisors at LSE, Professor Gunther Teubner and Mr. Damian Chalmers. I would also like to thank Professor Sol Picciotto for his comments on an earlier draft of this article.

77

and radical websites. The apparent unity of action, which seemed to conjoin these multiple acts of protest, is, however, highly misleading. In the first place, the image of a single-minded, homogeneous movement is clearly unfounded. Behind the protests at Seattle, Quebec, and Genoa lies an amalgam of different groups and multiple ideologies. But this apparent unity is misleading also in that it has projected a false picture of a unified global economic system. The description of the Bretton Woods triad and the multinational enterprises community as a kind of monstrous, anti-social and anti-environmental transnational cartel is clearly too simplistic as a characterization of the global economic field. This article rejects this simplistic binary story. It pursues a different narrative, which is based on the following thesis: the trade and environment conflict should not be seen as a uni-dimensional problematic, a clear binary discord, but, rather, as a reflection of multiple dilemmas – constituted and negotiated by a myriad of institutional and discursive networks.

Developing an understanding of this conflict requires a multi-dimensional perspective. One of the major blind spots of the current legal research in this context is its myopic focus on the World Trade Organization. The 'trade and environment' research programme has failed to take into account the pluralistic nature of the contemporary global legal sphere. Far from being homogenous, this sphere consists of multiple systems, which include, on the one hand, traditional, treaty-based legal structures (for example, the WTO or the IMF), and, on the other, a-national, or private legal networks (for example, the *lex mercatoria*); together, this diverse network constitutes a complex web of transnational governance.[1] The influence of this 'web' has not been confined, however, to the economic realm; it has encroached deeply into various aspects of our civic life – including the environment.

The thesis of global legal pluralism reconstructs the 'trade and environment' conflict, then, as a multi-faceted dilemma, which is not limited to the WTO. It makes clear that international trade – with its various ecological side-effects[2] – is governed by multiple systems of law rather than

1 These a-national, or private networks, are not made of the familiar legal sources of public international law, such as international treaties and state-practice, but are, rather. the result of (private) norm production by trade associations, independent professional organizations, commercial arbitrators, and multinational enterprises. See G. Teubner, '"Global Bukowina": Legal Pluralism in the World Society' in *Global Law Without a State*, ed. G. Teubner (1997) 3. The establishment of the WTO did not impede the growth of these a-national systems of law. On the contrary, the economic environment of expanded international commerce, which was facilitated and encouraged by the WTO, provided fresh stimulus to these processes of private rule-making.
2 For those who still doubt the existence of these side-effects, see, for example, R. Jha and J. Whalley, 'The Environmental Regime in Developing Countries' (paper presented at a NBER/FEW conference on 'Distributional and Behavioural Effects of Environmental Policy', Milan, 11–12 June 1999, available at <www.cid.harvard.edu/cidtrade> and W.D. Sunderlin et al., 'Economic Crisis, Small Farmers' Well Being, and Forest Cover Change in Indonesia' (2001) 29 *World Development* 767.

by any single system. A proper analysis of the trade-environment conflict must be sensitive, therefore, to the composite nature of contemporary global law. This article takes a closer look at one of the 'private' manifestations of this multi-faceted conflict: international construction law (the *lex constructionis*) – an important branch of the *lex mercatoria*.[3] The relevance of this field of law to environmental studies stems from the fact that construction activities – particularly those associated with large infra-structure projects – can generate significant environmental damage.[4] Any construction activity modifies the land or habitat in which it is taking place. This damage, is highly varied, and includes loss of biodiversity, reduction in the stability of land formations, and contamination of water resources. The large volume of waste generated by construction operations can cause further environmental degradation.[5]

The interference of the construction activity in the eco-system and human community, which hosts it, could give rise to bitter social disputes, driven by conflicting interests, values, and discourses. This article explores the way in which international construction law has confronted this construction-environment dilemma. While this exploration takes place in the context of a particular legal regime, its methodology and conclusions – in particular, the critique of the private/public regulatory separation and the cooperative regulatory model (which are developed in sections III.3 and III.4) – should be relevant to many other environmental dilemmas taking place at national or transnational levels. This alternative regulatory vision is consistent with the increasing recognition among environmental researchers that, to be successful, environmental policy must adopt a multi-dimensional strategy.[6]

The article proceeds as follows. Section I outlines the environmental world-view, which guides the discussion in the rest of the article. This world-view is based on a political interpretation of the ecological 'project'. Section II considers the nature of the *lex constructionis* as an autonomous system of law, and attempts to unravel the reflexivity structure of this legal system,

---

3 The term '*lex constructionis*' was first suggested in C. Molineaux, 'Moving Toward a Construction *Lex Mercatoria*: A *Lex Constructionis*' (1997) 14 *J. of International Arbitration* 55.

4 See, for example, the discussion in G. Ofori and P. Chan, 'Contractual Provisions For Sustainability in Construction in Singapore' (1999) 16 *International Construction Law Rev.* 241.

5 Construction activities also have indirect environmental effects, related to the impact of the construction activity on the general sustainability of the local or global economy, due to their intensive resource utilization and energy use. Ofori and Chan note, for example, that in monetary terms construction activity utilizes up to seven times as much wood, minerals, water, and energy as the rest of the economy (id., p. 242). This article focuses, however, on the direct effects.

6 See, for example, T. Tietenberg and D. Wheeler, 'Empowering the Community: Information Strategies For Pollution Control' (paper delivered at the Frontiers of Environmental Economics Conference, Virginia, 23–25 October 1998, available at the World Bank website, NIPR programme).

focusing on two key factors: its communicative patterns and its organizational features. This dual exploration points to two prominent features of the *lex constructionis*: that its main communicative channel is standard model-forms, and that its norm-production activity is controlled by few non-state actors. The article focuses on one key international player – the International Federation of Consulting Engineers (FIDIC) – which plays a dominant role in the international construction market.

Section III seeks to decode the linkage between the structural-cultural attributes of the *lex constructionis* and its environmental (in)sensitivity. It argues that the contractual tradition of the *lex constructionis*, in particular, its distinction between the 'public' and 'contractual' orders, have generated a legal culture that was highly inattentive to the ecological aspects of construction practice.[7] This has important practical consequences because of the deep environmental problematic of transnational construction projects. My goal is not confined, however, to an articulation of institutional 'blindness'. I am interested also in developing pragmatic alternatives. To this end, I draw a distinction between the contractual heritage of the *lex mercatoria* and a counter contractual vision, which depicts the construction contract as a semi-political mechanism, rather than a strictly private tool. This conceptual change seeks to break the traditional separation between the 'public' and 'private' realms – a division that characterizes most of the standard contracts in the construction market.

Of course, the main challenge lies in developing detailed normative/institutional configurations that would enable the realization of this 'political/constitutional' understanding of the contract. These configurations should have a reasonable 'fit' with the commercial constraints of the transnational construction market. The article offers some practical reflections, which seek to respond to this challenge.

---

7 In exploring this 'inattentiveness' I was guided by the idea that any communicative structure (for example, the legal system) is necessarily 'blind', or 'closed' to some features of the world. This blindness, or closure, reflects the fact that communication emerges as a product of coordinated selections at the level of inter-subjective interactions. It is, in other words, the result of a social process, by which a unique domain of possibilities is singled-out collectively, and provides a background for further selections. The emergence of communication (or societal meaning) thus comes, necessarily, at the expense of some other potential distinctions (or selections) which were successfully excluded. Any observer – whether a human being or a social system – by founding his or her observation on this distinction rather than any other, would fail to see what this distinction excludes. Only a second observer can view this failure – but he or she, also, would be subject to the limits of his or her own point of view. See N. Luhmann, '"What is the Case" and "What Lies Behind It?" the Two Sociologies and the Theory of Society' (1994) 12 *Sociological Theory* 126, 137. Note, however, that this closure is not all 'bad'. It also enables the system to act. Thus, changing too much can also be risky – it could undermine the capacity of the system to react to external perturbations.

I. THE POLITICS OF ECOLOGICAL CO-EXISTENCE

Construction activities constitute a highly visible ecological threat. Environmentalists tend to view this industry, primarily, as a source of ecological disturbance and disfigurement. Indeed, over the last years construction practice has been portrayed, increasingly, as an ecological culprit. This process of 'demonization' is at odds with the positive role that construction practice has played during human history – in providing basic human needs, such as safe dwelling and a tamed environment. The sharp contrast between these two articulations constitutes a difficult dilemma. In developing a legal response to this dilemma I want to contrast between two different environmental world-views, Both have emerged as a counter-response to the capitalist vision of 'nature-as-a-resource'. The first has been mostly associated with the 'deep-ecology' movement, which interprets the idea of 'environmentalism' as a new form of ethic, which 'gives to nature a social role beyond being a means for human well-being'.[8] This alternative, non-anthropocentric ethic sees the motif of 'domination of nature' as the main malady of modern society, leading to two possible resolutions of the nature/society opposition. The first seeks to replace the hierarchical approach to nature, which is characteristic of contemporary society, with an ideology of strict bio-egalitarianism. The second seeks to conflate the nature/society distinction, and to replace it by a holistic vision, in which the boundaries between humanity and nature are completely dissolved.

The practical implications of these interpretations remain unclear. Strict bio-egalitarianism can only lead to social paralysis. If both humans and nature are sanctified, how are we supposed to mediate between them if a conflict arises? The holistic vision is no less problematic. If humanity and nature are conflated into a unitary (non-hierarchical) whole, which becomes the primary object of moral deliberation, how should we understand its various components and envision their intricate relations (for example, in the context of a construction-induced conflict?). It seems that the only way in which these interpretations could be implemented in practice is through a strategy of strict 'social asceticism', which would call for a complete withdrawal from the industrial system and a return to a pre-capitalist society.[9] Only by adopting this vision of stern 'minimalism' could the idea of nature as the embodiment of non-instrumental moral value be given full effect

Bruno Latour's environmental philosophy evolved as a counter-thesis to the ideas of deep ecology. It offers, I believe, a more reasonable framework for thinking about the construction-environment dilemma. Instead of calling for bio-spherical egalitarianism or for the sanctification of nature, Latour

8 K. Eder, *The Social Construction of Nature: A Sociology of Ecological Enlightenment* (1996) 207. See, further, A. Naess, 'The Shallow and the Deep, Long-Range Ecology Movement: A Summary' (1983) 16 *Inquiry* 95.

9 See D. Forman, 'Putting the Earth First' in *Debating the Earth: The Environmental Politics Reader*, eds. J.S. Dryzek and D. Schlosberg (1998) 358.

argues that ecological dilemmas should be conceptualized as political dilemmas. This political vision is based on a radical shift in the way in which ecological dilemmas are observed; a shift from essences to relations. Latour is not interested in investigating the essence of things, in attributing a-priori labels to either humans or non-humans. His interest lies elsewhere: in developing rich articulations of the intricate ways in which humans and non-humans commingle and interact, and of the ways in which this commingling transforms them both (in terms of preferences, properties, and so on).[10] Construction activity is a rich source of such commingling: it provides the setting for a very 'tight' or 'intimate' (in terms of space and time) commingling between humans, eco-systems, and technologies.

But the move from essences to associations does not change just the way in which nature-society dilemmas are observed.[11] It also reformulates their resolution path – from the ethical to the political. To understand this change, Latour argues, 'one has to abandon the false conceit that ecology has anything to do with nature as such'. Rather, political ecology needs to be seen as 'a new way to handle all the objects of human and non-human collective life'; it is 'a collective experimentation on the possible associations between things and people without any of these entities being used, from now on, as a simple means by the others'.[12] By designating this new 'collective', Latour seeks to reformulate our understanding of politics and polity. He thus challenges not just the deep ecologists' dance between sanctification and equality, but also the traditional conceptions of politics and democracy, which have constructed these notions as exclusively human constructs.

Conceptualizing ecology as a political endeavour means – in contrast to the visions of bio-spherical egalitarianism or human domination of nature – that the rights of both humans and non-humans cannot be decided a priori. Rather, these rights can only emerge and be negotiated through a revised – 'ecologized' – political process. The main challenge lies, of course, in developing practical institutional structures in which this new 'ecologized'

---

10 You could feel, act, and be considered as a bourgeois, ecologically indifferent citizen for a long period but then the risk of a bulldozer transgressing on your neighborhood could turn you into a 'green warrior' or a green voter. And similarly, the bulldozer – once a 'neutral' technical artifact – could be transformed into an anti-nature token. See B. Latour, *Pandora's Hope: Essays on the Reality of Science Studies* (1999) 174–215.

11 This move does not mean that we have to abandon all our prior distinctions. One such basic distinction is between communicating beings, non-communicating beings, and societies (networks of communications). See N. Luhmann, *Ecological Communication* (1989). However, the political shift proposed by Latour provides one possible (and in no sense privileged) standpoint from which the relations between these distinct realms could be conceptualized.

12 See B. Latour, 'To Modernize or to Ecologize? That is the Question' in *Remaking Reality: Nature at the Millennium*, eds. N. Castree and B. Willems-Braun (1996) 221, 234.

polity could be realized.[13] It is on this point that the law and legal scholars can make their most substantial contribution. Devising regulatory structures is, after all, what the law has been doing from the moment it emerged into the social plane.

From this perspective, the solution to the construction-environment dilemma lies in the political domain. My critique of the *lex constructionis* follows this line of thought in that it does not attempt to proceed, deductively, from some universal solution to the trade and environment conflict. Rather, I explore the cultural and institutional features of this body of law, and examine how it could be transformed in order to facilitate a more inclusive 'ecological dialogue' which will give nature a more 'proper' voice *vis-à-vis* its human associates.

II. THE FEATURES OF THE *LEX CONSTRUCTIONIS* AS AN AUTONOMOUS LEGAL SYSTEM

1. *The basic structure of the international construction market*

The international activity in the construction market takes place in a limited segment of the global construction market – that which involves large-scale projects (such as airports, harbours, sanitary schemes, mines, petrochemical plants, and so on).[14] The international market for construction services has expanded substantially over the last decade;[15] supported by the conclusion, in 1995, of the WTO Agreement.[16] Construction projects are a multi-party operation. As such, they generate a complex web of contracts.[17] In international projects, the principal parties are generally the host nation's government, the project sponsors, lenders, contractors, operators, and insurers. The contractual framework can vary substantially between different

13 Latour, op. cit., n. 10, p. 214.
14 For a more detailed discussion see the WTO report 'Construction and Related Engineering Services: Background Note by the Secretariat' (1998).
15 id., para. 12. The size of this market is huge. In most industrialized economies the share of construction in total GDP is between 5 and 7 per cent (id., para. 7). Construction services are traded, primarily, through the establishment of commercial presence at the site of the works, either by local subsidiaries or through joint ventures between foreign and domestic firms. A good proxy for the scale of the trade in construction services is the total revenues of the top 225 international contractors. According to the WTO, total revenues have grown between 1994 and 1996 from $62,219.4 millions to $126,777.2 millions, a 104 per cent increase (id., table 1, p. 9). This economic expansion is likely to yield a parallel expansion in the legal universe that supports the global trade in construction services.
16 Particularly important in this context are the new General Agreement on Trade in Services ('GATS'), and the Plurilateral Agreement on Government Procurement (Annex 4 to the WTO Agreement), both signed at Marrakesh on 15 April 1994.
17 For a more detailed description of this complex contractual framework, see G.D. Vinter, *Project Finance* (1998).

83

project types, However, most construction projects include the following three basic types of contracts: a construction agreement, in which the project company and the contractor agree on the terms of the project; funding agreements between the project company and the lenders; and insurance contracts. Where the construction project concerns either an infrastructure service (public utility) or the extraction of natural resources, the contractual framework might include, in addition, a concession agreement in which the host government grants the project company a long-term right to engage in the relevant industry, and an operation agreement, which sets the conditions for the operation of the service.[18]

Of this complex contractual web, international construction law deals, principally, with the construction agreement. In that respect, the *lex constructionis* does not represent the whole legal complexity of the construction endeavour. However, from an environmental perspective, the construction agreement is probably the most interesting element of this contractual web, as this is the 'legal space' which deals directly with the ecological-physical aspects of the project. Any attempt to influence the environmental impact of a construction project should focus, therefore, on the structure and content of the construction agreement.

2. The emergence of the lex constructionis: basic communicative patterns

The *lex constructionis* is a product of standardized contracts, technical guidelines, and arbitration awards.[19] Standard contractual forms constitute, however, the most important element in this discursive universe: they form the principal communicative channel through which the *lex constructionis* evolves, and maintains its reflexivity.[20] While even the most popular forms are rarely used unamended,[21] they have a profound effect on the formation of normative expectations in this market. They underpin the negotiation process, and accompany the construction process from beginning to end. The common usage of standard contracts generates substantial economic advantages, which seem to ensure the durability of this practice. It has

18 A common type of operation agreement is an output purchase agreement which commits the host country, over a specified period, to purchase a minimum quantity of the project's output at an agreed price.
19 See B.J. Tieder, 'The Globalization of Construction – Evolving Standards of Construction Law' (1998) 15 *International Construction Law Rev.* 550, and Molineaux, op. cit., n. 3.
20 See J. Sweet, 'The American Institute of Architects: Dominant Actor in the Construction Documents Market' (1991) *Wisconsin Law Rev.* 317, and Tieder, id., p. 552. There are significant linkages and cross-dependencies between domestic-oriented forms and internationally-oriented standard contracts, see, for example, H. Lloyd, 'Prevalent Philosophies of Risk Allocation – An Overview' (1996) 13 *International Construction Law* 502. For reasons of space I do not consider these interlinkages here.
21 See W. Hughes and D. Greenwood, 'The Standardisation of Contracts For Construction' (1996) 13 *International Construction Law* 196, 204.

84

reduced the transaction costs of entering into an international project and has contributed to the evolvement of tendering as a conventional method of obtaining competing quotations.[22] Public international law (both customary and treaty law) has played, in contrast, a very limited role in the development of the *lex constructionis*.[23]

Standard model forms constitute, then, the main channel through which the *lex constructions* transforms itself. There are, however, several other important communicative channels. Of these the most important is international arbitration. Most of the transactions in the international construction market are subject to arbitration agreements. This means that the majority of construction-disputes are being adjudicated before private arbitrators, usually in one of the main international arbitration centres.[24] However, the capacity of the arbitration channel to instigate legal change is limited, due to several features of the international arbitration field: the lack of precedential practice, the absence of institutional cohesion (which prevents the evolvement of organizational custom), and the lack of a wide and timely circulation of judgments.[25] The increasing dominance of the International Chamber of Commerce (ICC) International Court of Arbitration might rectify, in the future, this lack of organizational cohesion, and could thus increase the role played by the arbitration channel in the evolution of the law.[26] The work of scholars constitutes another important communicative channel. Scholarly publications are a particularly important source of internal observation for the *lex constructionis* because, unlike

---

22 By ensuring a common basis for the evaluation of tenders, see N. G. Bunni, *The FIDIC Form of Contract: The Fourth Edition of the Red Book* (1991) 3. The WTO Agreement on Government Procurement, which is based on the idea of equal access to governmental contracts, has also contributed to the expansion of the tendering method.

23 The intervention of public international law in the construction market was generally limited to projects with transboundary effects. For a general discussion, see R. Lefeber, *Transboundary Environmental Interference and the Origin of State Liability* (1996) 19–46.

24 See Lloyd, op. cit., n. 20, p. 509. National courts, particularly in England and Wales, are another source of interpretation. Arbitration awards frequently refer to decisions of national courts, see the extracts of ICC arbitral awards on construction contracts, which appeared in the *ICC International Court of Arbitration Bulletin*, vols. 2(1), 9(1), and 9(2).

25 Whereas new electronic forms of storing legal data, such as *Lexis* and *Westlaw*, have changed significantly the pattern of communication in other legal spheres (particularly in the United States of America), in the arbitration world, awards are still available only in a printed form, with poor devices for sorting and ordering, and even that only after a substantial delay. As was noted above, the ICC has made some effort to rectify this problem by publishing extracts from ICC arbitral awards.

26 The prominence of the ICC arbitration centre seems to be guaranteed by the common stipulation in FIDIC's contracts that a contractual dispute should be submitted to ICC arbitration if it can not be resolved in a less contentious way: see C. Wade, 'FIDIC's Standard Forms of Contract – Principles and Scope of the Four New Books' (2000) 17 *International Construction Law Rev.* 5, 9. Other arbitration centres, such as the London Court of International Arbitration, have failed, so far, to establish themselves as prominent players in the construction arbitration market.

arbitration awards which tend to provide an extremely scattered and episodic portrait of the law, the work of scholars provides a comprehensive and updated observation of the law – particularly of new standard forms.[27]

Unlike domestic legal systems, in which legal change is effectuated through two different processes – legislation and judicial decisions – the *lex constructionis* changes principally through the channel of standard contractual forms. Its reflexivity structure is thus much more limited than that of domestic legal systems. This observation leads to two related predictions. First, that the *lex constructionis* would be much more influenced by its history: legal practices might persist even when the historical conditions in which they were formed cease to be relevant. Because of its limited reflexivity, we might reasonably expect such persistence to be more pervasive within the *lex constructionis* than in a domestic system of law. Second, the evolutionary path of the *lex constructionis* should be much more sensitive to the institutional nature and structure of the organizations which control the production of standard forms.[28] I will revisit these predictions in the course of the discussion of the openness of the *lex constructionis* to environmental considerations (section III below). The following section examines the institutional structure of the *lex constructionis*.

3. *The institutional setting of the* lex constructionis: *exclusion and dominance*

The international market for standard construction contracts is dominated by a small group of international organizations.[29] This private control of the norm-production process stands in contrast to the WTO realm in which the norm-production process is divided between a contractual, inter-state realm, and an independent judicial system. The main players are the International Federation of Consulting Engineers (FIDIC),[30] the International European Construction Federation (FIEC), the British Institution of Civil Engineers (ICE), the Engineering Advancement Association of Japan (ENAA), the American Institute of Architects (AIA),[31] and the International Bank for

27 See, for example, the commentaries on FIDIC's Red Book by E.C. Corbett, *FIDIC 4th – A Practical Legal Guide: A Commentary on the International Construction Contract* (1991), and Bunni, op. cit., n. 22. Forums like the *International Construction Law Review* fulfil a similar role. The capacity of scholarly publications to effectuate legal change remains, however, quite limited.

28 Neither of these predictions should lead, a priori, to a conclusion that the *lex constructionis* is inefficient or ecologically indifferent. One cannot rule out the possibility that a legal system will develop very sensitive private-legislative mechanisms that will compensate for the absence of judicial innovations.

29 For a recent survey of these organizations, see Tieder, op. cit., n. 19, pp. 554–79.

30 The acronym stands for the French title: the *Federation Internationale des Ingenieurs – Conseils*.

31 Although AIA model forms are not meant to be used in international projects, their widespread use in the United States market (Sweet, op. cit., n. 20) has turned them into a significant transnational benchmark.

Reconstruction and Development (the World Bank).[32] Other key
contributors are UNCITRAL and UNIDROIT, through their more general
work on universal contract models.[33] UNCITRAL was involved also in
specific work on the construction market.[34] International legal firms are
another important player.[35]

I would like to focus, however, on one prominent player in this group –
the International Federation of Consulting Engineers.[36] This does not imply
that the other players are not important, but FIDIC enjoys a dominant
position which justifies, I believe, this special attention. The discussion that
follows examines closely the structure of FIDIC's contractual products, and
the institutional framework that facilitates the norm-production process.[37] I
will nonetheless make comparative references to the contractual products of
two other organizations: ENAA and the ICE.

FIDIC was founded in Belgium in 1913.[38] It is an association of national

32 The World Bank's operational directives have a large influence on the operations of
    other public lending bodies such as the Asian Development Bank, see Tieder, op.
    cit., n. 19, p. 555. To some extent the World Bank also influences the lending
    practices of private financial institutions.
33 See Tieder, id., pp. 558–72. In that context, the publication, in 1994, of *UNIDROIT's
    Principles of International Commercial Contracts* was particularly important.
    UNIDROIT's principles set themselves with the ambitious task of creating a model
    contract law for cross-border transactions, see K.P. Berger, 'The *Lex Mercatoria*
    Doctrine and the UNIDROIT Principles of International Commercial Contracts'
    (1997) 28 *Law and Policy in International Business* 943. UNCITRAL's most
    important contribution was the adoption, in 1993, of the Model Law on Procurement
    of Goods, Construction and Services. This model law deals, however, only with pre-
    contractual selection practices, and does not address contract performance issues or
    the settlement of disputes (Tieder, id., pp. 561–2).
34 In 1988 UNCITRAL published its 'Legal Guide on Drawing Up International
    Contracts for the Construction of Industrial Works' (1988) which was quite widely
    used, especially by developing countries. Another and more recent contribution is a
    'Legislative Guide on Privately Financed Infrastructure Projects' (2001).
35 See Y. Dezalay and B. Garth, 'Merchants of Law as Moral Entrepreneurs:
    Constructing International Justice from the Competition for Transnational Business
    Disputes' (1995) 29 *Law and Society Rev.* 27.
36 For the central role of FIDIC in the construction market see ICC, 'Extracts of ICC
    Arbitral Awards on Construction Contracts Referring to the F.I.D.I.C. Conditions'
    (1991) 2 *ICC International Court of Arbitration Bull.* 15. The ICC notes in the
    introduction to this collection that: 'In recent years construction disputes have
    represented some 21 per cent of cases submitted annually to ICC arbitration. A
    significant portion of these construction cases is governed by the F.I.D.I.C. ...
    Contract (International) for Works of Civil Engineering Construction or on
    conditions modeled on the F.I.D.I.C. Conditions' (id., p. 15).
37 This aspect of FIDIC's work has received little attention in the legal literature. Most of
    the literature consists of legal analysis of FIDIC and other international standard forms.
38 The following description is based on a paper by John Bowcock who was the
    chairman of FIDIC's Contracts Committee at the time: J. Bowcock, 'The Four New
    FIDIC Forms of Contract – Introduction' (FIDIC New Contracts Launch Seminar
    Series, September – December 1998), available at <www.fidic.org>.

member associations; thus, it does not include as members individual firms of consulting engineers. The original founding countries were France, Belgium, and Switzerland. FIDIC's current membership circle transcends the limited European membership of its inception period. By September 2001 FIDIC's membership encompassed sixty-seven national member associations representing some 560,000 professionals.[39] FIDIC is governed by an executive committee and several specific committees and task groups.[40]

FIDIC has dominated the market for international construction documents since the 1960s, with its standard forms of contract for engineering construction and for the provision of mechanical and electrical plant. The first form, 'Conditions of Contract for Works of Civil Engineering Construction', which came to be known as the 'Red Book', was used mainly for large projects, such as infrastructure and hydropower. The second form, 'Conditions of Contract for Electrical and Mechanical Works including Erection on Site' (also called the 'Yellow Book') – was used mainly for the construction of industrial sites. Both forms have been in widespread use for several decades.[41] FIDIC's Red Book was particularly dominant in the world market.[42] The prominent status of the Red Book was affirmed by the World Bank, which has incorporated it into its standard bidding documents for procurement of works.[43] Other private associations, such as the British Institution of Civil Engineers and ENAA of Japan, have

---

39 The information was drawn from FIDIC's website, <www.fidic.org/federation/default.asp>, visited on 26 September 2001.

40 These include an Assessment Panel for Adjudicators, Business Practices Committee, Contracts Committee, Capacity Building Task Force, Integrity Management Task Force, Quality Management Task Force, Sustainable Development Task Force, and a Risk Management Forum. The data were drawn from FIDIC's website, <www.fidic.org/about/committees.asp>, visited 26 September 2001.

41 The Red Book was first published in 1957 and its fourth (and last) edition was published in 1987. The Yellow Book's third edition was published in 1987.

42 For a comprehensive commentary on the Red Book, see Corbett, op. cit., n. 27, and Bunni, op. cit., n. 22. The Red Book has been amended several times since 1987. In 1999 FIDIC published a new series of contracts, which replaced the Red Book. The detailed discussion below is based on FIDIC new contractual products which, as will be explained below, are quite different from their predecessors.

43 See the World Bank Standard Bidding Documents for Procurement of Works ('SBDW') May 2000, electronic version available at <www.worldbank.org/html/opr/procure/workspage.html>, visited 25 September 2001). The SBDW are based on the fourth edition of the Red Book (1987, reprinted 1992 with amendments) and thus do not reflect, as yet, FIDIC's most recent forms. See, also, Molineaux, op. cit., n. 3, p. 59. Additional indication of the normative status of FIDIC's model forms can be found in the recent decision of the World Bank to base its new trial edition (2000) of Bidding Documents for Procurement of Simple Works (of Small Value, Short Duration and Low Risk) on FIDIC's 'Short Form of Contract' (1999). A copy of this sample document is available on the World Bank website, id.

88

also produced important standard documents;[44] however, none of these documents has received the same kind of international stature that was achieved by FIDIC documents, in particular by the Red Book.

The process through which FIDIC has produced its most recent contractual products provides a good illustration to the institutional bounds of the *lex constructionis* (or, in other words, to the openness of the norm-production process). These bounds tend to perpetuate the ecological insensitivity, discussed in the following section. In 1994 FIDIC decided to update the Red and Yellow Books, by initiating a long and varied consultation process.[45] This consultation process was mainly restricted, however, to FIDIC's natural audience: its members and other relevant groups such as law firms, contracting groups, and financing institutions.[46] The consultation process did not extend beyond the limited circle of the potential users of FIDIC's forms. FIDIC has not consulted other groups, such as environ-mental and labour groups, despite the fact that international construction projects can have a large influence on the life of the people that these groups represent.

The institutional process behind the production of FIDIC's new contracts, reveals, therefore, a clear pattern of exclusion: the contracts were formulated in the closed organizational sphere of the construction industry (including related affiliates like financial institutions).[47] Groups which were not part of this closed circle were left out. The exclusion of other voices, such as those of environmental groups, provides one explanation for the environmental insensitivity of FIDIC contracts, which will be considered in more detail in section III below. However, it would be wrong, I believe, to explain this insensitivity simply in terms of cartelistic behaviour.[48] The cultural orientation of FIDIC cannot be reduced to the business interests of its members. This non-economic background (to which I shall return in section IV below) indicates that the organizational closure, which was sketched above, could be altered.

---

44 See Tieder, op. cit., n. 19, pp. 576–9.
45 See, Wade, op. cit., n. 26.
46 id., p. 7.
47 The drafting process within other professional associations seems to follow a similar pattern of exclusion. See, for example, the discussion of the American Institute of Architects model contracts in T.L Stipanowich, 'Reconstructing Construction Law: Reality and Reform in a Transactional System' (1998) *Wisconsin Law Rev.* 463, 526.
48 For this type of argument in the context of standardization, see G. Spindler, 'Market Processes, Standardisation, and Tort Law' (1998) 4 *European Law J.* 316.

III. ENVIRONMENTAL CLOSURE AND STANDARD CONSTRUCTION CONTRACTS

1. *FIDIC's model forms: a general exposition*

This section seeks to expose and criticize the environmental record of the *lex constructionis*. Whereas the domestic scene, particularly in the United States of America and Europe, has experienced a burgeoning wave of legal innovations, covering different aspects of the environmental problematic – from corporate liability (moving from traditional notions of individual liability to new forms of collective liability), pollution control (using market mechanisms rather than strict emission standards), to new regulatory tools (such as broad disclosure requirements and eco-labelling),[49] the *lex constructionis* has shown little 'environmental' innovation. It has maintained in general an attitude of indifference toward environmental problems. This section seeks to explore the nature of this indifference through a close examination of some of the model forms that dominate the global construction market, in particular the new series of contracts which was published by FIDIC in 1999. I will try to assess to what extent these model forms incorporate and give voice to general environmental concerns.[50] Two other model forms, ENAA's Model Form of International Contract for Process Plant Construction (ENAA Model Form) and the ICE New Engineering Contract (NEC) will be used as an additional comparative source. I have chosen these two model contracts as a second point of reference, because, although they do not enjoy the same universal stature as FIDIC's contracts, they are also used commonly in international projects.[51]

---

49 See, for example, G. Teubner, 'The Invisible Cupola: From Causal to Collective Liability' in *Environmental Law and Ecological Responsibility*, eds. G. Teubner, L. Farmer and D. Murphy (1994) 17–48, discussing new doctrines of collective liability, and Tietenberg and Wheeler, op. cit., n. 6, pointing to information strategies as a new form of environmental regulation.

50 The analysis of FIDIC's new forms does not intend to provide a comprehensive analysis of their provisions. For a more general analysis, see, for example, P.L. Booen, 'The Three Major New FIDIC Books' (2000) 17 *International Construction Law Rev.* 24, and Wade, op. cit., n. 26.

51 As was noted before, one indication of the international status of FIDIC's Red Book was its adoption by the World Bank. The ENAA's Model Form of International Contract for Process Plant Construction was also adopted by the World Bank, and is used in its 'Standard Bidding Documents for Supply and Installation of Plant and Equipment' (November 1997, revised January 1999), electronic version available at <www.worldbank.org/html/opr/procure/workspage.html>. For a commentary on ENAA's Model Form, see T. Wiwen-Nilsson, 'The 1996 Edition of the ENAA Model Form – International Contract for Power Plant Construction – A Brief Review' (1997) 14 *International Construction Law Rev.* 273. ICE's NEC series, which was first published in 1993 (a second edition was published in 1995), has also significant international profile: see M. Barnes, 'The New Engineering Contract –

Before proceeding to review the environmental aspects of FIDIC's new contracts it might be worthwhile to consider the general structure of the three model forms, which constitute the core of FIDIC's new contracts-series. FIDIC's new line of contracts[52] reflects a change of thought in FIDIC. The new contracts focus more on the apportionment of responsibilities between the parties, than on the project's type. Thus, the emphasis was shifted from 'civil' versus 'electrical and mechanical' works to 'works being designed by the Employer' versus 'works being designed by the Contractor'. Accordingly, the special task-group established for this purpose decided to develop a new construction book to be used for building/civil/ engineering works designed by the employer or by his representative, the engineer (henceforth, the Construction Contract). Conversely the new *Plant & Design-Build Book* was designed to be suitable for plant/building/ engineering works designed by (or on behalf of) the contractor (henceforth, the Plant Contract).[53] In addition, FIDIC issued a completely new model form, based on a two-party approach, entitled the EPC Contract.[54]

Both the new construction contract and the plant contract kept the traditional three-party structure, which was used in the contracts' previous editions. Within this framework, the engineer, whom the employer (the procurer of the works) employs for this purpose, administers the contract, monitors the construction work, and certifies payments. Whenever the engineer is required to determine any contentious matter or settle any claim for time extension or extra costs, he or she is first required to consult with each of the parties in an endeavour to reach agreement. If agreement is not achieved, the engineer is required to make a fair determination in accordance with the contract. If the engineer's determination is not agreed by either of the parties, or if a dispute otherwise arises, the parties can forward

An Update' (1996) 13 *International Construction Law Rev.* 89, 95. The NEC series comprises six different options, which all share the same core clauses. I will use the NEC option F: *Management Contract (November 1995)* as my reference document.

52 The contracts were published initially in 1998 in a test edition. All my comments refer to the 1999 edition of the contracts.

53 See Wade, op. cit., n. 26, p. 8. In the construction jargon the term 'employer' refers to the entity which initiated the project. In many cases this would be a governmental body of some sort; the term 'contractor' refers to the entity which would be responsible for the actual execution of the project.

54 These three short titles are used in FIDIC publications, the full names being: 'Conditions of Contract for Construction (for Building and Engineering Works Designed by the Employer)'; 'Conditions of Contract for Plant and Design-Build (for Electrical and Mechanical Plant, and for Building and Engineering Works, Designed by the Contractor)'; and 'Conditions of Contract for EPC Turnkey Projects' (EPC stands for engineering, procurement, construction). See FIDIC, 'New Documents Ready For Edmonton' (1998) 1998/2 *FIDIC Q. Report* 2. A fourth form, which was also published in 1999 – *Short Form of Contract* – deals mainly with small-value and simple projects. It is thus less relevant to the international market, and will not be referred to in the following.

the dispute to a dispute adjudication board (DAB).[55] If either party does not accept the DAB's decision and the parties fail to reach an amicable settlement, the matter must be finally settled by international arbitration, usually under the ICC Rules.[56]

During the work on updating the Red and Yellow Books it became apparent to the special task group that there is a demand in the market for a contract that takes a two-party approach, where the engineer plays a less prominent role in the administration of the contract resulting in the EPC contract.[57] This demand was a reflection of the increase in the number of privately financed international projects.[58] The move toward private forms of financing triggered the development of several new models of project delivery. These include the Build-Operate-Transfer (BOT) model, and the Build-Own-Operate (BOO) model. In these concession-type arrangements a private company[59] (the concessionaire) is granted the right and obligation to provide an infrastructure service, usually by the state or a municipality.[60] The service, whether gas, power, water, transport, sanitation, or telecommunications, is provided under terms and conditions specified in a contract or licence. The concessionaire takes over operational responsibility and at least part of the commercial risk of service provision.[61] By granting the concession the state eliminates the need to pay for the construction services once the work is completed.

In such projects, the concessionaire takes most of the responsibility for the financing, construction, and operation of the project. The uncertainty associated with BOO or BOT projects includes, in addition to the 'normal' risks associated with the construction process, also the risks associated with the project's future cash flow. In order to limit their risk exposure, the lenders seek to limit the uncertainties associated with the contract, both by

55 The DAB comprises one or three persons, which should be jointly appointed by the parties, either at the commencement of the contract or on an ad hoc basis. The concept of DAB was imposed on FIDIC by the World Bank, which was not happy with the original Red Book framework, which appointed the engineer – despite being paid by the employer – as the internal disputes-adjudicator of the contract. The DAB concept is discussed in more detail below.

56 See, Wade, op. cit., n. 26, pp. 8–9.

57 id., p. 9.

58 id., p. 10, and World Bank 'Privatization and Environmental Assessment: Issues and Approaches' in *Environmental Assessment Sourcebook Update No. 6.* (1994).

59 The construction company and the operator of the infrastructure service may be different entities.

60 I am interested here mainly in those concession arrangements, which include both a 'service' element (the operation and maintenance of the facilities and the supply of the infrastructure service) and a 'construction' element (the design and construction of the new infrastructure). However, some concession arrangements may include only a service element.

61 See P Guilaim and M. Kerf, 'Concessions – The Way to Privatize Infrastructure Sector Monopolies' *World Bank Public Policy for the Private Sector Series*, October 1995, 4 at <www.worldbank.org>.

eliminating the 'engineer' as an independent contractual persona with semi-arbitral powers, and by placing the majority of risks associated with the construction of the facility (for example, market and technical risks) on the construction contractor.[62] The EPC Contract reflects the special requirements of privately financed models by placing the total responsibility for the design and construction of the infrastructure or other facility on the contractor, and providing a higher degree of certainty that agreed contract price and time will not be exceeded.

2. Environmental concerns and FIDIC model contracts

The way in which FIDIC (and other) contracts deal with environmental issues reflects a commitment to a strict public/private dichotomy, and their understanding of environmental responsibility is very much a product of this dichotomy. In analysing the contractual treatment of environmental problems I will use the concept of environmental impact assessment (EIA) as my focal point. EIA constitutes today the preferred regulatory response to the construction-environment dilemma, aiming to provide a comprehensive framework in which the ecological impacts (including long-term effects) of construction activities can be assessed and dealt with. The EIA doctrine is based on the idea of ex-ante assessment – on the adoption of a forward-looking approach, which seeks to examine the environmental impacts of a project at an early stage. Because the EIA process is conducted before the commencement of the construction project – with all the financial commitments that come with it – it opens the way for an early detection of 'environmental' mistakes (for example, problems of location, or basic design flaws). EIA enables, therefore, the prevention of nonreversible actions and costly financial commitments. EIA also provides a mechanism for blocking those construction activities, which are completely untenable from an environmental perspective. The extent to which FIDIC's new contracts incorporate the concept of 'environmental impact assessment' can provide, therefore, a good indication of their ecological 'sensitivity'.

Before turning to the detailed assessment of FIDIC forms, it is important to make more explicit the ecological challenge that is faced by the *lex constructionis* (this would help us to assess the environmental 'failings' of this legal system). The scope of this challenge is determined by the sequential fashion in which the construction process is observed by the law. The standard construction contract (FIDIC's or any other) does not normally govern the contractual phase in which the EIA process takes place. The construction contract regulates the 'main phase' of the construction project, the detailed design and execution. In contrast, the EIA process is usually part of a 'pre-contract' evaluation process, in which the procurer of the works assesses the feasibility of the development plan and considers possible alternatives. This

62 See Wade, op. cit., n. 26, p. 11.

93

assessment process comprises, usually, in addition to the EIA element, other studies which examine, for example, the financial feasibility of the project, and its compatibility with local land-use requirements.[63] This stage is governed by a separate set of consultancy contracts, and by extra-contractual legal requirements.[64] The construction contract holds, then, a posterior position in this contractual sequence.

The legal separation between the different phases of the construction project creates two difficulties. The first concerns the issue of implementation and monitoring. the second has to do with unforeseen contingencies. The first problem points to the need for a contractual mechanism, which could ensure that the conclusions of the EIA are actually implemented. Proper monitoring procedures should form an essential element of any such mechanism. The importance of follow-up mechanisms stems from the fact that both the regulatory authority and the developer may find it tempting to use the EIA as a 'pseudo-analysis'.[65] From the authority's perspective, the EIA process could be perceived solely as a pre-decision mechanism, which culminates in the authority's final decision to grant (or refuse) a development consent, and as such has no post-decision (for example, monitoring) implications. From the developers' point of view, once the project is granted a formal consent, they have little interest in developing and implementing a monitoring and post-auditing programme, which would enable them to implement the EIA conclusions (and provide the authority with a convenient supervising mechanism). The EIA literature points, indeed, to that lack of proper post-EIA monitoring as one of the key problems in the current EIA practice, both in the developing and developed world.[66]

The issue of unforeseen contingencies points to a different problem, which stems from the (unwarranted) tendency to treat the conclusions of the EIA process as a closed and final set of prescriptions. This perception ignores the fact that the EIA process, which is conducted before the commencement of the project, cannot provide a complete description of the

63 See, for example, UNCITRAL (1988), op. cit., n. 34, pp. 9–13.
64 The separation between these two phases is further exacerbated by the fact that in most cases the preliminary studies will not be conducted by the contractor that would be engaged to construct the works, but by another firm (mainly because of the risk of conflict of interests). In complex projects this principle could, however, be compromised (id., p. 12).
65 'Pseudo-EIAs' indicates those EIAs which are carried out with the single objective of getting the project cleared. irrespective of the true environmental costs. See A.K. Biswas, 'Summary and Recommendations' in *Environmental Impact Assessment for Developing Countries*, eds. A.K. Biswas and S.B.C. Agarwal (1992) 240–1.
66 For a discussion of the problem of compliance monitoring in the context of the developing world see id.; and see, also, for example, B. Dipper et al., 'Monitoring and Post-auditing in Environmental Impact Assessment: A Review' (1998) 41 *J. of Environmental Planning and Management* 731, 735 (discussing the EU), and L. Canter and R. Clark, 'NEPA Effectiveness – a Survey of Academics' (1997) 17 *Environmental Impact Assessment Rev.* 313, 323–4 (discussing the United States of America).

project's ecological impacts. Once the project unfolds there are bound to be some environmental 'surprises'. Coping with the problem of unforeseen contingencies requires more than a mere implementing mechanism. It requires the development of reflexivity procedures, which would encourage the parties to reassess the environmental impacts of the project (even when such impacts have no functional implications), and would provide the parties with clear procedures through which the original design or work-programme could be updated in response to such contingencies.

The discussion so far has pointed to two main legal challenges (both related to the sequential nature of the construction process): post-EIA monitoring and unforeseen contingencies. None of these problems is treated by FIDIC contracts (or by the ENAA and NEC forms). For reasons of space I will not enter here into a detailed description of the contracts.[67] I will only make some brief references to the actual – and unsatisfactory way – in which FIDIC contracts deal with the environmental issue. A direct reference to environmental concerns can be found only in one clause, which is common to the construction, plant, and EPC contracts. Article 4.18, which is titled 'Protection of the Environtnent', provides that:

> The Contractor shall take all reasonable steps to protect the environment (both on and off'the Site) and to limit damage and nuisance to people and property resulting from pollution, noise and other results of his operations.
> The Contractor shall ensure that emissions, surface discharges and effluent from the Contractor's activities shall not exceed the values indicated in the Employer's Requirements, and shall not exceed the values prescribed by applicable Laws.[68]

While the inclusion of Article 4.18 in FIDIC's new forms does reflect an awareness of environmental issues, its limited coverage means that it cannot provide an adequate response to many environmental concerns. The duty of care imposed on the contractor by Article 4.18 is limited to the contractor's operations on and off the site; it does not cover the broader and long-term ecological impacts of the construction project as a whole.[69] Moreover, this provision makes no attempt to deal with the challenges of post-EIA monitoring or unforeseen contingencies. The ENAA's model form and the Institution of Civil Engineers NEC do not include even such a limited provision.

---

67 For a more detailed discussion, see O. Perez, 'Ecological Sensitivity and Global Legal Pluralism: Rethinking the Trade and Environment Debate' (PhD thesis, London School of Economics and Political Science, 2001) ch. 6.
68 Article 4.18 of the construction contract uses the term 'specification' instead of 'employer's requirement'.
69 Article 4.18 can be enforced, of course, only by the employer. The question is whether the employer will bother to enforce this provision in those cases in which its breach does not affect the successful completion of the project. I did not find examples for such litigation with respect to FIDIC contracts (which does not necessarily say that there were no such incidents).

95

FIDIC's new contracts do not include any other clear environmental provisions, or, to that extent, any direct reference to a pre-contractual EIA statement. This is also the case with respect to the NEC and ENAA's model form. The main other (indirect) route through which the 'environmental' issue enters into the contractual universe of the industry's standard forms concerns the contracts' general compliance provisions, which require the parties to comply with the applicable laws of the host country in the design and execution phases of the project.[70] These would include, of course, any environmental regulation, The underlying assumption behind these provisions is that it is the responsibility of the 'external' law to regulate the environmental aspects of the construction activity, including the EIA process, and any post-EIA requirements. The compliance provisions construct the ecological side-effects of the construction activity, as a 'public order' dilemma – a dilemma that lies outside the contractual realm – and as such should be regulated by the state which hosts the construction project.

3. Critique of the contemporary contractual response to the environment-construction dilemma

The response of the *lex constructionis* to the construction-environmental dilemma is, then, based primarily on a strategy of deference, which seeks to externalize the responsibility for regulating the environmental aspects of the construction activity to the 'extra-contractual' realm of the law of the host-state. This is achieved through the employment of 'compliance' provisions, which appear in most of the standard forms. The fundamental assumption behind the deference model is that the contract is a private ordering device. As such it cannot and should not interfere with the kind of issues that fall under the ambit of the 'public order'. Since environmental problems are seen as part and parcel of this 'public order' they are envisaged as falling outside the boundaries of the contractual regime. The contractual order has, under this vision, no original role to play in the field of public order. Its only contribution is to provide legally recognized addressees to which external orders may be directed. The environmental closure of the *lex constructionis* is a clear product of this private/public divide.

This sharp distinction between the private and public orders, which characterizes the *lex constructionis*, has strong roots within the *lex mercatoria*. The purpose of the *lex mercatoria* was understood, historically, as protecting business expectations; the primary task of the *lex mercatoria* was to render business relations more calculable.[71] The *lex mercatoria* was

---

70 See Articles 1.13, 2.2, of the construction contract, and Articles 1.13, 2.2, 5.4 of the plant and EPC contracts. See, also, Articles 9.3, 9.4, 10.3, and 10.4 of the ENAA model form, Articles 18.1, 31.2, 95.3 (health and safety requirements), and 19.1 and 21.2 (general compliance requirements) of the NEC.

71 See H. Collins, 'Formalism and Efficiency: Designing European Commercial Contract Law' (2000) 1 *European Rev. of Private Law* 211, 216–17.

seen, therefore, as having no interest in other forms of expectations. This 'interest' had to be imposed from the outside. The growing debate among scholars and practitioners of international arbitration with respect to the linkage between mandatory rules of law and the *lex mercatoria* is one example of the influence of this legal conception.[72] The question underlying this debate was to what extent mandatory rules of law, or issues of 'public policy', should interfere with the 'law of the contract', This question has usually arisen in proceedings for enforcement of foreign arbitral awards, where the 'public policy' argument was invoked as a ground for refusing enforcement. The question has become especially important in the field of competition law, An increasing number of cases deal with the question whether an international contract, which is seen as inconsistent with the competition laws of the country in which it was made or was intended to be executed, should be given effect.[73]

While there are varying opinions with respect to how far mandatory rules can interfere with the realm of the *lex mercatoria*, and how the content of these rules should be determined,[74] the legal debate is, nonetheless, based on the shared and uncontested assumption that the private realm of the *lex mercatoria* can make no positive contribution to the realm of public order. The debate has focused exclusively on the question whether public law can (and should) encroach into the private order of the contract. The opposite question has never been discussed.[75] As one ICC arbitrator has put it: 'Agreements and contractual obligations may not be extended to the field of public orders'.[76]

---

72 The New York Convention on the Recognition and Enforcement of Foreign Arbitral Awards recognizes the violation of public policy (or *ordre public*) as a ground for refusing recognition/enforcement of foreign awards (see Article V.2). A similar provision is included in *UNCITRAL Model Law on International Commercial Arbitration* (1985), see Article 36.

73 The two leading cases are the US Supreme Court decision in *Mitsubishi* v. *Soler* 473 US 614 (1985), a case involving the applicability of the US Sherman Act to an arbitration conducted under Swiss law, and the European Court of Justice decision in Case C-126/97 *Eco Swiss China Time Ltd.* v. *Benetton International NV* [1999] ECR 1–3055, where the ECJ considered this question in light of the EU competition rules. For a more detailed discussion of these cases, see A. Sheppard and N. Nassar, *Final Report on Public Policy as a Bar to Enforcement of Arbitral Awards* (2000) 19–20, and D. Hochstrasser, 'Choice of Law and "Foreign" Mandatory Rules in International Arbitration' (1994) 11 *J. of International Arbitration* 57, 75–9.

74 For a detailed discussion of this debate see Sheppard and Nassar, id, and Hochstrasser, id.

75 This question was discussed, however, in the domestic context, see, for example, note, 'Private Law Making by Trade Associations' (1949) 62 *Harvard Law Rev.* 1346, 1367 and M.C. Dorf and C.F. Sabel, 'Constitution of Democratic Experimentalism' (1998) 98 *Columbia Law Rev.* 267.

76 See S. Jarvin, 'International Chamber of Commerce Court of Arbitration: Award Rendered in Case No. 3902 in 1984' (1984) 2 *International Construction Law Rev.* 49, 52 (which includes a report of the case).

97

However, the translocation of the distinction between the contractual and public orders from the *lex mercatoria* to the *lex construcionis* is highly problematic from an environmental perspective. Indeed, it undermines the capacity of the *lex constructionis* to 'see' the deep environmental problematic of the construction practice. There are two aspects to this legal 'blindness'. The first is political; the second is functional. From a political perspective, there is a problematic gap between the fragmented legal image that is generated by the *lex constructionis*, and the actual socio-environmental intimacy that characterizes the construction endeavour. Construction activities, which encroach deeply into the social and ecological localities in which they take place, are highly contextualized activities; they are 'webbed' into their social and ecological surroundings. This embeddedness is highly incongruent with the image of an isolated 'business relation', which underscores the contractual tradition of the *lex mercatoria*. The fragmented discourse of the *lex constructionis* is 'blind', in other words, to the community that is fabricated by the interference of the construction endeavour in a particular geographical space and a delimited time horizon.

This 'blindness' of the *lex constructionis* provides a convenient setting for the externalization of the project's environmental costs to the extra-contractual community. In that respect the contractual tradition of the *lex mercatoria* goes hand in hand with the economic constraints that surround the construction market. Economists view the legal contract as a tool for enhancing the economic value of the business deal for its parties. This economic vision, as its legal counterpart, provides no basis for the consideration of those interests, which are not parties to the 'deal'.[77] The notion of 'efficient risk allocation' further illustrates how this logic of externalization operates. In order to maximize its economic value the contract is expected to provide the parties with an efficient risk-allocation scheme. This should be achieved by allocating particular risks to the party best able to manage them.[78] Any other allocation would inhibit the realization of a surplus-maximizing transaction. The economic vision clearly encourages the parties to allocate environmental risks to the extra-contractual community, when they can do it without any external consequences.[79]

---

77 Under this economic vision, a perfect, or complete contract is that which 'fully realize[s] the potential gains from trade in all states of the worlds', see I. Ayres and R. Gertner, 'Strategic Contractual Inefficiency and the Optimal Choice of Legal Rules' (1992) 101 *Yale Law J.* 729, 730.

78 See L.W. Carter and G. Bond, *Financing Private Infrastructure* (1996) 67.

79 Indeed, the idea that 'third parties' might need protection from such externalization is used to justify in the national context – the encroachment of the 'freedom of contract' ideal by mandatory rules. A prominent example is antitrust laws, which restrict the power of private parties to enter into exclusive dealing agreements.

98

But the private/public dichotomy, and the sharp apportionment of roles that accompanies it within the contractual discourse of the *lex constructionis*, is problematic also from a functional perspective. The assumption that the extra-contractual realm can provide the regulatory services that are expected from it under the deference model is highly questionable. The complexity of the construction endeavour requires a cooperative regulatory strategy, which would bring together the problem-solving capacities of the constructing agents, the regulatory establishment, and the community that hosts the project. Thus, for example, successful environmental assessment might require the involvement of both local knowledge and highly technical capabilities. Assessing the environmental and social impacts of a project is a 'fuzzy' and unbounded task. There is no clear candidate to whom this task can be delegated on exclusive terms. The sharp distinction between the internal and external orders inhibits the evolvement of such flexible, trans-domain collaborations. The fact that the regulative capacities of many developing countries are highly limited further emphasizes the need for such collaborations.[80] It is important to note in this context, that the existing international regulatory framework cannot, in its current form, fill the regulatory void that characterizes the developing world.[81]

4. *A different contractual vision?*

Any attempt to incorporate environmental concerns into the *lex constructionis* would require, then, a change in the current conception of the construction contract. I believe that viewing the construction contract as a semi-political mechanism, rather than a strictly private tool, can provide a useful basis for transforming the current environmental insensitivity of the *lex constructionis*. This transformation should seek to break the traditional

---

80 Thus, for example, in many developing countries EIA is not required, and, even when it is required, tends to be poorly implemented and monitored. See Biswas and Agarwal, op. cit., n. 65, and the World Bank, op. cit., n. 58, p. 4. The EIA issue is, of course, only one aspect of this institutional weakness. Similar regulatory problems exist in the supervision of industrial pollution, see, for example, S. Pargal et al., 'Formal and Informal Regulation of Industrial Pollution: Comparative Evidence from Indonesia and the United States', World Bank Policy Research Working Paper 1797 (1997).

81 First, the activities of transnational corporations are not subject to a general (and binding) system of international supervision. Second, the issue of EIA itself is subject to a limited international regulation. Even when there is some sort of international regulation, it is limited, usually, to projects with substantial transboundary effects. As it currently stands, international environmental law does not seek to regulate those construction projects which are contained within the boundaries of one jurisdiction, even when they involve multinational cooperation: C. Klein-Chesivoir, 'Avoiding Environmental Injury: the Case for Widespread Use of Environmental Impact Assessments in International Development Projects' (1990) 30 *Virginia J. of International Law* 517, 527.

division (between the public and private realms) that characterizes the regulatory spectrum of the modern welfare state. The cornerstone of this alternative vision is the idea that any construction activity creates, through its interference in a singular geographical space, a micro 'polity', which consists of the inhabitants (humans and non-humans!) of this space.[82] This micro-polity is not just a reflection of common space/time boundaries but, more importantly, of a common dilemma: how to cope, collectively, with the potential impacts of a proposed construction project. Indeed, the fact that this dilemma requires a collective solution is what makes it political.

Under this view the construction contract should constitute an integral part of the constitutional' framework through which this collective dilemma is resolved, The construction contract is conceptualized, then, as one of the tools through which the project of 'ecologizing' our political life could be realized. 'Ecologizing' is interpreted in the spirit of Bruno Latour – not as the sanctification of nature but as the invention of new political procedures for managing this construction-induced 'collective'.[83] The deference model and the private/public dichotomy that informs it are, of course, inconsistent with this constitutional vision. This constitutional vision fits nicely with the idea of EIA, which is perceived by many observers not just as a technocratic decision-making tool but as a consensus-building mechanism that aspires to bring within its boundaries all those who might be affected by a construction activity.[84]

The more difficult question, of course, is how to translate this abstract vision into a set of realizable institutional practices. This question is explored in the remaining part of this section. In seeking possible implementation paths I focus on two key points, which seem to me to be the most promising. The first argues for the incorporation of an environmental management system (EMS) into the construction contract. The second seeks to modify the dispute resolution model that dominates the construction world. Consider first the issue of environmental management. The main advantage of the EMS concept is that it provides a way to integrate the environmental cause, in a systematic way, into the decision-making structure of a business endeavour. As such, it provides a way to bring some of the 'externalized

---

82 As a 'micro-constitution' the construction contract should develop deeper sensitivity to the details of the social situation in which it is embedded, where 'social situation' depicts the totality of societies, living organisms, and physical environment, which interact in the context of a particular ecological problem.

83 See Latour, op. cit., n. 12, pp. 234–5.

84 See, for example, O. Renn et al. (eds.), *Fairness and Competence in Citizen Participation: Evaluating Models for Environmental Discourse* (1995). The World Bank adopted a similar cooperative vision, which views the process of EIA as a cooperative effort that involves the borrower, the Bank, the affected populations, and local NGOs; see the World Bank, 'Public Involvement in Environmental Assessment: Requirements, Opportunities and Issues' in *Environmental Assessment Sourcebook Update No. 5* (1993).

100

parties' into the contractual universe of the *lex constructionis*. The environmental management system of the International Organization of Standardization, the ISO 14001, is the most likely candidate for such incorporation, since it is currently the most widely used global EMS.[85]

The ISO 14001 standard and its most important rival, the European EcoManagement and Audit Scheme (EMAS)[86] are based on a similar vision, which is to create a framework that will encourage the certified organization to improve, continuously, its overall environmental performance.[87] ISO 14001 attempts to achieve this goal through a very simple scheme, which is based on five general principles: commitment and policy, planning, implementation, measurement and evaluation, and finally, review and further implementation. What links these principles together is a general commitment to a dynamic cyclical process of 'plan, implement, check and review'.[88] Linking this cyclical process to the environmental objectives that were set out in the pre-contractual EIA should provide a mechanism for implementing and reviewing the conclusions of the EIA.

The integrative and reflexive vision of the ISO 14001 and EMAS seems to provide a good setting for confronting some of the key problems of the *lex constructionis*. As was noted before, these problems emanate from the discontinuity between the 'pre' and 'post' phases of the contractual project.

---

85 In 1998 there were 5,637 ISO sites against 2,141 sites for the competing European scheme (EMAS), see Anonymous, 'ISO 14001 and EMAS Sites World-Wide' (1998) 5 *J. of the Institute of Environmental Management* 3, 6. By the end of 2000 the total number of ISO 14000 certificates has risen to 22,897; see 'ISO Survey of ISO 9000 and ISO 14000 certificates – Tenth cycle: up to and including 31 December 2000', available at <www.iso.ch>.

86 ISO 14001 (1996) Environmental Management Systems – Specification with Guidance for Use is the actual management system. A second standard, the ISO 14004 (1996) Environmental – Management Systems – General Guidelines on Principles, Systems and Supporting Techniques is a guidance manual. The European scheme was established in 1993 by Council Regulation (EEC) 1836/93 29 June 1993, OJ L168, 10 July 1993, 1, and became operative in 1995. The 1993 scheme was revised in 2001 by the Regulation (EC) No. 761/2001 of the European Parliament and of the Council of 19 March 2001 allowing voluntary participation by organisations in a Community eco-management and audit scheme, OJ L114, 24 April 2001, 1 (henceforth EMAS II Regulation). The EMAS II Regulation incorporates ISO 14001 as its environmental management system (see Annex 1 of the revised regulation). EMAS II imposes, however, several additional obligations that go further than the requirements of ISO 14001, particularly in the areas of environmental improvement, external communication, and employee involvement. For a review of the ISO 14000 series, see the ISO website at <www.iso.ch>, and P.C. Murray, 'Inching Toward Environmental Regulatory Reform – ISO 14000: Much Ado About Nothing or a Reinvention Tool?' (1999) 37 *Am. Business Law J.* 35; for a review of the EMAS II Regulation, see the EMAS website: <www.europa.eu.int/comm/environment/emas>.

87 See the ISO 14001 introduction at vi, and Article 3.1, and Article 1(2) of the EMAS II Regulation.

88 ISO 14001, Annex A.1, at 6; Murray. op. cit., n. 86, pp. 45–8.

This discontinuity tends to impede the efficient implementation of a pre-contractual EIA, and, as such contributes to the culture of 'externalization' which characterizes the *lex constructionis*.[89] In order to create a temporal continuity between the different phases of the construction project, the main contract should provide both a monitoring mechanism, which would guarantee that the conclusions of the preliminary EIA are actually implemented (in both the design and execution of the works), and a mechanism for coping with the problem of unforeseen contingencies. A possible response to the latter challenge might be to create a mechanism of second environmental review. This contractual mechanism should fulfill two goals. First, it should provide an opportunity for re-evaluating the conclusions of the preliminary environmental assessment in light of any new information (for example, unforeseen changes to the original design or unpredicted environmental effects). Second, it should provide clear procedures for programme revision, which would enable the parties to incorporate the conclusions of such a 'second review' into the working programme.[90] These two tasks fit quite naturally into the management cycle of the ISO 14001 standard.

Some features of the ISO 14001 standard are, however, inconsistent with the constitutional vision that was promulgated above. In the first place, the ISO 14001 is designed to operate mainly within a given organizational structure – usually a business corporation. In contrast construction activities involve, usually, a multiplicity of agents (owner, designers, constructors, sub-contractors, suppliers, and future operators) who operate either simultaneously or in a sequential fashion. The ISO 14001 system does not provide an adequate answer to this institutional complexity, and it would have to be modified accordingly.[91] A second shortcoming of the ISO 14001 standard, is that it gives the organization a wide discretion, both in devising its environmental plan and in designing the environmental indicators according to which it will measure its performance.[92] If the basic 'regulatory level' is

---

89 The emphasis on the post-EIA problematique is consistent with the World Bank understanding of the EIA process, which views the idea of post-EIA auditing as an integral part the EIA process. See Articles 12, 13, 15 of *Operational Directive 4.01 on Environmental Assessment* (1991, updated 1996), and Annex C to OD April 2001 (*Environmental Mitigation or Environmental Management Plan*).

90 Article 13 of the new FIDIC forms, which deals with 'Variations and Adjustments', can provide some guidance to the way in which such a review mechanism could be designed. However, Article 13 is based on an either/or risk allocation that is, again, at odds with the cooperative vision that is advocated here. The provisions of the NEC that deal with programme revision (Articles 31, 32) can also provide useful guidance for devising such procedures.

91 For example, the notion of continuous improvement would have to be interpreted as project-specific rather than organization-specific.

92 See Murray, op. cit., n. 86, pp. 49–50. The introduction to ISO 14001 provides that: '... this international standard does not establish absolute requirements for environmental performance beyond commitment, in the policy, to compliance with applicable legislation and regulations and to continual improvement', ISO 14001,

102

low, as might be the case in many developing countries, the commitment to continual improvement might not mean much.[93] One of the challenges of the *lex constructionis* and the construction industry as a whole is, indeed, to fill this gap. The integrity of the initial EIA has a crucial role in this context.

A final weakness of the ISO 14001 framework, is its undemanding position with respect to public participation. The ISO 14001 standard does not view the notion of public consultation as an integral element of the environmental management system.[94] The involvement of the public is, however, a key element of the contractual vision, which was promulgated here. Public participation is important both in the context of post-EIA monitoring, and in the context of second environmental review. In that respect the revised EMAS regulation provides a more progressive model, both by introducing demanding disclosure requirements,[95] and by requiring any certified organization to

introduction, at vi. Organizations certified under EMAS II will face higher demands. This was achieved by introducing the concept of significant environmental aspects. Article 1(2) of the EMAS II regulation states that 'The objective of EMAS shall be to promote continual improvements in the environmental performance of organisations ...'. Article 2(b) defines 'continual improvement of environmental performance' as 'the process of enhancing, year by year, the measurable results of the environmental management system related to an organisation's management of its *significant environmental aspects*, based on its environmental policy, objectives and targets ...' (my emphasis). The notion of significance is defined in Annex VI (Article 6.4).

93 Note, also, that under the ISO 14001 scheme, a firm can legitimately respond to nonconformance by reducing the stringency of its declared goals on the ground that the initial goals were 'inappropriate' (as long as the new goals comply with regulatory guidelines): J. Switzer and J. Ehrenfeld, 'Independent Environmental Auditors: What Does ISO 14001 Registration Really Mean?' (1999) *Environmental Quality Management* 17, 27.

94 Article 4.4.3 of ISO 14001 requires the organization only to '*consider* processes for external communication on its significant environmental aspects and [to] record its decision' (my emphasis). Furthermore, the ISO 14001 standard does not require the publication of an annual environmental statement (see ISO 14004, Article 4.3.3.1). This of course raises the question of the public accountability of the scheme. This approach to the disclosure issue reflects mainly the concern of the United States business community that such extensive disclosure would act as a platform for criminal or civil litigation, and not as a platform for constructive dialogue; see Murray, op. cit., n. 86, pp. 53–4. Responding to these concerns, several US states have made an attempt to provide firms with certified EMS programmes with either a statutory immunity from liability or a qualified privilege. For a more detailed discussion, see Murray, id., pp. 53–62.

95 The organizations that will register under the new scheme will be required to publish, on a yearly basis, an environmental statement, which should provide details of the environmental performance of the organization against its environmental objectives and targets (Art. 3, sub-paragraphs (2)(c) and (c) and (3)(b) of the EMAS II regulation). The environmental statement shall be verified by 'environmental verifier' (Art. 3(2)(d)). Further details with respect to the objectives, structure (including data requirements), and modes of publication, of the environmental statement are given in Annex III. Art. 3.6, which deals with the issue of public availability, encourages the certified organizations to use various communicating channels – including electronic publication, libraries, and so on.

103

engage in true and open dialogue with its employees and the public at large.[96] The revised EMAS regulation thus makes an attempt to go beyond a purely 'disclosure' model, in which the deliberation is perceived only as an ad hoc exercise, toward a model in which the dialogue between the organization and the public is perceived as a continuous process. This approach fits nicely with the construction context, where it is critical that any deliberation would take place before the project is completed.

It is important to understand that this proposal does not seek to transform the construction contract into some monstrous, all-embracing instrument. Thus, I do not believe that the construction contract should provide a detailed environmental performance schedule, or act as an environmental management manual. Rather, this proposal seeks to encourage a greater use of the construction contract as a coordination mechanism. As a coordinating device the contract can, and should, refer to external sources such as the World Bank's EIA guidelines or the ISO 14001 standard, only modifying them when required.[97] The technical modalities of such incorporation are not complicated. Indeed, FIDIC model forms already use this 'legislative' method, albeit in relation to quality assurance.[98] I believe that this idea could find some support within FIDIC, which has been involved over the last few years in an initiative to introduce the concept of EMS to the construction industry.[99]

A second area, which could be used to advance my 'constitutional' vision, concerns the issue of dispute settlement. As was noted above, most of the model forms include an arbitration agreement. This means that most of the

96 Thus, Article B(3) of Annex 1 of the Revised Regulation, entitled 'external communication and relations', requires that the organization shall be able 'to demonstrate an open dialogue with the public and other interested parties including local communities and customers with regard to the environmental impact of their activities, products and services in order to identify the public's and other interested parties' concerns'. Article B(4) of the same Annex requires certified organizations to involve their employees in the operation of the environmental management system, through, for example, suggestion-book systems, project-based working groups, or environmental committees.

97 As the EMAS II regulation does with respect to ISO 14001.

98 Article 4.9, which appears in almost identical form in the construction, plant, and EPC contracts, provides that: 'The Contractor shall institute a quality assurance system to demonstrate compliance with the requirements of the Contract. The system shall be in accordance with the details stated in the Contract. The Employer shall be entitled to audit any aspect of the system, ...' This is the EPC version. The construction and plant contracts differ only in that they use the term 'Engineer' instead of the 'Employer'. A similar provision could be used to introduce an 'environmental management system' ('EMS') into the contract.

99 FIDIC published in 1995, in cooperation with UNEP and the International Chamber of Commerce, a resource training kit on environmental management, which was inspired, largely, by the ISO 14001 standard and EMAS. However, FIDIC has viewed the concept of EMS as a purely managerial notion, and has made, so far, no attempt to incorporate it into its model forms.

disputes in the global construction market are adjudicated before private arbitrators, usually in one of the main international arbitration centres. The arbitration universe is, however, a closed world; it gives no voice to those parties who are external to the contractual order. This closure, which means that non-parties can raise claims against the contractual order only through the 'external' court system, supports and perpetuates the private/public separation which was criticized earlier. Breaking this separation clearly requires an alternative dispute settlement structure.

The idea of Dispute Adjudication Board (DAB), which was adopted by FIDIC's new model contracts, can provide a useful starting point for thinking about such an alternative structure.[100] The DAB is constructed as an internal adjudicator/mediator, which should deal with any dispute before it is forwarded to an external formal arbitration.[101] The main advantage of the DAB concept is that by being in place at the outset of the project, before the emergence of any dispute, it 'is able to have personal and contemporaneous familiarity with the development of the work under the contract' and to establish regular communication with the parties.[102] This close contact with the project's 'reality' distinguishes the DAB from a post-dispute legal adjudicator, who necessarily relies, in constructing her judgement, on documents and witnesses, rather than on a direct knowledge of the project. It is this close contact, which makes the DAB's opinion with respect to any disagreement more acceptable to the parties. Of course, to create this distinction between the DAB and a legal adjudicator, it is essential that the 'DAB' be appointed by the parties at the commencement of the contract, and will familiarize itself with the project before the occurrence of any dispute.[103]

Under the current construction contract the DAB members are appointed by the parties.[104] This arrangement is unsatisfactory from my

---

100 See Article 20 to FIDIC new model-forms. The DAB shall comprise either one or three persons.

101 Both parties have the right to submit the dispute to formal arbitration, usually under the ICC Rules, if they do not accept the DAB's decision, and fail to reach an amicable settlement (Article 20.6 of FIDIC's new forms).

102 G.L. Jaynes, 'FIDIC's 1999 Editions of Conditions of Contract For "Plant and Design-Build" and "EPC Turnkey Contract": Is the "DAB" Still a Star?' (1999) 17 *International Construction Law Rev.* 42, 45.

103 The construction contract establishes explicit procedures to enable the DAB to familiarize itself with the project prior to any dispute. These include regular visits to the site and allowing the DAB to request different documents (such as a copy of the contract documents, progress reports, variations instructions, and so on). See Articles 1–4 to the 'Procedural Rules' annex to the 'General Conditions of Dispute Adjudication Agreement' appendix of the construction contract.

104 Article 20.2 provides that 'If the DAB is to comprise three persons, each party shall nominate one member for the approval of the other party. The parties shall consult both these members and shall agree upon the third member, who shall be appointed to act as chairman'.

perspective, because it does not provide a voice to the extra-contractual community. A possible solution would be to appoint a public representative to the DAB, The power to appoint this member could be conferred upon an acceptable third party.[105] This member should have the right to accept complaints from the public and initiate internal discussions within the DAB. A more difficult question is how to link this transformed DAB with the arbitration world. To make this proposal more appealing, it might be more realistic to limit any public-initiated deliberation to the informal discussions at the DAB, and not to carry them further to the arbitration phase. While this would formally give the contractual parties the right to overrule any public-initiated DAB decision, I believe that it would not stop the DAB from having some impact on the social reality of the project. It is clear, however, that this idea requires further experimentation.[106]

The alternative contractual vision that was suggested in this section could find some support in the new contractual paradigms that appeared recently in the construction market. Both the ICE managerial model, which views the contract as a stimulator of 'good management',[107] and the 'partnering ideology' of the Egan report[108] indicates an increasing willingness within the industry to adopt novel contractual models. The concept of partnering provides a useful counter-metaphor to the public/private image; the ICE model, for its part, includes several interesting ideas on the question of how to use the construction contract as a management tool. Particularly interesting is the attempt of the ICE NEC series to create a flexible framework, which would encourage the parties to seek 'win-win' solutions to unexpected problems.[109] However, while these new paradigms do signal a willingness to experiment with alternative contractual models, they do not

---

105 Such procedure already exists in the contract for cases where the parties fail to nominate a member or chairman to the DAB. See Art. 20.3.

106 For a more detailed discussion of the DAB concept, see Jaynes, op. cit., n. 102, p. 45, and C.R. Seppala, 'Letter to the Editor (Reply to Jaynes)' (2000) 17 *International Construction Law Rev.* 1.

107 See Hughes and Greenwood, op. cit., n. 21, p. 197 and Barnes, op. cit. n. 51, for a discussion of the ICE new engineering contract.

108 J. Egan, *Rethinking Construction: Report of the Construction Task Force to the Deputy Prime Minister, John Prescott, on the Scope for Improving the Quality and Efficiency of UK Construction* (1998). For a further discussion of the 'partnering' paradigm, see B. Colledge, 'Obligations of Good Faith in Partnering of UK Construction Contracts' (2000) 17 *International Construction Law Rev.* 175–7, and Stipanowich, op. cit., n. 47, pp. 568–9.

109 See, Barnes, op. cit., n. 51, p. 93. The NEC includes (Article 16) an 'early warning' procedure which obliges the contractor and project manager to give an early warning with respect to any matter that could increase the total cost, delay completion or impair the project. It then provides that either the contractor or the project manger can initiate an 'earning warning meeting' in which solutions to the unexpected problem should be sought.

provide, in themselves, an appropriate constitutional framework, since their structures still retain a strong private/public perspective.[110]

IV. THE ENGINEERING ETHOS AND OTHER CONTRIBUTING FACTORS

The alternative contractual vision, which was sketched in the previous sections, could face strong resistance. The 'externalization' culture of the *lex mercatoria* is driven by strong economic interests, which cannot be disregarded. The contractual changes, which were proposed above, are likely to increase the cost of the construction project, and as such are highly inconsistent with the economic perspective of the contract.[111] What I would like to do in this concluding section is to point to some social processes, which, together, could overcome this economic power. The first process is internal to the construction market. It has to do with the cultural context in which FIDIC operates what we might call the 'engineering milieu'. I believe that this unique institutional ethos – a product of special values, technical competencies, and accumulated experience – could be conducive to an attempt to change the environmental contours of the *lex constructionis*. This unique ethos distinguishes FIDIC from business organizations, in which the edict of profit-maximizing has a much more dominant role.

The engineering ethos is primarily a product of the unique training path of civil engineers. Civil engineers are trained to provide solutions to very pragmatic problems: how to construct bridges, high roads, chemical plants, and so on. Traditionally, it was not their job to guarantee the profitability of the project on which they were employed. Rather, as one commentator put it, 'their prime responsibility is to ensure the *safety* and *functionality* of their projects. Economics are important but slightly lower than safety in the typical engineer's hierarchy of values'.[112] The pragmatic orientation of civil

---

110 The new partnering initiatives, both in the United States and the United Kingdom, still perceive their audience as the construction community, that is, the owner, contractor, subcontractors, and design professionals. The inhabitants who populate the project surroundings are still not conceived of as part of this emerging 'partnership', see Egan, op. cit., n. 108, paras. 36–37, and C.L. Noble, 'Friend of the Project – A New Paradigm for Construction Law Services in a "Partnered" Construction Industry' (1998) 15 *International Construction Law Rev.* 79.

111 The introduction of an environmental management system and the establishment of a Dispute Adjudication Board (DAB) would increase the cost of the contract. See, for example, Murray, op. cit., n. 86, p. 43, fn. 48 (for the cost of ISO 14001 certification) and Seppala, op. cit., n. 106 (discussing the cost implications of the DAB). These costs should be shared by the contractual community as a whole. Placing all the costs on one party (for example, the contractor) would not only be inconsistent with the political vision promulgated above, but would probably be untenable from a financial perspective.

112 D.S.O. Russell, 'Insights From the Three Gorges Study' (1994) 21 *Cnd. J. of Civil Engineers* 541, 545.

107

engineers means that environmental concerns can be incorporated quite naturally into the set of technical objectives and constraints that constitute a particular 'engineering problem'. From an environmental perspective, the weaker commitment of the engineering community to the edict of profit making constitutes a convenient setting for an agenda of ecological transformation. The cultural framework in which FIDIC operates offers, then, a receptive terrain for green ideas;[113] it distinguishes FIDIC from economic-oriented organizations such as the WTO.[114] Indeed, over the last decade FIDIC has made a substantial effort to develop greater awareness of environmental issues among its members.[115]

The recent environmental awakening within FIDIC has not found its way yet to its normative products. It would be wrong, however, to dismiss

113 A similar process occurred in the chemical industry. In the wake of the Bhopal tragedy in 1984, the chemical industry established a voluntary programme, the Responsible Care Programme, which sought to improve environmental standards in the chemical industry worldwide. See F.L. Reinhardt, 'Bringing the Environment Down to Earth' (1999) 77 *Harvard Business Rev.* 149, 152–3.

114 While one of FIDIC's principal tasks is, indeed, to stand 'as the rightful spokesperson for the *business interests of the industry* in the global forum' (FIDIC, *Engineering Our Future* (1998) i, my emphasis) the business perspective is not the main ethos by which the organization orients itself. Thus, in the same 1998 report we can also find the idea that FIDIC's mission should be 'To promote the business interests of members in relation to the provision of technology-based intellectual services for the built and natural environment, and while doing so, *accept and uphold our responsibilities to society and the environment*' (id., p. 25, my emphasis). Of course, to what extent these broader commitments are realized in practice is a matter for empirical analysis.

115 This effort was reflected by a series of pro-environmental documents and statements. In 1990 FIDIC published a policy statement titled 'Consulting Engineers and the Environment', which promulgates the environmental commitments of a consulting engineer (it calls, for example, on each engineer, to 'evaluate the positive and negative environmental impacts of each project ... [and] suggest alternatives to [his] clients if environmental risks emerge' (Art. 8)). Another recent report, FIDIC, id. – a strategic action plan that should guide FIDIC into the twenty-first century – states that one of the objectives of the organization would be to promote the commitment of FIDIC's members to environmental sustainability. Institutionally, this effort is coordinated by a special task force for sustainable development. In 1999 the sustainable development task force issued another strategy paper, 'Sustainable Development in the Consulting Industry' (1999). The paper is particularly interesting in our context because it is guided by a participatory outlook. It encourages FIDIC members to contribute to the involvement of key stakeholders in the construction process, to be willing to engage in a dialogue with the general public in large and complex projects, and to contribute to the development of new institutional structures in which this participatory outlook can be advanced (id., p. 8). While the paper does not make any references to FIDIC contractual products, its general message seems to be consistent with the contractual vision proposed in this article. All of the documents referred to above are on FIDIC's website: <www.fidic.org>.

FIDIC's green initiatives as mere cheap talk.[116] I believe that as a locus of technical expertise and professional pride, FIDIC has a real potential (much more than business oriented organizations such as the WTO) to act as a bridge between the environmental and business communities. Several recent social developments make this scenario more reasonable. These developments could provide the necessary counterforce to the economic motivations which lie behind the externalization praxis. They include an increased environmental awareness within the realm of international finance,[117] the increasing international presence of environmental NGOs and the news media,[118] and the growing impact of transnational environmental litigation.[119] These different phenomena present a common threat to the discourse of externalization, in that they encourage the participants in construction activities (through different means) to consider more seriously the ecological consequences of their activities.

A final point. It is important to emphasize that the proposals made in this article do not seek to achieve some kind of 'perfect internalization'. While adopting new procedures for project management and dispute settlement should extend the discursive horizon of the *lex constructionis*, they could also create new blind spots. Although I believe that in a transformed form FIDIC's contracts could be more attentive to environmental considerations, some undesired effects are unavoidable. In particular, the reliance on standard eco-management systems such as the ISO 14001 could subscribe the contractual parties to a certain way of constructing and understanding environmental problems. The technical outlook which characterizes the ISO 14001 standard means that environmental dilemmas would be constructed, primarily, as technical problems of management and engineering. This technocratic bias could be further exacerbated by the cultural background –

116 'Cheap talk': a costless signal or communication. It should be noted in this regard that FIDIC's environmental awakening is supported also by economic considerations. The report *Engineering Our Future* argues that the increasing demand for new environmentally related services, such as enviromnental assessment and environmental management, offer new business opportunities to the engineering profession (FIDIC, id., p. 22).
117 See the discussion in P. Thompson, 'Bank Lending and the Environment: Policies and Opportunities' (1998) 16 *International J. of Bank Marketing* 243; S. Williams, 'U.K. Ethical Investment: A Coming of Age' (1999) 8 *J. of Investing* 58; and K.A. Strasser and D. Rodosevich, 'Seeing the Forest for the Trees in CERCLA Liability' (1993) 10 *Yale J. on Regulation* 493.
118 See the discussion in G. Jordan. 'Indirect Causes and Effects in Policy Change: the Brent Spar Case' (1998) 76 *Public Administration* 713, and P. Wapner, 'Politics Beyond the State: Environmental Activism and World Civic Politics' (1995) 47 *World Politics* 311.
119 See the discussion in F.K. Juenger, 'Environmental Damage' in *Transnational Tort Litigation: Jurisdictional Principles*, eds. C. McLachlan and P. Nygh (1996) 199, and A. Rosencranz and R. Campbell, 'Foreign Environmental and Human Rights Suits Against U.S. Corporations in U.S. Courts (1999) 18 *Stanford Environmental Law J.* 145.

the engineering milieu – in which this concept would be invoked. This interpretative 'bias' could lead to the marginalization of other points of view, which offer different understandings of the relationships between humans and nature.

There is no clear answer to this problem. For me, the most plausible response lies in expanding the reflexivity of the contractual package. Flexible participatory procedures should play a prominent role in this effort. These procedures should enable the public to participate, in a meaningful way, in the assessment (and management) of construction projects.[120] Only a genuine commitment to involve the public in the assessment and management of the construction endeavour could guarantee the necessary 'plurality of thoughts' which is needed to overcome/supplement the technocratic orientation of the eco-management concept and the engineering milieu.

---

120 There is an increasing recognition within international bodies of the importance and value of public participation, see the World-Bank, op. cit., n. 84 and UNCITRAL, op, cit., n. 34, p. 202. See, further, Dorf and Sabel, op. cit., n. 75.

JOURNAL OF LAW AND SOCIETY
VOLUME 29, NUMBER 1, MARCH 2002
ISSN: 0263-323X, pp. 111–36

Competition Law in the International Domain: Networks as a New Form of Governance

IMELDA MAHER*

Central to the internationalization of competition law has been the emergence of transnational networks of competition officials and experts. These networks have operated in three main areas: co-ordination on enforcement; technical assistance; and moves to develop overarching competition principles at the level of the WTO. The debate over the nature of internationalization of competition norms has fallen into three phases: early failures mainly due to the lack of any network; politicization of competition policy within a UN context followed by the emergence of a network primarily focused on the OECD. The current phase concerns coordination and the attempt to develop a competition law regime at the WTO level. This process is spearheaded by the European Union, with the United States of America favouring bilateral agreements on enforcement and technical assistance only. The way the debate has changed over the past ten years and how the two main protagonists have modified their positions, is indicative of the influence and importance of networks which, while they may give rise to formal agreements, can operate through soft power and persuasion. What emerges from the analysis is the centrality of these networks to this important aspect of contemporary international governance. They supplement rather than replace more traditional forms of internationalism and, while they may fundamentally regard themselves as technocratic, deriving legitimacy from outputs, current pressures on international policy making require them to attend to the process aspects associated with legitimacy of democratic regimes.

* *Law Program, Research School of Social Sciences, Australian National University, Canberra, ACT 0200, Australia, and Law Department, London School of Economics and Political Science, Houghton Street, London WC2A 2AE, England*

Earlier versions of this paper were presented at a workshop at the European University Institute, Florence, 6 May 2000 and at University College London, November 2000. Thanks to the participants, John Braithwaite, Sol Picciotto, and Colin Scott for comments. The usual disclaimer applies.

INTRODUCTION

The ministerial meeting of the World Trade Organization in Doha in early November agreed that the negotiations will take place in two years time at the next ministerial meeting, on multilateral competition rules.[1] This compromise reflects the division between the United States of America and the European Union on how and to what extent competition law[2] is and should be internationalized. The United States government has consistently advocated a bilateral approach organized around antitrust officials liaising primarily over enforcement issues with their counterparts in other states, and with United States officials carrying out an educative and assistance function for those states with embryonic or non-existent competition regimes. The EU on the other hand, while sharing the educative ambitions of the United States, has actively advocated a multilateral approach towards the development of international competition norms, most recently under the aegis of the WTO.[3] The EU initially and ambitiously proposed global competition norms.[4] It has gradually modified its position and now calls for a Global Competition Network with a wide membership of competition agencies as well as non-governmental organizations, representatives of consumer interests, business, the legal professions and academics.[5] This proposal, following more than a year of talks, is supported by the United States[6] and thus represents a compromise by both the United States and EU. The United States has agreed to the establishment of a plurilateral body albeit one that lies outside any formal international organization, while the EU has not insisted on competition policy being on the agenda for the Doha talks. This body will supplement the newly established OECD Global Forum on Competition which has a narrower membership[7] and will address specified (and, according to the United States), fairly narrowly drawn competition problems while the EU sees it as creating a 'competition culture'.

1 Ministerial Declaration, 14 November 2001.
2 Discussion of competition law here is limited to the regulation of private market behaviour which restricts competition, including restrictive agreements and abuse of dominance.
3 Communication from the EC and its Member States WT/WGTCP/W/152, 25 September 2000.
4 EC Commission, Communication to the Council: Towards an International Framework of Competition Rules COM(96) 284, final.
5 M. Monti, Opening Speech, First OECD Global Forum on Competition Policy, OECD Paris, 17 October 2001.
6 C.A. James, 'International Antitrust in the 21st Century: Co-operation and Convergence', speech to the OECD Global Forum on Competition, Paris, 17 October 2001.
7 Thirty OECD states, five observers, and twenty-one invited non-members, see press release, 'OECD Organises First Global Forum on Competition', 17 October 2001. Significantly, the Forum had its first meeting shortly before Doha.

Though they face common problems in addressing the difficulties of regulating multinational enterprises (MNEs) in the competition sphere, the starting points of the United States and EU reflect a fundamental difference in approach. The EU position, predicated on the success of its own regional competition law, is that of liberal internationalism which attempts to develop a framework of international institutions while respecting national sovereignty as the bedrock of the international legal order.[8] The United States position represents the alternative response to the threat of globalization – transgovernmentalism – with its emphasis on functional coordination by national officials.[9] As the issue of the internationalization of competition law crept up the political agenda in the 1990s, there has been to some degree a blurring of positions between the two camps. Thus the horizontal functional coordination (favoured by the United States), and the more traditional vertical coordination by foreign ministries through international organizations and treaties (favoured by the EU), are blurred through the compromise on the Doha declaration.

Characterized by horizontal, decentralized, and informal coordination by government officials sharing common functional interests, trans-governmentalism is sometimes presented as an alternative paradigm to the traditional liberal model of internationalism where the state is a unitary actor advancing its own interests through diplomatic channels and international organizations and treaties.[10] Slaughter has challenged this view pointing out that, like all paradigms, the purity of the transgovernmental model of global governance is quickly stained. She does point to international competition regulation as an area where a real choice is emerging between government networks and existing or new international organizations.[11] However, recent developments suggest that, while policy networks seem to be in the ascendancy, they do not supplant more traditional forms of international governance, in this instance, the WTO Working Group on Trade and Competition and the possibility of increased harmonization and formality arising out of institutions created both as part of, and independent from, the OECD. As Mortensen notes, the emergence of such networks is not inconsistent with centralization of governance specifically through the WTO.[12] One of the strengths of the GATT is that it is not really a rule-of-law

---

8 See, generally, S. Picciotto, 'Networks in International Integration: Fragmented States and the Dilemmas of Neo-Liberalism' (1996–97) 17 *North-western J. of International Law and Business* 1014.

9 See, generally, A-M Slaughter, 'Governing the Global Economy through Government Networks' in *The Role of Law in International Politics: Essays in International Relations and International Law*, ed. M. Byers (2000).

10 Picciotto, op. cit., n. 8, p. 1019 and following.

11 Slaughter, op. cit., n. 9, p. 200.

12 J.L. Mortensen, 'The Institutional Requirements of the WTO in an Era of Globalization: Imperfections in the Global Economic Polity' (2000) 6 *European Law J.* 176, at 194.

regime. The credibility of the GATT rules is established through effective (which in the international context may mean flexible) enforcement.[13] Thus, if a competition code were to be adopted, it would not have the force of the rule of law until such time as the most powerful members (the United States and the European Union in particular) were convinced that the rules were sound enough to be interpreted as legally binding. Thus the issue is whether the closer contact among enforcement officials can really generate common perspectives, and, if so, to what extent can such common perspectives underpin more formal processes of coordination. In short, are the networks ends in themselves, signifying a new form of governance with a limited remit and of uncertain influence over the medium term, given the level of informality? Or can such networks constitute an important form of governance in themselves, with coordination leading to changes in formal processes of coordination?

This article first considers the drivers for transnational networks before exploring the analytical framework for policy networks and epistemic communities. It then examines the linkages between trade and competition before looking at the internationalization debate in the 1990s. The shared perspectives are then explored before concluding that networks are a prerequisite to any greater internationalization although they can operate as an alternative to traditional internationalism.

WHY TRANSNATIONAL NETWORKS?

There are three drivers for the emergence of transnational government networks: perceptions of globalization (even if not verifiable statistically); the changing nature of international trade and the operation of MNEs as the key agencies within that context; and a mirroring of the trend towards the regulatory state with increased delegation of regulatory authority to specialist agencies.[14] While increases in international trade can be quantified,[15] such figures are difficult to analyse because statistics either are not available for some sectors or are not collated in the same way. Picciotto points out that the quantity of international transactions when calculated in proportion to local or national transactions do not generally show any significant relative increase but what seems to be important is the increased potential for such flows.[16] Irrespective of the figures, Hay and Rosamond argue that once policy makers assume globalization then they will

13 J. Braithwaite and P. Drahos, *Global Business Regulation* (2000) 185.
14 Picciotto, op. cit., n. 8, p. 1018.
15 See, for example, H. Anheier, M. Glasius, and M. Kaldor (eds.), *Global Civil Society* (2001) Table R1. <http://www.lse.ac.uk/Depts/global/Yearbook/outline.htm>.
16 S. Picciotto, 'Fragmented States and International Rules of Law' (1997) *Social and Legal Studies* 259, at 260.

114

act in a manner consistent with it, whether or not it is absolutely verifiable. In other words, the discourse of globalization is a powerful rhetorical device and it can be used strategically to legitimate or advance specific courses of action.[17] The rhetorical force of globalization makes it what Snyder calls a characteristic of our time, a multifaceted, uneven, and often contradictory economic, political, and social process.[18] As such, it leads to the reconstruction of economic and institutional structures and hence raises the issue of the governance of the integrating global market.[19] The growing disjunction between traditional conceptions of the law governing international transactions, especially trade, and the shape of economic networks emerging in the international sphere, calls for a re-evaluation of global governance, and it is within this reconceptualization that the debate on the internationalization of competition law occurs.

There is a growing emphasis on legal pluralism in the light of economic networks dominated by MNEs, the key agents in the globalization of international trade. This globalization can be identified in a number of increasingly related spheres:[20] trade – following the removal of tariff and non-tariff barriers in successive GATT agreements; financial markets – prompted by the oil shocks and OPEC surpluses, the Japanese surplus in the 1980s, and further liberalization of markets spearheaded by the Reagan/ Thatcher deregulation ethos; and finally, the current phase which has led to the increasing internationalization of so-called flanking policies like consumer policy, environment policy, and competition policy that traditionally have been seen as exclusively in the domestic realm.[21] In this third phase, there has been an increased integration in business activities. Research and development has grown in importance with MNEs seeking new networks through various forms of strategic alliances. The independent but related development of information technology has fed into globalization of international trade flows with technology a key factor in business growth. In more traditional traded sectors, production can occur across several states with sales requiring local presence to ensure adequate and appropriate marketing and service thus giving firms increased incentives towards multiple locales.

---

17 C. Hay and B. Rosamond, 'Globalization, European Integration and the Discursive Construction of Economic Imperatives' (2002) 9 *J. of European Public Policy* (forthcoming).
18 F. Snyder, 'Governing Economic Globalization: Global Legal Pluralism and European Law' (1999) 5 *European Law J.* 334, at 335.
19 Mortensen, op. cit., n. 12, p. 177.
20 id., p. 181. M.J. Trebilcock, 'Competition Policy and Trade Policy: Mediating the Interface' (1996) 30 *J. of World Trade* 71 citing S. Ostry, 'Beyond the Border: The New International Policy Arena' in *Competition Policy in an Interdependent World Economy*, eds. E. Kantzenbach, H.-E. Scharrer, and L. Waverman (1993) 261.
21 Trebilcock, id. p. 71, quoting a discussion paper presented to the Canadian Bureau of Competition Policy by D. Ireland in November 1992.

Because business activity takes place beyond the boundaries of the state, norms are being devised outside the scope of the state through private behaviour. Teubner's work based on systems theory[22] looks to mercantile law as an example of how non-hierarchical and even non-legal forms can govern behaviour within a particular industry: identifying the contract as the key mechanism of private law-making and considering state institutions either as being excluded altogether or having a secondary role. His work emphasizes the fragmentation of control and authority at all levels, exploring the perceived weakening of state institutions in the context of globalization.[23] Away from this exclusively private sphere governed by notions of contract and conventional practice within industry, global governance is also characterized by different sites of governance with networks of government officials emerging in response to the perceived increase in international transactions and the transnational nature of MNEs. In order to overcome the bounded territoriality of their own powers, with its constraints on their ability to control behaviour which has an impact within the state but originates outside their jurisdiction, officials operating in the same functional spheres see the advantages of new forms of contact and cooperation. Semi-formal arrangements can create a significant potential for the exercise of power through new channels, networks which act as conduits for credible information flows, policy learning, and policy transfer.

This shift at the international level reflects a trend at the state level where there is a shift from 'government' to 'governance',[24] with a decentring of the state. The policy boom area of the 1990s – privatization – was not generally accompanied by deregulation.[25] Instead, state command and control has given way to the regulatory state with the rise of new specialized regulatory institutions, from individual utility regulators to nursing-home inspectorates.[26] As the state has become more fragmented domestically, this has created incentives for informal contact and coordination between officials across state boundaries, particularly when faced with similar problems. Crisis management – either arising out of a common problem (for example, an international cartel), or a difference in approach (for example, towards mergers[27]) may lead to initial contact and prompt the development of

---

22 G. Teubner, *Law as an Autopoietic System* (1993), see Snyder, op. cit., n. 18, for a comment and critique on Teubner's work, pp. 341 and following.
23 '"Global Bukowina": Legal Pluralism in the World Society' in *Global Law without a State*, ed. G. Teubner (1997) 3–28.
24 Picciotto, op. cit., n. 8, p. 1018.
25 H. Feigenbaum, J. Henig, and C. Hamnett, *Shrinking the State: The Political Underpinnings of Privatization* (1998).
26 J. Braithwaite, 'The New Regulatory State and the Transformation of Criminology' (2000) 4 *Brit. J. of Criminology* 222, at 224.
27 See the recent debate between the US and EU over the application of portfolio theory to conglomerate mergers such as the failed GE/Honeywell merger: Monti, op. cit., n. 5; James, op. cit., n. 6.

networks through which knowledge is exchanged, and trust increased, so that common problems can be discussed such that later conflicts are pre-empted or are more easily resolvable.

The problems which prompt discussion of international competition laws are fourfold and arise in the context of growing international trade: anti-competitive practices outside the control of any single state; enforcement conflicts between national competition authorities; unnecessary compliance costs; and market access. Tarullo suggests that while international competition problems are real they are still modest and any response is in the spirit of pre-emptive action.[28] Such action, most evident in the last ten years, occurs primarily in three inter-related spheres: bilateral coordination in competition enforcement; technical assistance; and steps to develop common substantive and procedural competition principles within the context of the WTO. Each sphere is underpinned by the operation of networks with varying levels of formality, either achieved (in the case of bilateral agreements on competition enforcement) or aspired to indirectly in the case of technical assistance or more directly in steps taken in relation to multilateral initiatives particularly through the WTO.

POLICY NETWORKS AND EPISTEMES

Actors in a network are interdependent and have incentives to share resources (including knowledge), as all are interested in the overall success of the policy and none has the power, funding or legitimacy to enact a particular policy alone, especially where there is an international dimension.[29] Networks that meet regularly and communicate both in person and through correspondence build trust over time, allowing for informal information exchanges and creating the potential for evolutionary policy formation or, at a minimum, reducing the risk of jurisdictional conflicts. The functional nature of the networks can mean that their technocratic nature insulates them from 'high' politics. However, even in the absence of any power to create laws, or without any formal institutional setting, such networks can have an agenda-setting role and as such may frame the nature of the debate, and decide which ideas are currently 'in' or 'out'. Thus the culture of a network can both provide an opportunity and act as a constraint for its actors.[30] Behaviour becomes routinized, path dependencies are

---

28 D.K. Tarullo, 'Competition Policy for Global Markets' (1999) *J. of International Economic Law* 445, at 447.

29 E. Bomberg and J. Peterson, 'Policy Transfer and Europeanization: Passing the Heineken Test?' Queen's University Belfast, on-line papers on Europeanization, no. 2/2000.

30 D. Marsh and M. Smith, 'Understanding Policy Networks: Towards a Dialectical Approach' (2000) 48 *Politics* 4.

117

created for problem solving that simplify processes but also reduce the number of acceptable alternatives.

Actors may use the network strategically in order to advance particular policy objectives. For example, as one of the key players on the international trade stage, the EC Commission may be fairly confident, given its experience, the access it has to expert knowledge, and its commitment to the issue of international competition rules, it is in a position to influence the proposed Global Policy Network. The United States has also agreed to participate in this broader policy network, albeit that its influence may be used to limit the likelihood and scope of an international competition law. The participation of the United States in such networks shows how they can be sites of struggle between competing interests and hence often riven with contradictions. Thus, continuation and development of a network depends on the interests articulated by the actors within it, those actors, and the power and resources they have to maintain the network and work towards a policy outcome.

The informal nature of these networks means that knowledge is an important source of power within them. Yet, as Keohane and Nye note, with the exponential increase of free information, there is a paradox of plenty. With so much information readily available, the attention of policy makers and government officials is a very scarce resource. The source of knowledge becomes important, with credibility one of the key factors in determining the extent to which such knowledge will secure attention. With a credible dissemination of information through such networks, theoretically it is possible to exercise soft power: using persuasion through the effective and credible dissemination of knowledge to achieve a particular outcome because others want what you want, rather than through the use of coercion or rewards.[31] The status of the information provider therefore becomes critical.

Adler and Haas identify epistemic communities as an important source of expert knowledge that in turn can define the alternatives and policy outcomes for policy makers.[32] Haas defines an epistemic community as a knowledge-based network of specialists who share beliefs in cause-and-effect relations, validity tests and underlying principled values, and who pursue common policy goals.[33] Such communities are capable of exerting considerable influence on policy debates at the national and international level where there is a need for expert knowledge in order to elucidate the technical aspects of a particular problem. Epistemic agreement and the operation of such a community is generally only possible in areas where the

31 R.O. Keohane and J.S. Nye Jr., 'Power and Interdependence in the Information Age' (1998) 77 *Foreign Affairs* 81, at 86.
32 E. Adler and P.M. Haas, 'Conclusion: Epistemic Communities, World Order, and the Creation of a Reflective Research Program' (1992) 1 *International Organization* 367.
33 P.M. Haas, 'Introduction: Epistemic Communities and International Policy Co-ordination' (1992) 46 *International Organization* 1, at 3.

118

very technicality of the topic to some extent insulates the community from some of the strategic behaviour commonly found in the political whirl, in particular lobbying.[34] While an epistemic community can feed into policy-making, policy choices remain highly political in their allocative consequences.[35] The community, by definition, does not make such choices, so it is suggested that its influence may tend to diminish once the debate shifts to the policy domain.

Its fluidity and capacity to interact with, and to some extent include, policy-makers conflates the notion of an epistemic community with that of a policy network. Alternatively this characteristic can be indicative of what Drake and Nicolaïdis in their rich narrative of the emergence of the GATS, describe as a two-tier epistemic community. In the first tier are individuals who work for organizations with direct interests in alternative policy solutions. The second tier is removed from the policy domain and consists of academics, journalists, lawyers, and those with an interest, either purely intellectual, or one based on professional entrepreneurship.[36] This study notes that as the idea of international rules for trade in services became institutionalized and moved into the negotiating sphere directly, there were two effects on the role of the epistemic community. First, once the issue started to be examined within the GATT, the ideas and concepts of the community acquired direct access to that forum. The drawback was this meant that they were reshaped and redefined in order to fit the culture of the GATT and its existing principles and procedures. In some ways, this made the issue of common rules for services even more complex, as certain regulatory notions which were important to understanding the links between trade and services could no longer be addressed. Secondly, as negotiations started and became focused on policy development, then the gap between the first and second tiers of the community grew with the 'pure' epistemic group becoming more remote. In fact, for some of them, once the issue reached the negotiating phase, their intellectual and professional interests moved on to other issues. From the perspective of policy makers, they had less need of the community's expertise once the questions of state interests and trade-offs came to the fore and the main battles of relevance and importance had been 'won'.

In relation to the nature of epistemic communities itself, the distinction drawn by Drake and Nicolaïdis between the two tiers is indistinct, and requires clarification of the difference between an epistemic community and a policy community. This is an issue that has dogged the literature.[37] Stone

34 G.J. Ikenberry, 'Knowledge, Power, and International Policy Co-ordination' (1992) 46 *International Organization* 289.
35 Haas, op. cit., n. 33, p. 11.
36 W.J. Drake and K. Nicolaïdis, 'Ideas, Interests, and Institutionalization: "Trade in Services" and the Uruguay Round' (1992) 46 *International Organization* 37, at 39.
37 See, for example, D. Toke, 'Epistemic Communities and Environmental Groups' (1999) 19 *Politics* 97 and C. Dunlop, 'Epistemic Communities: A Reply to Toke' (2000) 20 *Politics* 137.

has suggested that as distinct from epistemic communities, policy networks emphasize the extent to which policy formation is the outcome of a struggle over resources among groups, so interests and agency are to the fore. For the epistemic community literature, the emphasis is on knowledge and uncertainty – uncertainty as to the scope of the community (even if it is possible to identify the criteria for membership or to draw up a definitive list of members), and uncertainty as to the exact nature of the influence the community can exert over policy formation. For Stone, an epistemic community can constitute a sub-group of a policy network, in which the policy community consists of actors bound together by a common interest in a particular policy field, and is composed of interest groups, government officials, ministers, parliamentarians, consultants, and journalists.[38] If the epistemic community advocates policy at odds with that of the policy community, it will not be part of it. This reflects the view that policy networks tend towards continuity of membership and purpose while epistemic communities, with their characteristic of uncertainty and to some extent insulation from political agendas, can be agents of innovation and change arising out of their commitment to shared principled beliefs which to some extent are linked to their validity tests.

It is important to explore the difference between epistemic communities and policy networks, especially as the conflation of the knowledge community with the policy community can in turn mix issues of power based on knowledge and political power.[39] An epistemic community's role in indirectly influencing policy debates rests on claims to knowledge supported by tests of validity such as scientific expertise, which create barriers to membership of the group and help to inure the community to influence from other actors. They rely on quasi-autonomous or independent organizations outside government such as universities, policy institutes, laboratories, and international organizations, both to develop and to sustain their expertise and their authority.[40] These external measures of validity, and with them, the community's primary social power resource, become questionable when it is difficult to differentiate the epistemic community from the policy community. This distinction was perhaps historically easier to maintain when the technical issue was one of so-called hard science (although the validity tests that render expert advice in some sense objective and immune from politics can be called into question).[41] In short, while a glance at the vast academic literature means it is arguable that there is an epistemic community which has contributed to the debate on the

38 D. Stone, *Capturing the Political Imagination: Think Tanks and the Policy Process* (1996) 91.
39 See Picciotto, op. cit., n. 8, pp. 1036–7.
40 Stone, op. cit., n. 38, p. 95.
41 See, for example, G. Little, 'BSE and the Regulation of Risk' (2001) 64 *Modern Law Rev.* 730.

120

internationalization of competition norms, the theory does not adequately differentiate between the multiplicity of actors who at various junctures influence decision-making and policy formation.[42]

THE COMPETITION POLICY NETWORK

The debate on international competition law has three distinct phases – early failures; a politicization of competition policy; and suggested but faltering formalism spearheaded by the EU. While any analogy with the GATS negotiations has to be carefully drawn, the observations of Drake and Nicolaïdis on the nature and role of epistemic communities are relevant to the competition sphere. The early failures in the twenty years following the Second World War[43] were perhaps partly because policy making did not benefit from the kind of homogeneity of approach associated with the existence of an epistemic community. The defeat of the 1948 Havana Charter for a proposed International Trade Organization in the US Congress, in part because of the presence of competition provisions,[44] was a major setback for any multilateral development in the competition law sphere. The GATT did not include any specific competition provisions and when the issue was revisited in the late 1950s, it was concluded that it would be impractical.[45] Few states had competition laws in the 1950s and 60s, and there was a tolerance of cartels even in industrial countries[46] while competition policy was not relevant in state-socialist economies. The United States of America, the state with the most highly developed competition law, did not strenuously advocate an international competition law regime, partly because its very contentious 'effects doctrine'[47] extended the jurisdictional scope of its antitrust laws albeit beyond what was generally accepted in international law.[48]

In the second phase, from the 1970s, competition policy re-emerged at the international level at the United Nations. As part of an attempt to create a

---

42 Dunlop, op. cit., n. 37, p. 137.
43 For a summary of developments, see D.P. Fidler, 'Competition Law and International Relations' (1992) 41 *International and Comparative Law Q.* 563, at 578; Trebilcock, op. cit., n. 20, p. 88.
44 M.-C. Malaguti, 'Restrictive Business Practices in International Trade and the Role of the World Trade Organization' (1998) 32 *J. of World Trade* 117, at 120.
45 Decision of 18 November 1960, BISD 9S/28 see Malaguti, id. p. 121. F. Roessler, 'Should Principles of Competition Policy be Incorporated into WTO Law through Non-Violation Complaints?' (1999) *J. of International Economic Law* 413.
46 See J. Davidow, 'The Relevance of Antimonopoly Policy for Developing Countries' (1992) 37 *Antitrust Bulletin* 277; D.J. Gerber, *Law and Competition in Twentieth Century Europe: Protecting Prometheus* (1998).
47 For example, *In re Westinghouse Elec. Corp Uranium Contracts Litig.* 563 F. 2d 992 (10th Cir 1977).
48 Braithwaite and Drahos, op. cit., n. 13, p. 214.

121

new international economic order by changing the hierarchy and patterns of power, developing countries linked competition policy to questions of international economic justice through the UN Conference on Trade and Development (UNCTAD).[49] They sought to label as restrictive business practices any behaviour that did not facilitate their development. Negotiations on guidelines were long and difficult but the final product, the Set of Multilaterally Agreed Equitable Principles and Rules for the Control of Restrictive Business Practices, was a fairly conventional statement of competition principles, although export cartels were noticeably absent due to opposition from industrialized countries to their inclusion.[50]

While formally, the outcome of the process was limited to this non-binding, and largely ineffectual, set of principles, the process also marked an important stage in the development of transnational competition policy networks, and determined the locus of those networks. The way competition policy had been employed in a radical attempt to re-define the international order and the hierarchies within it, meant that the major industrial countries turned to the Organization for Economic Co-operation and Development (OECD) as the favoured plurilateral forum, in preference to the UNCTAD where developing countries have a much more prominent role. Thus the OECD has dominated debates on competition policy at the international level since the 1980s although its efforts have been limited to soft law measures such as the guidelines on Hard Core Cartels[51] and guidelines for MNEs.[52] It is a key forum for policy networks to develop with non-governmental groups, formalized through the consultative role of bodies such as the Business and Industry Advisory Committee, which act as a channel for private sector and professional views. The primacy of its position is reflected in the recent establishment of the Global Competition Forum within it.[53] While it is an important forum, its position is weakened because of its limited membership, limited to developed economies. This means there is an overlap in function with the UNCTAD Intergovernmental Group of Experts on Competition Law and Policy, set up to monitor the UN Set of Principles. For example they both act as sources of information on national competition laws and they both have published guidelines on competition law. At the same time, the UNCTAD group has more inclusive membership and hence provides a forum for discussion between industrialized and developing countries.[54]

---

49 Fidler, op. cit., n. 43, pp. 580–2.
50 5 December 1980, UNCTAD Doc. TD/RBP/Conf. 10/Rev. 1.
51 C(86)65(final) amended and updated by Recommendation of 25 March 1998 C/M (98)35/final.
52 These call on MNEs not to abuse their dominance such as to affect competition. Last revised in 2000. See <http://www.oecd.org/pdf/M000015000/M00015419.pdf>.
53 See Introduction above.
54 A.D. Melamed, 'International Cooperation in Competition Law and Policy: What can be Achieved at the Bilateral, Regional, and Multilateral Levels' (1999) *J. of International Economic Law* 423, at 431.

These events in the 1980s, helped to create an extensive, if not global, epistemic competition community[55] that has been essential to the policy network and developments through the 1990s, discussed below. Networking occurs through various forms of cooperation, including the exchange of ideas and/or technical assistance; case-specific case assistance between enforcement agencies and finally, as a result of learning, the evolution of common views.[56] The exchange of ideas occurs informally through international conferences and organizations such as the OECD Committee on Competition Law and Policy and the UNCTAD intergovernmental group of experts; through conferences such as the Annual Fordham Corporate Law Institute series; and as part of the day-to-day enforcement of competition laws which, in the context of globalization necessitates such contact across national boundaries.[57] Consumer policy issues are aired through the International Society of Consumer and Competition Law Officials.[58] A number of non-governmental organizations also participate, although the extent to which they are characterized as lobby groups suggests they may be seen more as part of the policy network than the epistemic community. Notably, the International Chamber of Commerce set up a Joint Working Party on Competition and International Trade in 1995 combining their trade and competition commissions and they have made representations to the WTO Working Group.[59] The American Bar Association Task Force also participates in debates and issued an influential report advocating an international agreement on basic competition principles, for example, in relation to cartels and unification of filing laws in relation to mergers.[60] Key academic figures also emerge such as Eleanor Fox, Barry Hawk, and E.-U. Petersmann who participate in conferences such as that held at Fordham. The community can also meld into a more hybrid form, having a quasi-formal status and combining private, academic, and professional expertise with policy-makers as in the OECD Business and Industry Advisory Committee, the US Department of Justice International Competition Policy Advisory

55 Braithwaite and Drahos, op. cit., n. 13, p. 212.
56 Melamed, op. cit., n. 54, p. 425.
57 R. Pitofsky, 'Competition Policy in a Global Economy' (1999) *J. of International Economic Law* 403, at 406.
58 Set up in 1998, see Braithwaite and Drahos, op. cit., n. 13, p. 622.
59 C.S. Goldman and B.A. Facey, 'Antitrust and Trade Policy: International Business Perspectives' in *International Antitrust and Policy*, ed. B. Hawk (1998) 280.
60 American Bar Association, *Report of the ABA Antitrust Section Special Committee on International Antitrust* (1991), see the ABA, *Report of the Section of Antirust Law of the ABA* (March 1993), reprinted in (1993) 64 *Antitrust and Trade Regulations Report* (BNA). See M. Matsushita, 'Reflections on Competition Policy/ Law in the Framework of the WTO' in Fordham Corporate Law Institute, *International Antitrust Law and Policy*, ed. B. Hawk (1997) 36. Its ideas in relation to filing requirements are reflected in the OECD report on this topic, see Committee on Competition Law and Policy, *Report on Notification of Transnational Mergers* 5 February 1999, DAFEE/CLP(99)2/final.

Committee[61] and now, and most significantly, the proposed Global Competition Network. In fact, the strategy of the EU can be seen as continuing to build and draw on that community's expertise.

TRADE AND COMPETITION

Competition and trade liberalization policies are inter-linked but serve different purposes. Competition policy is aimed at limiting market power, while trade policy expressly aims to allow market power to be used to shift rents away from foreign producers. Imports act as a competitive discipline, theoretically removing the need for competition law especially for small open economies either developed or industrializing. This implies that a liberal trade policy and a domestic competition policy are substitutes (in a loose sense). However, such a substitution argument does not work for non-tradable sectors, where there is product differentiation that works in favour of domestic producers, and where distribution arrangements are designed expressly to exclude imports.[62] Given these caveats, and the risk that trade liberalization will result in a shift in lobbying towards a protectionist use of competition policy, the need for an effective domestic competition law remains. In fact, Iacobucci argues that an effective competition policy in itself reduces the likelihood of lobbying because single firms have only an attenuated interest in lobbying to protect the entire sector from foreign competition, and rivalry between domestic firms makes coordinated lobbying more difficult, less likely, and less successful.[63]

Anti-dumping and competition policies are also closely related and at cross-purposes.[64] Dumping, whereby goods are exported at prices below cost or below those charged on the domestic market (or, if none, on a third-country market), is prohibited under the GATT. Dumping, as a form of price discrimination, represents unfair competition, restricts market access, and breaches the principle of reciprocity that pervades international trade. Anti-dumping rules are well entrenched and widely used even though they are seen as little more than disguised protectionism, save where addressing the rare occurrence of predatory pricing.[65] The emphasis on fair competition

61 See P. Stern, 'Working Toward New US Competition Policy Related to Trade' (1999) 4 *Economic Perspectives* <http://usinfo.state.gov/journals/ites/0299/ijee/stern.htm>.

62 O. Cadot, J.-M. Grether, J. De Melo, 'Trade and Competition Policy: Where Do We Stand?' (2000) 34 *J. of World Trade* 1, at 3–7.

63 E. Iacobucci, 'The Interdependence of Trade and Competition Policies' (1997–98) 21 *World Competition* 5, at 14.

64 M.J. Trebilcock and R. Howse, *The Regulation of International Trade* (1999, 2nd edn.) ch. 7.

65 I. De León, 'Should We Promote Antitrust in International Trade?' (1997–98) 21 *World Competition* 35, at 36 and following.

(and trader interests) rather than consumer welfare, is at odds with competition policy. The EU and the United States make extensive use of anti-dumping measures and there is much concern among members like Hong Kong and Japan (whose firms are often the focus of such measures), and among developing countries that proposals on international competition law are designed to sidestep any reform of the anti-dumping rules. Even those who advocate reform of the anti-dumping rules[66] recognize that that reform has to be part of an overall package.[67] Hence, while there is much concern among developing countries in particular over further liberalization proposed at Doha,[68] the inclusion on the WTO agenda of negotiations to clarify and improve the anti-dumping rules does represent some attempt to address these concerns.

The UNCTAD Set of Principles were not sufficient to pave the way for the inclusion of competition policy in the Uruguay Round of GATT negotiations by developing countries, because of opposition from the United States and other industrial countries.[69] However, competition policy was included on the list of possible topics for future WTO work at the ministerial round at Marrakesh that finalized the protracted Uruguay round in 1994.[70] In addition, there were some fragmentary references to competition in the GATT itself, mainly in relation to protecting the non-discrimination principle where firms are granted special or exclusive rights by states.[71] Potentially of greater significance, sectoral competition rules are to be found in other agreements such as the Agreements on Trade-Related Services (GATS),[72] and on Trade-Related Intellectual Property Rights (TRIPS).[73] These sectoral rules highlight the close relations between trade and competition in the context of liberalization of markets, especially those where state intervention and regulation has traditionally been extensive. They reflect the well-established ideas on market liberalization that had been developed and used by the policy community prior to, and during the

---

66 Report of the Working Group on the Interaction between Trade and Competition Policy to the General Council, 1999 WT/WGTCP/3, 17. See, also, P. Holmes and R. Read, 'Competition Policy, Agriculture and the WTO' in *Trade and Agriculture: Negotiating a New Agreement?*, ed. J. McMahon (2001).

67 E.-U. Petersmann, 'International Competition Rules for Governments and for Private Business' (1996) 30 *J. of World Trade* 28 and following.

68 G. de Jonquières and F. Williams 'Poor nations lead moves against new trade round' *Financial Times*, 8 November 2001.

69 A.-M. Van den Bossche, 'Liberalization, Globalization and Competition Law and Policy' (1998) 18 *Yearbook of European Law* 67, at 85.

70 id., p. 118.

71 Malaguti, op. cit., n. 44, p. 123. See Article XVII; Article 11.1(b) of the Safeguards Agreement

72 Article VIII.2. Restrictive business practices are also mentioned but only to the extent that members should accede to consultation when requested to by another member, see Article IX.2.

73 Article 40 recognized that members can adopt measures to limit the anti-competitive effects of licensing.

125

negotiation of the GATS.[74] They were measures adopted in a trade rather than a specifically competition policy network.

While the existence of some provisions on competition pointed to an acceptance of a role for the WTO and a multilateral framework for competition after the Uruguay round, that acceptance seemed limited, since general competition principles – and the public good ethos which underpins them – were eschewed in favour of a sectoral approach which focused on the interests of the particular industry.[75] This sectoral approach marks a disjuncture between trade and competition, with United States trade officials favouring the former because of concerns that a general competition regime might adversely affect some local trade interests.[76] This reflects a broader concern among competition officials about competition falling into the hands of trade experts, because this could change the debate from one about international competition (and the consumer welfare it is designed to promote) to one about market access, which is primarily focused on advancing traders' interests. While market access can be of concern in competition policy (for example, the extent to which there are barriers to entry is an important element in the analysis of the contestability of markets), it has a broader scope. For example, market access focuses on questions of discrimination in relation to foreign firms rather than the intensity of competition within the important market.[77] As the WTO is predominantly a trade body, it is questionable whether it is suited to competition regulation which is primarily the regulation of private market behaviour. Hence, Tarullo suggests the inclusion of competition within the WTO framework would lead to a focus on only one aspect of competition – that of market access.[78]

The trade versus competition issue is reflected in the fact there are competing policy networks, with trade officials dominating the WTO. However, because of the intersection of the issues, the trade and competition networks overlap. Thus both the OECD and the WTO have set up working groups on trade and competition. Membership of more than one group can be used strategically to influence the agenda and frame the debate of one or both networks. The way ideas can become refracted when a network becomes more formalized within a particular context can be seen in the agenda and deliberations of the WTO working group on competition and trade. The group was to explore the objectives of competition law and what they should be; the existence (if any) of common substantive principles; what further initiatives should be taken in the interests of cooperation and

74 Drake and Nicolaïdis, op. cit., n. 36.
75 Public-choice theory is a useful analytical frame in relation to the intensive lobbying and capture in international trade: see, generally, D.A. Farber and P.P. Frickey, *Public Law and Public Choice: A Critical Introduction* (1990).
76 Braithwaite and Drahos, op. cit., n. 13, p. 189.
77 Holmes and Read, op. cit., n. 66.
78 Tarullo, op. cit., n. 28, p. 450.

comity; and finally, whether there should be a dispute resolution mechanism.[79] Following its first report,[80] the group undertook further work in three areas: the relationship between competition and fundamental principles of the WTO; the role of competition in promoting international trade; and how to develop cooperation between WTO members in this area.[81] Thus, it highlights the conceptual ambiguity surrounding the relationship between competition and trade, while framing and narrowing that conceptual question within the framework of the GATT. The question of how to develop cooperation seems to fall far short of any suggestion of an international agreement, but also can be seen as a quid pro quo for any such agreement. The establishment of this working group was an important stepping stone towards further formalization of the debate within the WTO and marks a critical juncture in the third phase of the debate on internationalization of competition policy.

THE THIRD PHASE: COMPETITION POLICY IN THE 1990s

By 1991, the OECD Trade Committee Symposium concluded that competition policy was likely to be one of the major new issues on the international trade policy agenda in the 1990s.[82] The EC Commission, emboldened by the success of its own regional competition policy, appointed a group of experts to explore the issue of international competition law[83] as a precursor to its aggressive promotion of an international competition law within the framework of the WTO, as suggested by this expert report. This report to some extent mirrored the 1993 Munich Code,[84] an (over) ambitious proposal for a World Competition Code setting out minimum standards to be incorporated into the GATT and enforceable by an international competition authority operating under the WTO, with an antitrust panel hearing disputes.[85] These proposals, along with the early proposals of the EC Commission, are the zenith reached so far by any international competition model. In line with the argument of Drake and Nicolaïdis, as ideas have become more prominent in the policy sphere, the more radical ideas – in this case for a strong multilateral approach – are weakened. This is because, in addition to the usual complexity of negotiating any international agreement

---

79 WT/MIN(96)/DEC/W, concluding the WTO Ministerial Conference, Singapore 9-13 December 1996.
80 WT/WGTCP/2.
81 See, also, the 2000 Annual Report, WT/WGTCP/4, 30 November 2000.
82 Trebilcock, op. cit., n. 20.
83 EC Commission, op. cit., n. 4.
84 International Antitrust Code Working Group, *Draft International Antitrust Code as a GATT/WTO Plurilateral Trade Agreement, Antitrust and Trade Regulation Report* (1993) (BNA) vol. 64, no. 1628 (special supplement).
85 Trebilcock, op. cit., n. 20, p. 94.

127

attributable to state interests, there are particular difficulties posed by the harmonization of competition norms, (as with other forms of business regulation). First, at the international level the emphasis is on negative integration (prohibition of some national norms), while harmonization of competition norms would require positive integration (requirement to introduce particular norms). Secondly, in international law the subject is normally the state, while the focus of competition norms is the behaviour of private actors.

At the WTO ministerial meeting in Singapore in 1996, as a result of EU advocacy, the Working Group on Trade and Competition Policy was set up. This body, chaired by the eminent French expert, Frédèric Jenny, reports annually and has become a key forum for the exploration of competition law issues, albeit through an international trade lens, between developing and industrialized countries. By the end of the decade, the debate had become more institutionalized within the WTO, with the Chair's statement at the Quadrilateral Trade Ministers Meeting in Tokyo in 1999 stressing that competition laws necessarily complemented trade liberalization and that the WTO could make an important contribution in that sphere.[86] This shift in the locus of the debate is in part a result of the importance the EU has given to the issue. In 2000, it proposed a Multilateral Framework Agreement on Competition which would involve the adoption of three core principles by members. First, to have a competition authority with adequate enforcement powers and a commitment to due process; to have national competition laws based on the principle of non-discrimination on grounds of nationality; and to prohibit hard-core cartels.[87] This is a much watered down version of the first EU proposal put forward prior to the setting up of the working group and reflects the ongoing opposition of the United States to multilateral actions and fora and also the opposition of developing countries which is multi-faceted.[88]

Excluded from the primary competition policy network of the OECD, developing countries were concerned about what Slaughter calls the politics of insulation (where networks are restricted to the powerful), and policy imposition (where powerful states attempt to impose their particular models of governance on weaker states).[89] These concerns have been addressed to some extent during this ongoing third phase by the inclusion of developing countries within the WTO working group. This has served to raise their awareness of competition policy as an increasingly important issue in international debates. Importantly, also, it has allowed them to link

---

86 The ministers of the United States, Japan, the EC, and Canada, see Van den Bossche, op cit., n. 69, p. 111.
87 Communication from the EC and its Member States, WT/WGTCP/W/152, 25 September 2000.
88 Holmes and Read, op. cit., n. 66.
89 Slaughter, op. cit., n. 9, p. 180.

128

the debate to the reform of anti-dumping rules, putting the onus on the EU in particular to show that such international rules are not simply about giving American and European firms unlimited access to foreign markets. The fact that only about half of the WTO members have a competition law has become a major issue,[90] so that developing countries, who represent two-thirds of the 142 members, concerned about the regulatory costs of having an effective competition law, have emphasized the importance of technical assistance. The Doha Declaration recognizes the needs of developing countries for enhanced support for technical assistance and capacity building, and promises to provide strengthened and adequately resourced assistance to respond to those needs. Promises of assistance and flexibility may not be enough to assuage developing countries' concerns particularly when the balance of advantage that was supposed to emerge post-Uruguay has not been achieved. The burden of setting up a competition regime is considerable and yet they argue that there is limited improvement of access to industrialized markets notably in agriculture and textiles. Given these concerns, the EU and the United States of America, as the main protagonists in the WTO in general, and in the competition debate in particular, will need to adopt a common approach if the negotiations are to open at a formal level in the WTO on competition policy.[91] This raises the question of the extent of differences between the EU and the United States, and whether the increased interaction through the competition networks has reduced the extent to which they differ on the question of internationalization of competition norms.

THE UNITED STATES OF AMERICA AND THE EUROPEAN UNION: SHARED PERSPECTIVES?

The debate on international competition policy concerns bilateral cooperation on enforcement, technical assistance, and the development of common competition principles pluri- or multi-laterally. These are not mutually exclusive alternatives although Tarullo argues that if competition policy falls within the WTO remit, then organic cooperation between national competition authorities will be thwarted.[92] He suggests that the adversarial nature of the WTO panels would undermine the mutual trust which goes to the heart of any coordination on enforcement. This analysis would depend in part on the frequency of such disputes and perhaps

---

90 *Annual Report of the WTO Working Group on Trade and Competition Policy*, WT/ WGTCP/4, 30 November 2000.
91 K. Chutikul, 'Much will be asked of Members in Doha: The Prospect that Member countries will Emerge from the Conference Dancing to the same tune looks bleak' *Financial Times*, 7 November 2001.
92 Tarullo, op. cit., n. 28.

underestimates the extent to which in practice most disputes are resolved informally in the WTO. More importantly, it is the United States and the EU which are most likely to initiate WTO dispute procedures and they already have strong bilateral links on competition enforcement – despite or perhaps because of high-profile conflicts such as over the Boeing/McDonnell Douglas merger.[93] Tarullo's analysis emphasizes the perceived importance of horizontal coordination between officials but sees it in stark contrast to any attempt at multilateralism.

Fox advocates a more nuanced approach, seeing the merits of bottom-up intitiatives involving technical assistance and cooperation between enforcement officials, combined with sectoral rules (as favoured by the United States) and regional agreements (the EU being the primary example). United States caution is reflected in the limited provisions on competition law in the NAFTA agreement,[94] regarded as necessary but not sufficient. These approaches, in her view, all need to be guided by a concept from the top which, in an effort to secure maximum agreement, she limits to antitrust rules designed to ensure market access and applied through the WTO either on a plurilateral or multilateral basis,[95] thus adopting more modest aims than the EU. This all encompassing approach aims to satisfy both the EU and the United States. The EU strongly advocates transnational competition principles within the WTO framework,[96] following the success of its own regional competition regime, while the United States is extremely wary of any multilateral regime,[97] instead strongly advocating bilateral approaches with an emphasis on cooperation on enforcement of existing competition rules. Fox's proposal emphasizes that the three strands of the debate are not mutually exclusive and that, as the events preceding Doha indicate, there has been a considerable shifting of position by the United States – which has agreed to the Global Forum on competition as an extra-WTO but nonetheless quasi-formal network, while the EU has moved away from the idea of an

93 [1997] OJ C 336/16. A. Fiebig, 'International Law Limits on the Extraterritorial Application of the European Merger Control Regulation and Suggestions for Reform' (1998) *European Competition Law Rev.* 323; J.P. Griffin, 'Antitrust Aspects of Cross-border Mergers and Acquisitions' (1998) *European Competition Law Rev.* 1. Or, more recently, the GE/Honeywell merger which has prompted a discussion as to the appropriateness of portfolio theory in merger analysis, see Introduction above.

94 Trebilcock, op. cit., n. 20, p. 91.

95 E.M. Fox, 'Toward World Antitrust and Market Access' (1997) 91 *Am. J. of International Law* 1. In the WTO, the plurilateral agreements are optional, while all members must adhere to all the organization's multilateral agreements.

96 Communication from the EC and its Member States, WT/WGTCP/W/152, 25 September 2000; M. Monti, 'The EU Views on Global Competition Forum', speech to the ABA Forum, Washington, 29 March 2001.

97 See, for example, J.I. Klein, 'Anticipating the Millennium: International Antitrust Enforcement at the End of the Twentieth Century' in *International Antitrust Law and Policy*, ed. B.E. Hawk (1998) 1, at 9; Pitofsky, op. cit., n. 57.

international competition agency towards the more limited idea of common principles, while taking on board the problems of introducing a competition regime for developing countries. It is arguable that the shift in perspectives and a recognition that perspectives are not exclusive, is primarily as a result of the operation and embedding of the competition network at the three levels of debate.

First, and most formally, procedural cooperation through bilateral agreements has been enthusiastically pursued by the United States, and also by the EU, to a more limited degree.[98] Such agreements form part of, and reinforce policy networks as well as acting as a form of policy learning, because enforcement authorities exchange ideas and methods, as well as concrete information where agreements allow. Bilateral treaties regularize discussions with the main trading partners of the United States, that is, Australia, Brazil, Canada, the EU, Germany, Israel, Japan, and Mexico.[99] The Canadian, EU, and Israeli agreements go furthest by allowing for positive comity. Positive comity operates whereby one state may request another to investigate anti-competitive behaviour within that other's boundaries which is affecting firms located in the requesting state.[100] The United States also has more than forty mutual legal assistance treaties in international cartel matters.[101] Pitofsky sees such positive comity as an alternative to the extraterritorial jurisdiction advocated by the United States courts and thus a means of avoiding international friction through coordination. These treaties are underwritten by the American International Antitrust Enforcement Assistance Act 1994 which allows for the exchange of information and evidence with other competition authorities in civil and criminal actions. Thus, the emphasis for the United States is on retaining tight control on coordination by providing assistance and entering into bilateral agreements for the enforcement of competition laws. While the United States does participate in regional and multilateral fora, it advocates an evolutionary approach with case-by-case cooperation on a bilateral level and discussions and exchanges of ideas on the multilateral level. Such an approach is both 'congenial and sensible' according to Melamed, an official in the Department of Justice.[102] Pitofsky of the Federal Trade Commission echoes this view, advocating a similar evolutionary approach based on 'learning', the main strength of which he sees as flexibility.[103] The discourse of evolution is very much within the frame of policy networks where actors with considerable political power (the United States and the EU in the international context), can exert influence and use their power to fix the agenda.

98 For a list of countries with which the EU has agreements, see <http://europa.eu.int/comm/competition/international/bilateral/>.
99 For texts of the agreements, see <http://www.usdoj.gov/atr/public/international/docs/>.
100 Pitofsky, op. cit., n. 57, p. 408.
101 James, op. cit., n. 6, p. 3.
102 Melamed, op. cit., n. 54, p. 432.
103 Pitofsky, op. cit., n. 57, p. 411.

While the EU sees coordination with the United States through their agreement as absolutely essential,[104] the kind of highly formal coordination provided by such treaties is regarded as inadequate – a point conceded by the United States Department of Justice at the inaugural meeting of the OECD Global Competition Forum.[105] Despite months of coordination, the United States and EU competition authorities still disagreed substantively over the GE/Honeywell merger, which was rejected by the EU Commission, apparently because of their disagreement on views of competition based on portfolio theory. The conclusion taken from the exercise however was not to reduce coordination but rather to increase it, with a view to reaching common ground. Indeed, it is arguable that the GE/Honeywell experience was an important factor in the United States agreeing to the EU initiative of the Global Competition Network. In fact, it was suggested that the issue of portfolio theory could be taken up by the network, thus supplementing bilateral meetings between United States and EU officials.[106]

The second approach, technical assistance – involving policy learning and transfer – can range from informal discussions of enforcement strategies to the wholesale exportation of a particular competition model to another state. Policy learning and transfer can only arise where there are pre-existing networks and are most effective where there is a common discourse and shared objectives. Policy transfer occurs when knowledge about policies, administration, institutions, and so on in one time or place are used in the development of policies, administration or institutions in another time or place.[107] Policy transfer can occur in three different ways. Emulation is where transfer is voluntary. Regionalization has led to the development of similar competition rules or principles.[108] For example, most EU member states have voluntarily incorporated Articles 81 and 82 EC which prohibit restrictive practices and abuse of dominance into their laws.[109] Coercive transfer is where there is some sort of external inducement for the adoption of a particular policy. For example, the World Bank has given advice on implementation of competition laws as part of structural adjustment programmes[110] while the International Monetary Fund has required enactment or reform of competition regimes as a

104 See B.J. Rodger, 'Competition Policy, Liberalism and Globalization: A European Perspective' (2000) 6 *Columbia J. of European Law* 289, at 314.
105 James, op. cit., n. 6.
106 id.
107 D.P. Dolowitz and D. Marsh, 'Who Learns from Whom: A Review of the Policy Transfer Literature' (1996) 44 *Political Studies* 343.
108 For example, the NAFTA Agreement, Mercosur, and the New Zealand/Australia agreement, see Trebilcock, op. cit., n. 20, p. 90.
109 I. Maher, 'Alignment of Competition Laws in the EC' (1996) *Yearbook of European Law* 223.
110 WTO Working Group on the Interaction Between Trade and Competition Policy, *1999 Report*, WT/WGTCP/3 (11 October 1999) 12.

condition for loans in some circumstances.[111] The adoption of laws modelled on the EC Treaty's Articles 81 and 82 by candidate countries for membership of the EU, specifically those from the former Communist bloc, is also an example.[112] The third category of policy transfer is where there is convergence as a result of structural change, for example, in response to some unexpected or large-scale event such as a health scare. Policy learning is conceptually different from policy transfer though they are related. Learning is voluntary and can lead to transfer but not necessarily. It could also lead to innovation or termination of a particular policy process.[113] In the OECD, policy learning occurs between industrialized countries with an emphasis on cooperation, with recommendations passed encouraging cooperation between competition authorities on anti-competitive practices that affect international trade.[114] Its Committee on Competition Law and Policy continues to promote co-operation between competition authorities, and it also explores ways of improving coherence between trade and competition policies through the Joint Group on Competition and Trade.[115]

Policy learning and policy transfer can be seen, and are advocated by the United States, as desirable alternatives to a multilateral international competition law. The United States has an extensive technical assistance programme.[116] While the American approach is couched in terms of technical assistance, the spirit with which assistance is proffered is almost evangelical: Van der Bossche refers to their 'almost colonial attitudes'[117] and Braithwaite and Drahos cite a United States official referring to the missionary zeal about spreading antitrust.[118] Whether the adoption of competition rules by developing countries is coercive or voluntary is

---

111 For example, Indonesia, see E.M. Fox, 'Equality, Discrimination, and Competition Law: Lessons from and for South Africa and Indonesia' (2000) 41 *Harvard International Law J.* 579, at 589.

112 J. Fingleton, E. Fox, D. Neven, and P. Seabright, *Competition Policy and the Transformation of Central Europe* (1995).

113 D. Stone, 'Learning Lessons and Transferring Policy across Time, Space and Disciplines' (1999) 19 *Politics* 51, at 52.

114 1995 Recommendation of the Council concerning Co-operation between Member Countries on Anticompetitive Practices affecting International Trade 27 July 1995, (95)130/FINAL, updating earlier Recommendations dating back to 1967. See S. Shelton, 'Competition Policy: What Chance for International Rules?' (1999) *OECD J. of Competition Law and Policy* 59, at 67.

115 See, for example, Joint Group on Trade and Competition, International Options to Improve the Coherence between Trade and Competition Policies 11 February 2000, COM/TD/DAFFE/CLP(99)102/final.

116 Melamed, op. cit., n. 54, notes there were more than 200 missions 'to dozens of countries', both short- and long-term, as well as the Department of Justice and Federal Trade Commission hosting hundreds of officials and running intern programmes (p. 426).

117 Van Den Bossche, op. cit., n. 69, p. 69.

118 Braithwaite and Drahos, op. cit., n. 13, p. 216.

133

debatable: Braithwaite and Drahos argue that they seem to enact competition laws because a competition regime is seen as part of an efficient and successful economy and also because if the issue is linked to trade, better they enact their own laws before the issue is moved onto the international stage where they effectively lack any voice.[119] The extent to which policy transfer is a success is debatable. While one could argue like Pitofsky that the idea of competition law is catching on, with over eighty states now having competition laws,[120] this still leaves about half the members of the WTO without any.[121]

Thus far, developments have been a combination of creating and strengthening policy networks and promoting policy learning especially among developing countries in order to reduce their anxieties about issues of market access. Coordination in enforcement can only occur between states with relatively similar competition regimes making greater consistency between regimes a prerequisite to greater internationalization. As long as there is a policy network continuing to build trust and mutual respect, the possibility of a plurilateral if not multilateral competition regime remains possible. At the same time, the existence of a network does not automatically imply that further integration will follow. To some extent the fact of coordination and interaction may create a momentum towards the development of a common discourse and even common principles. Such functional cooperation can however only translate into more formal governance provided there is convergence not just between the perspectives of functional government officials but also between the national interests, more broadly expressed and as advocated by the traditional international players, notably foreign ministries and international institutions.

CONCLUSION

The internationalization of competition law is a fluid process. We have seen a number of developments along the lines of cooperation on enforcement, technical assistance, and an increase in the number of states adopting competition laws. The creation of international competition institutions is an uncertain prospect, with regional and bilateral initiatives dominating. Central to further developments, as they have been to the pattern already observed, are networks of competition law officials and the wider community of competition experts. They represent a key aspect of enterprising global governance wielding power based on knowledge.

---

119 id., p. 190.
120 Pitofsky, op. cit., n. 57.
121 *Annual Report of the WTO Working Group on Trade and Competition Policy*, WT/WGTCP/4, 30 November 2000.

One of the concerns that arises out of the emergence of such networks is the extent to which they are accountable, accountability being seen as a key aspect of legitimacy. International law regimes have always suffered from a legitimacy problem, in the sense that any democratic accountability is indirect at best.[122] The concern with the fragmentation of government in the international sphere is that traditional forms of accountability are lost. Informal groupings can be opaque, little more than old-boy networks where those with either credible knowledge or more traditional forms of power have access while less privileged actors in the international scene are excluded. The experience of developing countries lends some validity to this claim. At the same time, the efforts to address their concerns, however limited, also show the limitations of such networks and their essentially bounded nature within the international order. Such groupings, while seeking to address their own difficulties, operate fundamentally within the power structures of the state and hence within the power structures of the international legal order.

While technocracy may serve to insulate them, they ultimately remain accountable through existing national channels.[123] As long as they operate informally, and exercise no explicit power, the question arises: to what extent do they need to be accountable? If, as a result of their discussions, practices are adopted because they are perceived to be best practice then this seems an effective and efficient exercise of government. This argument of legitimation on the basis of outputs holds good as long as those outputs are consistent with those of the state and those securing them are agencies entrusted with the responsibilities of protecting the defined public good. Some competition authorities can be equated with courts or central banks as bodies that command respect and that need to be insulated to some degree from the body politic so they can properly carry out their functions. The embeddedness of a competition ethos within states varies fundamentally and hence so does the status of the agencies – an issue that has become all too apparent through the WTO working group.

Finally, the critique that technocratic networks displace international institutions does not hold in the competition sphere where internationalization is a theme across a number of fora, including the WTO. If anything, much of their activity can be seen as shoring up the state, ensuring more effective compliance with existing norms and, because the officials responsible for implementation are involved in discussions, any rules that do emerge are likely to be better grounded domestically.[124] The challenge for competition officials and others participating in this new form of governance is to ensure that the discourse of legitimacy, however flawed and however impossible of realization, becomes enmeshed in their

122 Picciotto, op. cit., n. 16, p. 263.
123 Slaughter, op. cit., n. 9, p. 195.
124 id., p. 201.

135

discussions of issues such as the extent to which portfolio theory should apply to conglomerate mergers. In competition policy this is relatively easy given the presence of a powerful theory – ordo-liberalism – emphasizing the importance of competition law in order to ensure that there is a balance between public and private power, such that the former can never intervene too much within the market place so as to curb individual freedom unnecessarily, and the latter never grows so as to alienate the citizenry from the state.[125]

---

125 See generally, Gerber, op. cit., n. 46; I. Maher, 'Re-imagining the Story of European Competition Law' (2000) 20 *Ox. J. of Legal Studies* 155; Rodger, op. cit., n. 104.

JOURNAL OF LAW AND SOCIETY
VOLUME 29, NUMBER 1, MARCH 2002
ISSN: 0263-323X, pp. 137–62

Technical Cooperation and the International Coordination of Patentability of Biotechnological Inventions

LOUISE DAVIES*

Within the formal international framework, the coordination and harmonization[1] of substantive patentability is currently of a limited nature, confined to the level of general principles, in contrast to the greater degree of procedural coordination. This involves increased costs and a lack of legal certainty for those seeking patents in multiple jurisdictions, mainly transnational corporations in some research-based industries such as pharmaceuticals. The problems encountered in achieving even a basic level of international consensus have encouraged informal cooperation through what could be conceptualized as 'global patent networks'. Furthermore, the interrelationship between procedural and substantive patent law issues has led the Trilateral Patent Offices, an informal, transgovernmental regulatory network of technical specialists, to undertake projects relating to the harmonization of procedural and substantive patent law issues primarily in contentious areas of patentability such as biotechnology.[2] This raises the possibility of developing convergent interpretations of the patentability rules, although with implications for accountability and legitimacy.

* Lancaster University Law School, Lancaster University, Lancaster LA1 4YN, England

I would like to acknowledge the helpful comments of Professor Sol Picciotto, Lancaster University Law School, and the assistance of the European Patent Office in the preparation of this paper. The sponsorship of the ESRC in this research is also gratefully acknowledged.

1 In this article the terms 'coordination' and 'harmonization' will follow the definitions of S.H. Jacobs, *Regulatory Cooperation for an Interdependent World: Issues for Government* (1994) 32. 'Coordination' is therefore '... the gradual narrowing of relevant differences between regulatory systems, often based on voluntary international codes of practice ...' and 'harmonization' '... the standardisation of regulation in identical form'.

2 For the purposes of this paper, the term 'biotechnological inventions' refers to nucleic acid molecule-related inventions.

I. INTERNATIONAL COORDINATION OF PATENTABILITY

1. The formal framework and beyond

Negotiators currently attempting to harmonize substantive patent law within the formal international framework[3] must overcome similar problems to those faced by their predecessors. Profound tensions caused by north-south differences in the ideological basis of patent law[4] and the reluctance of national governments to cede what they perceive to be a portion of national sovereignty to create a global, harmonized regime[5] simmer beneath the outwardly tranquil exterior of international negotiations. Each negotiating party realizes that only by harmonizing substantive patent law will they be able to reduce the workload and costs of each of their national/regional patent offices whilst simultaneously reducing the costs of global patent protection and providing greater legal certainty for applicants. However, attempts to reach agreement within the formal international framework may end in failure, or at best, in a semi-satisfactory compromise, following a protracted period of negotiation.

As it stands, the formal framework for the international coordination of patentability affords a high level of procedural coordination[6] but provides only

---

3 The World Intellectual Property Organization's (WIPO) Standing Committee on the Law of Patents (SCP) is currently discussing a new Substantive Patent Law Treaty (SPLT).

4 S.K. Sell, *Power and Ideas: North-South Politics of Intellectual Property and Anti-Trust* (1998) ch. 4.

5 A.D. Sabatelli and J.C. Rasser, 'Impediments to Global Patent Harmonisation' (1995) 22 *Northern Kentucky Law Rev.* 579–620.

6 Procedural and substantive patent law issues were dealt with separately (by the Council of Europe) after World War II through the Formalities Convention (1953) and the Strasbourg Convention (1963). Their key provisions were incorporated into the Patent Co-operation Treaty (PCT) and European Patent Convention (EPC) respectively (W. Paterson, *The European Patent System* (1992) 15–20). The PCT provides a single process for filing multiple international applications and grants national rather than international patents. Its substantive provisions are not binding upon its member states, see, for example, Articles 27(5) and 33(5). (S. Uemura, 'Programs and Activities for the Reduction of Patent Costs', symposium paper presented at 1999 Summit Conference on Intellectual Property, University of Washington <http://www.washington.edu/Casrip/> accessed 11 September 2001). WIPO's Patent Law Treaty (PLT) concluded in June 2000 harmonizes the procedural requirements for filing national and regional international applications and included provisions for electronic filing. With the exception of the filing date provisions, it establishes *maximum* standards which patent offices need apply and retains consistency with both the Paris Convention and the PCT. (See AIPLA Conference paper by P. Baechtold, 'Summary of the Patent Law Treaty and Plans for the Future' 15 February 2001 <http://www.c:\windows\profiles\rsagara\desktop\staff\mike kirk\webcontent\paris symposium\baechtold.doc> last accessed 6 June 2001). At the time of this paper, the PLT has still not entered into force.

138

a limited degree of substantive coordination. Formal international coordination is provided by two multilateral conventions: first, the Paris Convention of 1883, which has been administered by the WIPO since 1967. However this Convention did not establish minimum levels of substantive patentability, it also lacked effective enforcement and dispute settlement mechanisms and left member states with a large margin of discretion as to the implementation of its provisions.[7] Secondly, the Agreement on Trade Related Aspects of Intellectual Property (TRIPs), part of the package of agreements establishing the World Trade Organization (WTO) in 1995. This is now the principal international instrument of harmonization, having introduced minimum standards of intellectual property protection backed by the WTO's powerful dispute settlement mechanisms. However, TRIPs has only harmonized substantive patentability at the level of general principles. Article 27(1), the key substantive provision, specifies only that patents should be available for all inventions and in all spheres of technology provided that they fulfil the criteria of novelty, inventive step, and industrial application. No indication is provided as to how those criteria should be interpreted and the exclusionary clauses contained within Articles 27(2) and (3) are optional. Member states may implement this agreement in accordance with their national law, which does little either to ensure legal certainty within different patenting jurisdictions or to reduce the costs of obtaining patent protection.[8]

The European Patent Office (EPO), the 'executive-administrative arm' of the European Patent Organization (EPOr), provides a centralized system for the examination and grant of European patents[9] which are issued in the form

7 See H.P. Kunz-Hallstein, 'The United States Proposal for a GATT Agreement on Intellectual Property and the Paris Convention for the Protection of Industrial Property' (1989) 22 *Vanderbilt J. of Transnational Law* 265–84. Its principal achievements were to introduce national treatment (Art. 2), a right of priority (Art. 4), restrictions on penalties for non-working of the invention (Art. 5) and the right for member states to enter into special agreements to promote further co-operation provided that they were not in contravention of the principles of that Convention (Art. 19). See K. Curesky, 'International Patent Harmonisation through WIPO: An Analysis of the US Proposal to Adopt a "First-to-File" Patent System' (1989) 21 *Law and Policy in International Business* 289–308. The revisions of this Convention between 1900 and 1967 produced a patchwork of differing legal obligations for its member states because it was not compulsory for them to ratify the new version, E.T. Penrose, *The Economics of the International Patent System* (1973) 64–71.

8 TRIPs requires WTO member states to apply the basic principles of the Paris Convention (Article 2), but goes beyond both the Paris Convention and the EPC by laying down detailed standards involving strong international harmonization and enforcement procedures rather than substantive patentability. In contrast, Part III of TRIPs sets out in considerable detail the procedures states must establish for enforcement of intellectual property rights, ranging from *ex parte* provisional measures, to criminal penalties for wilful infringement.

9 G.B. Doern, 'The EPO and European Intellectual Property Policy' (1997) 4 *J. of European Public Policy* 388–403. The EPO is arguably the most important of the regional intellectual property institutions which include: North American Free Trade Association (NAFTA), African Regional Industrial Property Office (ARIPO),

of a 'bundle of national patents'[10] to states that have acceded to the European Patent Convention (EPC).[11] Within the framework of the European Union (EU)[12] the controversial Biotechnology Directive[13] has introduced a more harmonized approach towards the patentability of biotechnological inventions.

African Intellectual Property Association (OAPI) and Eurasian Patent Organization (EAPC).

10 European patents are subject to the national substantive rules of states designated on the application. This can lead to conflicting decisions in proceedings for validity and infringement. Article 69 EPC and the Protocol on Interpretation were intended to ensure some uniformity of patent claim interpretation in such cases. See J. Straus, 'Patent Litigation in Europe – A Glimmer of Hope? Present Status and Future Perspectives' (2000) 2 *Washington University J. of Law and Policy* 403, at 404–5; R. Lunzer, *The European Patent Convention* (1995) 253. P. Leith, 'Judicial or Administrative Roles: The Patent Appellate System in the European Context' (2001) 1 *Intellectual Property Q.* 50–99 notes that decisions of the EPO's Boards of Appeal exercise a considerable influence upon national courts' decisions. The lack of legal certainty and translation costs incurred under Art. 65(1) EPC, the second principal problem for European patents, are being addressed by the EPO. The Optional Protocol on Litigation is still under discussion, see second draft at <http://www.ige.ch/E/jurinfo/pdf/j14105_prop.pdf> accessed September 2001. The 'London Protocol' is intended to reduce translation costs, <http://www.ige.ch/E/jurinfo/pdf/epc65_e.pdf> last accessed September 2001. See, also, P. Cole, 'Centralised Litigation for European Patents: New Proposals for Inclusion in the EPC Revision Package' (2001) 5 *European Intellectual Property Rev.* 219–23. These discussions are being carried out in parallel to the EU's attempts to create a Community Patent, see n. 12 below.

11 The EPO extends the cover of European and Euro-PCT patents by issuing extension certificates to states that have not yet acceded to the EPC. See *Annual Report of the EPO 1996* <http://www.european-patent-office.org/epo/an_rep/hmlfiles/intcop.htm> s. 6, International Affairs and Cooperation, accessed 4 May 2000.

12 Attempts to create a unitary Community Patent using the Community Patent Convention ('CPC') (1975) failed for two reasons: i) the costs incurred when translating Community patents into the languages of each Community member and ii) lack of legal certainty since the invalidation of a Community patent by one national court would have resulted in Community-wide invalidation (Proposal for a Council Regulation on the Community Patent COM(2000) 412 Final 5.) The EU's Agreement Relating to Community Patents (1989) OJ 30 December 1989 L401, 1–27 and the Protocol on the Settlement of Litigation OJ 30 December 1989 L401, 34–44 did not resolve the situation. Discussions for a Community patent were revived in the EU Green Paper COM(97) 314 final 24 June 1997, but progress on the Proposed Regulation for a Community Patent depends upon the resolution of issues regarding language translation and the creation of a central Community Intellectual Property Court to deal with infringement and validity. 'Everyone Agrees the EU needs its own Patent System. So why is it so difficult to create one?' *Financial Times*, 8 October 2001. Cole, op. cit., n. 10 asks whether legal certainty will result if the EPO and EU operate two separate courts.

13 Directive 98/44/EC OJ 30 July 1998 L213, 13–31. Certain of its provisions have been incorporated into Ch. VI of the EPC's Implementing Regulations which will be discussed later in this paper. On the 9 October 2001 the European Court of Justice dismissed Case C-377/98 which attempted to annul this Directive.

However, beyond the formal framework of coordination through international treaties, extensive cooperation has developed informally, but directly between the three principal Patent Offices, the United States Patent and Trademark Office (USPTO), the Japanese Patent Office (JPO) and the EPO, the Trilateral Offices. The activity amongst technical specialists in this sphere of regulation bears some of the characteristics of Haas's[14] concept of an epistemic community. The work of the Trilateral Offices was initially aimed at coordinating and harmonizing procedural aspects of the patent granting process but, contrary to Cheek's view,[15] their comparative studies have also extended to substantive patentability in contentious areas such as computer software related inventions, business methods and biotechnology, the latter being the focus of this paper. The argument put forward by Haas and echoed by Slaughter[16] is that the work of technical specialists such as Trilateral officials merely facilitates governmental policy decisions at national and international level. For others, however, this type of globalized technocracy raises questions of accountability and legitimacy.

2. Technical and political issues in regulating patentability

Some discussions of international coordination and harmonization of patent law appear to suggest that this is a technical debate to be resolved solely through technical cooperation. Although questions concerning substantive patentability may be referred to as 'technical', they inevitably contain an element of a 'political' or 'policy preference'.[17] Patents are state-backed monopoly rights which regulate the balance between the rights of appropriation by the patent-owner and the possibility of diffusion of innovation, purportedly to the benefit of competitors and the general public. The scope of the protection given is determined by the breadth of applicants' claims and the interpretation of the criteria for patentability. As such, a patent is neither solely 'technical' nor 'political', but a combination of both. Importantly, this form of economic regulation is only a prima facie right, because even after it is officially 'granted', it is open to challenge by competitors through formal procedures of opposition which may result in

---

14 P.M. Haas, 'Introduction: Epistemic Communities and International Policy Coordination' (1992) 46 *International Organization* 1–35.

15 M.L. Cheek, 'The Limits of Informal Regulatory Cooperation in International Affairs: A Review of the Global Intellectual Property Regime'(2001) 33 *George Washington International Law Rev.* 277–322

16 A.-M. Slaughter, 'Governing the Global Economy through Government Networks' in *The Role of Law in International Politics*, ed. M. Byers (2000) 178–205. More recently, Slaughter does seem to acknowledge that some networks raise accountability issues: A.-M. Slaughter, 'The Accountability of Government Networks (2001) 8 *Indiana J. of Global Legal Studies* 347–69 <http://ijgls.indiana.edu/vol8/no2/slaughter.pdf> last accessed August 2001.

17 M. Shapiro, 'The Problems of Independent Agencies in the United States and the European Union' (1997) 4 *J. of European Public Policy* 276–91, at 280.

revocation; or simply through imitation requiring legal action for infringement.

The interrelationship between technical and political issues manifests itself in several ways within the patent granting process. One such example, which is directly relevant to the work of the Trilateral Patent Offices, discussed further below, is the interrelatedness of procedural and substantive patent issues.[18] Procedural matters inevitably require consideration of substantive issues and vice versa. This interrelationship may also mean that international negotiations to coordinate procedural issues may be used as a means of securing harmonization of substantive patent law. WIPO's 'Basic Proposal' for a Patent Harmonization Treaty provides some evidence of this practice. WIPO's director-general established a committee of experts in June 1983 to investigate the possible introduction of an international grace period.[19] Those involved in negotiations quickly realized that it was not possible to consider the grace period without a harmonized approach to identifying the inventor and the filing date of the patent application.[20] As the scope of WIPO's plans broadened, a total of eleven preparatory meetings preceded the publication of their 'Basic Proposal' on 21 December 1990, which included provisions on patentability, the scope of protection, and extending patent protection to all fields of technology.[21] The linkage between the introduction of an international grace period and the transition to a first-to-file system precipitated the collapse of the treaty negotiations on 27 January 1994 because the United States of America decided to retain its first-to-invent system of filing due to opposition by 'independent investors'.[22]

Harmonizing the substantive criteria for patentability will also have a global political impact through the 'intellectual property trade-off' in which these criteria play a key role in balancing the inventor's monopoly right against the degree of public benefit resulting from the dissemination of the invention. How this balance is struck depends on many social and economic factors. National and international institutions, private parties, and technical

18 One such example is the presence/absence of a grace period upon the novelty and inventive step criteria.
19 A grace period is an interval before filing in which inventors can make a non-prejudicial disclosure of their invention. See report of Prof. Joseph Straus for the EPO. He attributes the decision to consider a grace period to an international intellectual property NGO; the International Association for Intellectual Property (AIPPI) <http://www.european-patent-office.org.news/pressrel/2000_07 _25_e.htm> accessed 4 February 2001.
20 See document PCT/DC/5, p. 100, paras. 2 and 3 – WIPO publication no. 351(e), *Records of the Diplomatic Conference for the Conclusion of a Treaty Supplementing the Paris Convention as Far as Patents are Concerned* vol. 1 (1991).
21 R.C. Moy, 'The Patent Harmonisation Treaty: Economic Self-Interest as an Influence' (1993) 26 *John Marshall Law Rev.* 457–95; see, also, H. Bardehle, 'A New Approach to Worldwide Harmonisation of Patent Law' (1999) 81 *J. of the Patent and Trademark Society* 303–10.
22 Bardehle, id., p. 304.

specialists may all contribute to this process. Each of these participants are subject to a variety of influences including national governments, industry and intellectual property professionals[23] who all have different perspectives as to how the trade-off should be decided. However, the international coordination and harmonization of patentability may ultimately result in a global patent system which imposes a socio-economic and cultural homogeneity that may be inappropriate given the wide diversity of social and economic conditions, especially between developed and developing countries and particularly in relation to the patentability of biotechnological inventions.

The interrelationship between technical and political issues tends to be understated because certain conventions within the formal international framework have been broadly labelled as either 'procedural' or 'substantive'[24] when in fact the principal intellectual property treaties incorporate both elements. However, the current level of procedural coordination suggests that it has generally been easier to reach agreement on those issues.[25] WIPO recognized the problems of attempting to harmonize procedural and substantive issues within a broad-based treaty and subsequently remodelled its Basic Proposal into the procedural PLT discussed above. WIPO has recently recommenced negotiations for a separate Substantive Patent Law Treaty (SPLT) which it hopes will remedy the lacunae in the current intellectual property conventions including TRIPs.[26] At the meeting of WIPO's SCP in November 2000, the negotiating parties decided to focus the agenda for the SPLT on six basic issues; definitions of prior art, novelty, inventive step/non-obviousness, industrial applicability/utility, sufficiency of disclosure, and the structure and interpretation of claims.[27] However, much work remains to be done before any consensus is reached upon the general principles of patentability and the regulations to give guidance on their interpretation. These negotiations strike a cautionary note since a parallel can be drawn between the current negotiations and those for the Basic Proposal.[28] Once more, the United States has declared itself willing to negotiate on the first-to-invent issue, but only as part of a wider programme of harmonization and only after progress has been made in relation to the six basic substantive issues.[29]

23 B.G. Doern, *Global Change and Intellectual Property Agencies* (1999) 8.
24 Hence WIPO negotiations to streamline procedural issues culminated in the PLT and substantive issues are currently being discussed for a Substantive Patent Law Treaty.
25 However, the current dispute over translation issues for the Proposed Regulation for the Community Patent, op. cit., n. 12, and the first-to-file/first-to-invent debate illustrate the political nature of procedural issues and the problems which beset negotiators.
26 WIPO document SCP/4/2, fourth session, 6–10 November 2000, p. 3, para. 7.
27 WIPO, id, para. 9.
28 'Third Session of Committee of Experts on the Harmonisation of Certain Provisions in Laws for the Protection of Inventions' (1987) 26 *Industrial Property* 204–34.
29 WIPO Report adopted by the Standing Committee on the Law of Patents SCP/4/6, 7 December 2000, agenda item 4. The meeting of the SCP in November 2001 is attempting to create a harmonized interpretation of prior article.

143

As this brief account has indicated, there has been considerable progress in developing the international coordination of patenting in recent years, although greater progress has been made on the procedural aspects. Clearly, however, significant obstacles remain to achieving harmonization, especially of the substantive criteria for patentability. In this context, it is instructive to consider the contribution made by the growth of networks of technical experts within closed regulatory communities who work to create closer coordination and harmonization. The following section of this paper will attempt to ascertain whether closer coordination can occur through technical cooperation, with reference to Trilateral cooperation, and the implications of informal cooperation for accountability and legitimacy.

II. TECHNICAL COOPERATION AND INTERNATIONAL POLICY COORDINATION

1. International regulatory coordination

Certain authors have suggested that understanding regulatory cooperation within the global marketplace requires a fresh approach to that advocated by the realist state-centred international relations paradigm and the Westphalian system of international law[30] in which the multilateral convention was the principal tool of coordination.[31] Slaughter characterizes the shift from national government to global governance in terms of a 'disaggregation' of the state which suggests key roles for government institutions and agencies within transgovernmental regulatory networks. Others see this process in terms of the 'fragmentation' of the state, with non-governmental organizations (NGOs),[32] professionals, and other sub-state actors,

---

30 See, for example, K. Jaysuria, 'Globalisation, Law and the Transformation of Sovereignty: The Emergence of Global Regulatory Governance' (1999) 6 *Indiana J. of Global Legal Studies* 425–55 and see, also, B.L. Walser, 'Shared Technical Decision-Making and the Disaggregation of Sovereignty: International Policy, Expert Communities and the Pharmaceutical Industry' (1998) 72 *Tulane Law Rev.* 1592–1699; Slaughter, op. cit. (2000), n. 16, p. 178. J. Kelsey, 'Globalisation, State and Law "Towards a Multi-Perspectival Polity"' (1996) 14 *Law in Context* 31–51 describes the need to reconceptualize sovereignty, state, and the law in the face of globalization.

31 A.-M. Slaughter, 'The Real New World Order' (1997) 76(5) *Foreign Affairs* 183–97 and Slaughter, id. Disaggregation of the state does not involve its disappearance, but suggests that an increasingly prominent role is played in international fora by '... administrative agencies, courts and legislatures' which was formerly the sole domain of '... foreign ministries and heads of state'.

32 See, for example, R. Hofman (ed.), *Non-state Actors as New Subjects of International Law* (1999) and J. Mertus, 'From Legal Transplants to Transformative Justice: Human Rights and the Promise of Transformative Justice' (1999) 14 *Am. University International Law Rev.* 1335–9.

144

comprising 'global civil society', increasingly forming part of the regulatory web from which global governance is fashioned.[33]

Cheek argues that with the exception of the Stockholm Group, an informal forum where policy-makers from industrialized countries meet to discuss copyright protection, no transgovernmental regulatory networks[34] for intellectual property exist. She also suggests three factors, which may prevent the growth of such networks in the future. First, governments do not wish to usurp the role of WIPO as a consensus building inter governmental organization. Secondly, international treaties already exist which provide for national treatment, mutual recognition, and harmonization in specific areas of intellectual property. However the current negotiations for the SPLT would appear to challenge this point since they acknowledge the need to move beyond harmonizing patentability at the level of general principles and to produce globally coherent interpretations of those criteria. Cheek's third point suggests that the aggressive involvement of the TRIPs Council and US Trade Representative in intellectual property enforcement issues together with a high degree of executive involvement by the US State Department, has done little to foster an environment of consensus, trust, and cooperation which is vital to the development of transgovernmental networks. The third section of this paper will address her argument through an analysis of the activities of the Trilateral Patent Offices.

Epistemic communities,[35] transnational advocacy coalitions, and advocacy coalition frameworks[36] have all been cited as active phenomena

---

33 S. Picciotto, 'The Regulatory Criss-Cross: Interaction between Jurisdictions and the Construction of Global Regulatory Networks' in *International Regulatory Competition and Coordination*, eds. W. Bratton et al. (1996) 95; see, also, S. Picciotto, 'Networks in International Economic Integration: Fragmented States and the Dilemmas of Neoliberalism' (1996–97) 17 *Northwestern J. of International Law and Business* 1014–56.

34 Cheek, op. cit., n. 15, suggests a hierarchy of four types of network which vary in the degree of harmonization: cross-fertilization networks, coordination networks, mutual recognition networks, and harmonization networks but acknowledges that the participation of bureaucratic, intellectual property professionals could lead one to expect the development of transgovernmental networks of intellectual property specialists, some of whom may be characterized as an 'epistemic community'.

35 Haas, op. cit., n. 14, p. 3.

36 id., p. 18 distinguishes epistemic communities from interest groups, pressure groups and transnational advocacy coalitions (TACs) the latter being motivated by principled ideas and values. TACs attempt to influence the policy-making process by acquiring leverage over specific actors and institutions rather than their authoritative claim to knowledge (M.E. Keck and K. Keck, *Activists beyond Borders: Advocacy Coalitions in International Politics* (1998) 1–2. The advocacy coalition framework analyses the policy process through a policy sub-system containing coalitions of actors drawn from public and private organizations, each with a hierarchically ordered model of beliefs (P.A. Sabatier, 'The Advocacy Coalition Framework: Revisions and Relevance for Europe' (1998) 5 *J. of European Public Policy* 98–130).

in the process of international regulatory coordination. The concept of an epistemic community, as developed by Haas, is particularly relevant because it is primarily concerned with cooperation by networks of technical experts and professionals with a shared worldview whose 'authoritative claim to policy-relevant knowledge'[37] may facilitate international policy coordination.[38] This concept has been described as 'methodologically pluralistic', since it draws upon '... neorealism, liberal institutionalism, neo-functionalism and cognitive analysis',[39] and has been applied to case studies in both the natural and social science.[40] Many authors have used the concept to analyse the political impact of international policy coordination in several different spheres, including international environmental policy,[41] food aid,[42] and the incorporation of EMU into the Maastricht Treaty.[43] Interestingly, Ryan[44] describes WIPO as having a:

> ... flat organizational structure, with staff members who belong to transnational professional communities, share world views, and communicate through institutionalised internal mechanisms.

These characteristics are reminiscent of Haas's definition of an epistemic community, although Ryan suggests that the WIPO merely interacts with, rather than functions as, an epistemic community. This paper conceptualizes WIPO as being a key node in what could be conceptualized as the 'global patent networks'.

---

37 Epistemic communities also have common views on '... cause-and-effect relationships, truth tests to assess them and ... common values.' (P.M. Haas, *Saving the Mediterranean: The Politics of International Environmental Cooperation* (1990) 55.)

38 Haas, op. cit., n. 14, suggests that the increased range of policy issues confronting decision makers, the interdependence of domestic and international concerns, and the ensuing uncertainty may lead decision makers to seek advice from epistemic communities.

39 E. Adler and P.M. Haas, 'Conclusion: Epistemic Communities, World Order and the Creation of a Reflective Research Programme' (1992) 46 *International Organization* 367–90, at 368.

40 Haas, op. cit., n. 14, p. 3, acknowledges similarities between epistemic communities and Kuhn's scientific community, such as their cohesiveness and work within a paradigm, but E.B. Haas, *When Knowledge is Power: Three Models of Change in International Organizations* (1990) 221 acknowledges that T.S. Kuhn, *The Structure of Scientific Revolutions* (1970, 2nd edn.) intended his theory to apply only to the natural sciences.

41 See, for example, A.R. Zito, 'Epistemic Communities, Collective Entrepreneurship and European Integration' (2001) 8 *J. of European Public Policy* 585–603.

42 R.F. Hopkins, 'Reform in the International Food Aid Regime: The Role of Consensual Knowledge' (1992) 46 *International Organization* 225–64.

43 A. Verdun, 'The Role of the Delors Committee in the Creation of the EMU: An Epistemic Community?' (1999) 6 *J. of European Public Policy* 308–28.

44 M.P. Ryan, 'Adaptation and Change at the World Intellectual Property Organization' (1998) 1 *J. of World Intellectual Property* 507–23, at 508.

146

The international coordination of patentability takes place within the broader construct of a global regulatory web. This web is a flexible framework, binding multiple nodes in intersecting networks,[45] a 'regulatory criss-cross'.[46] This facilitates a regular interchange of ideas and views at informal gatherings and within formal international fora, some of which may entail epistemic community action. Participation in the global patent networks is not confined to IGOs; public interest NGOs, professional and business associations and groups, academic institutions,[47] and even individual academics[48] can play important roles. International coordination by networks of technical experts has been characterised by its *ad hoc* nature together with its speed, flexibility, and informality. This is reflected by the networks' preference that their arrangements take the form of non-legally binding documents such as the Memorandum of Understanding (MOU) rather than a formal international agreement. Examples of similar modes of cooperation are provided by Zaring[49] and Slaughter,[50] who focus on the regulation of banking and finance. These kinds of activities raise certain key issues:

(i) The technocratic nature of their cooperation.
(ii) Their lack of democratic accountability.

---

45 Castells provides a useful description of networks as '... open structures, able to expand without limits, integrating new nodes as they are able to communicate within the network, namely as long as they share the same communication codes.' See M. Castells, *The Rise of the Network Society* (1996) 470–1.
46 Picciotto, op. cit. (1996), n. 33, p. 95.
47 The Max Planck Institute, Munich has NGO observer status at WIPO, see, for example, WIPO Standing Committee on the Law of Patents First Session 15–19 June 1998 <http://www.int/eng/document/scp_ce/scp1_7.htm> last accessed 10 September 2001. According to J.J. Brinkhof, 'Extent of Protection of European Patents' (1991) 21 *International Rev. of Industrial Property and Copyright* 488–97, the Institute took the initiative in organizing annual symposia for patent law judges which were intended to create a forum for discussing European patent law and to impress upon them the need for uniformity of interpretation and rulings.
48 Professor Dr. Joseph Straus, Professor of Law and Head of Department, Max Planck Institute for Foreign and International Copyright and Competition Law is one such example. He has, for instance, chaired the Biotechnology Committee of the AIPPI and currently chairs their Programme Committee. He sits on the Human Genome Organization's Intellectual Property Rights Committee and the Nuffield Council Roundtable discussions regarding the ethical and legal issues raised by patenting DNA and proteins.
49 D. Zaring, 'International Law by other Means: The Twilight Existence of International Financial Regulatory Organizations' (1998) 33 *Texas International Law J.* 281–327.
50 Slaughter, op. cit. (2000), n. 16, pp. 181–9.

(iii) Do technical experts usurp the role of politically accountable actors by narrowing the policy agenda?[51]

Technocracy in its purest form raises the spectre of 'rule by experts', especially in a post-industrial society in which technical knowledge and information have become key political resources.[52] As a synthesis of professionalism, technical control, and bureaucracy, technocracy is inextricably linked to its seventeenth-century Enlightenment roots and the dominance of scientific rationality over social institutions.[53] Technocracy's neopositivistic and rationalist epistemology lays claim to it being *the* way to achieving a 'true knowledge' which is both value-free and neutral. It also promotes the idea that political problems should be 're-classified' as technical problems thus depriving them of their relevant social and political values.[54] Landfried[55] believes that one question which should be addressed is why politicians choose to classify questions as technical. She suggests that this may ultimately work in the politicians' favour, since they can avoid having to justify why certain problems may be resolved by the executive. An alternative explanation is that politicians may be able to shift responsibility for undesirable consequences to technical specialists.[56]

The technical rationality perspective exemplified by Weberian bureaucracy, is based on the claim that power derived from technical expertise makes bureaucracy an efficacious instrument of domination. Rule by a technocratic elite who legitimize their actions through legal-rational authority[57] is therefore inevitable. Deflem[58] has noted the implications of this technical rational perspective when examining the development of international cooperation between police institutions. His central argument is that international cooperation was only possible when the police institutions

---

51 Picciotto, op. cit. (1996–97), n. 33, p. 1037 responds to Adler and Haas's claim, op. cit., n. 39, that an epistemic community facilitated agreement on the Bretton Woods monetary system by narrowing the subjects on the negotiators' agenda to certain key issues, leaving others such to be resolved by political means. He states that the memoirs of Raymond Mikesell show that the experts negotiating the Bretton Woods monetary policy included 'highly political individuals' such as Harry White.

52 F. Fischer, *Technocracy and the Politics of Expertise* (1990) 14.

53 B.H. Burris, *Technocracy at Work* (1993) 21.

54 Fischer, op. cit., n. 52, p. 42.

55 C. Landfried, 'The European Regulation of Biotechnology by Polycratic Governance' in *EU Committees, Law and Social Regulation*, eds. C. Joerges and E. Vos (1999) 176–7.

56 Haas, op. cit., n. 14, p. 16.

57 H.H. Gerth and C. Wright Mills, *Essays in Sociology* (1974) 28; A. Giddens, *Capitalism and Modern Social Thought: An Analysis of the Writings of Marx, Durkheim and Weber* (1971) 158; and D. Beetham, *Max Weber and the Theory of Modern Politics* (1974) 65.

58 M. Deflem, 'Bureaucratisation and Social Control: Historical Foundations of International Police Cooperation' (2000) 34 *Law and Society Rev.* 739–78.

had reached a point of bureaucratic autonomy. This meant that the police bureaucracies were applying means-end rationality in an attempt to produce the most *technically*, rather than *politically*, acceptable goals. Landfried[59] has examined Weber's definition of a technical question within the context of the regulation of biotechnology within the EU and suggests that the distinction between 'technical' and 'political' is tenuous at best. She argues[60] that, '... a question is technical only if the means chosen are neutral with respect to the purpose of the action' and that few purely 'technical' questions remain in relation to biotechnology.

There could therefore be significant implications for governance if the patentability of biotechnological inventions were to be coordinated through transnational networks of technical experts adopting a purely technocratic approach to policy-making. Biotechnology should be considered as an interacting set of practices, namely, science, economics, morality, culture, and (patent) law, and could thus be likened to what Rabinow[61] describes as a 'purgatorial zone of contestation, where claims to knowledge, forms of economic organization and social values have found variant formulations'. If technical experts consider themselves free to classify the criteria for patentability solely as 'technical' rather than 'political' issues, this could reduce the transparency of the policy-making process for biotechnology and ultimately deprive the criteria for patentability of the relevant political, ethical, social, and economic values. This raises issues of legitimacy and accountability.

Certain authors support a more moderate view of technocracy. Haas[62] acknowledges that the concept of an epistemic community is open to the criticism that it perpetuates technocracy to the detriment of politically accountable actors. Although such communities may frame the issues for the political agenda, Haas[63] argues that epistemic community influence '... remains conditioned and bounded by international and national structural realities'.[64] Slaughter[65] argues similarly, stating that since transgovernmental regulatory networks consist essentially of government officials, their actions do not lack legitimacy since they operate within powers delegated to them by their national states, and hence within the framework of national democratic

59 Landfried, op. cit., n. 55.
60 id.
61 P. Rabinow, *French DNA: Trouble in Purgatory* (1999) 9.
62 Haas, op. cit., n. 14.
63 id., p. 7.
64 Some support for this perspective comes from M.J. Peterson's 1992 case study on whaling policy in which the actions of the epistemic community of cetologists was limited by political processes and internal conflict. See 'Whalers, Cetologists, Environmentalists and the International Management of Whaling' (1992) 46 *International Organization* 147–86.
65 See Slaughter, op. cit. (2000), n. 16, p. 195.

149

accountability. As Alston[66] notes however, Slaughter's analysis is confined to *transgovernmental* networks and she fails to consider the implications for networks comprised of other sub-state actors including NGOs[67] which have increasing involvement in areas of state concern. In the patent field, the highly influential International Association for Intellectual Property (AIPPI), provides an example of the latter category, since it institutionalizes a network whose membership is composed principally of professionals and academics, but includes some Patent Office officials, judges, academics, and industrialists.[68] This organization is quite open about its use of networking to achieve its objectives, both at meetings of the AIPPI and by representation of its members at national and international meetings,[69] principally to 'improve and promote the protection of intellectual property on both an international and national basis'.[70] It is also concerned with harmonizing intellectual property laws and developing existing intellectual property agreements and conventions. There is an affinity between the AIPPI and the Paris Convention[71] that can be understood on one level as being almost paternal. This is because the forerunners of the AIPPI were instrumental in establishing the framework for the Paris Convention of 1883[72] and that organization has been closely involved in the development of the convention. However, transnational networks of sub-state actors such as the AIPPI lack the veneer of democratic accountability which Slaughter ascribes to transgovernmental regulatory networks. By playing an active role in the development of the Paris Convention, the AIPPI has drawn a measure of influence and accountability from its relationship with key decision-makers in WIPO, where it currently enjoys observer status in international intellectual property negotiations. The organization presents itself as a politically neutral intellectual-property NGO, which operates democratically in accordance with specific statutes and regulations. In practice, however, its membership is dominated by professional intellectual-property practitioners, whose clients are mainly the research-intensive business sectors, which deploy patents. Thus, it could be argued that the views and interests that the AIPPI represents in discussions with WIPO are not politically neutral but

---

66 P. Alston, 'The Myopia of the Handmaidens: International Lawyers and Globalisation' (1997) 8 *European J. of International Law* 435 <http://www.ejil.org/journal/Vol8/No3/art4.html>, last accessed May 2001.
67 Mertus, op. cit., n 32.
68 AIPPI, <http://www.aippi.org.aims.html>, accessed 10 January 2001.
69 id.
70 id.
71 Articles 2(a)-(c) of AIPPI's Statutes and Regulations <http://www.aippi.org/reports/statutes-e-ed-95–revised-25-5-98.htm> accessed 10 January 2001.
72 See AIPPI, 'The Forerunners' in *AIPPI and the Development of Industrial Property Protection 1897–1997* (1997) 16–21. Prior to 1967, the AIPPI drafted the 'reform proposals' for consideration at the revision conferences for the Paris Convention (J. Clark, 'The Role of GATT/TRIPs, of WIPO and of AIPPI in the Further Development of Intellectual Property Protection', id., p. 148.

150

reflect a generally pro-patent viewpoint, developed by its membership in the course of their activities on behalf of their corporate clients.

Any optimism that networks of transnational civil society actors open up a new forum for the debate of global issues must therefore be weighed against the degree of transparency, responsibility, and accountability with which such networks conduct their business.[73]

2. Trilateral cooperation

Trilateral cooperation evolved from informal, bilateral contacts initiated by the USPTO Commissioner, Gerald J. Mossinghoff, with his counterparts at the EPO and JPO.[74] The informal nature of their cooperation was reflected by their decision to use bilateral and subsequently, trilateral MOUs rather than a treaty[75] to formalize their agreement. These documents established a broad framework for technical cooperation including the introduction of automated patent filing and search procedures, the exchange of technical or 'other specialists' information, and making patent information and other documents available in both paper and electronic format.[76] The overall objective underpinning these actions was to ensure that their respective industrial property systems fulfilled '... the needs of their fostering nations and industries'.[77] Participation in trilateral activities extends from the Heads of the Patent Offices to the Trilateral Coordinators[78] and any other Patent Office employees, all civil servants, who may be invited to contribute. The three offices can therefore draw upon and indeed supply when required, a large interchangeable body of expertise, including technical specialists and WIPO officials who are well-versed in procedural and substantive areas of patent law.

The initial focus of activities in 1982 was to establish an infrastructure within which the administrative and procedural differences in the patent granting procedure could gradually be harmonized and common problems

---

73 S. Picciotto, 'Democratizing Globalism' in *The Market or the Public Domain*, ed. D. Drache (2001) 335–59.

74 Commissioner Mossinghoff raised the possibility of cooperation with Commissioner van Bentham of the EPO in a letter dated 24 November 1981 and with Kazuo Wakasugi of the JPO in January 1983. See 'Symposium Proceedings for the Tenth Anniversary of Trilateral Cooperation' (1994) 23. However, the three Patent Offices had cooperated on matters of common concern before 1982 (interview at the EPO 5 July 2001).

75 Bilateral MOUs were signed between the USPTO and the EPO and the USPTO and the JPO in June 1982 and January 1983 respectively. The first Trilateral MOU was signed on 18 October 1983 at the First Annual Trilateral Conference in Washington D.C.

76 Exchanges of information included PCT search results, document classification and indexing, and patent documents. First MOU on Trilateral Cooperation, *First Annual Trilateral Conference Proceedings* (1983) 15–18.

77 *Proceedings of the Second Annual Trilateral Conference* (1984) 57.

78 The Trilateral Coordinator at the EPO is also responsible for EU liaison.

addressed. These initiatives were directed to two main areas: the automation of the patent filing process and the improvement of search quality.[79] Trilateral projects were therefore established to standardize patent applications and to develop and apply techniques for the capture, processing, storage, and exchange of textual and image data (projects 1, 3, and 4). Secondly, the Trilateral Offices worked to improve the quality of prior art searches by developing common, automated databases, some of which were intended to hold details of all existing patents (project 2) and others to contain coding standards for various technologies, for example, chemical data standards (project 5). The three offices also decided to share search results (project 8) and to consider developing a common patent classification system (project 7). A more general desire to create joint information resources and to foster greater awareness of their work within the public and private sectors was reflected by the decision to create common sets of statistics relating to the number and type of patent applications received by each of the offices (project 9), and to make automated patent data, which previously had been accessible only to the respective Patent Offices, more widely available (project 10).

The scope of the common projects has gradually been expanded over the last nineteen years and they now fall into four broad categories following reclassification in 1997: network and data exchange, search and examination, patent information dissemination, and legal issues associated with electronic filing. These activities should be considered within the context of the Trilateral Offices' 'Kyoto Action Plan',[80] a three-stage plan which does not aspire to create a global patent system, but to reduce costs for applicants and Trilateral Offices.[81] This involves: first, the creation of a secure trilateral network for the electronic exchange of search record data, examination records, and new applications as priority documents; secondly, trilateral concurrent search and examination to build mutual trust and increase search effectiveness in specific technical areas; and thirdly, the establishment of a trilateral website. The latter facility could be said to serve three functions. One is purely practical, since the three offices can use the site to disseminate patent information, including the Trilateral Statistical Reports and software products developed by them.[82] It could also be argued that the web site has the function of diffusing the Trilateral Offices' views in relation to substantive issues to a wide variety of recipients since it also

---

79 The JPO's efforts to automate the patent granting procedure preceded those of the EPO and USPTO. Its 'Paperless Project' was launched in 1984 and became operational in 1990.

80 See joint press release 14 November 1997 <http://www/jpo.go.jp/saikine/tws/gen-3–1.htm> accessed 5 May 2000.

81 T. Isayama, 'Japan's views on a Desirable IP System for the Global Economy' (1999) 2 *J. of World Intellectual Property* 679–96.

82 These include PATENTIN V2 which complies with WIPO ST25 for filing amino acid sequences.

152

carries reports of some of the comparative studies conducted by the three offices, including those relating to biotechnology. Finally, Slaughter[83] quite correctly states that websites can be used to increase the transparency and the legitimacy of transgovernmental networks; however, this will necessarily depend upon the degree of disclosure and range of documents which are made available.

The degree of commercial influence upon the Trilateral Offices' activities could also challenge the claims of accountability and legitimacy that have been made for transgovernmental networks. As previously discussed, when discharging their regulatory function, patent offices balance the rights of the patentee against the public interest when determining the intellectual property trade-off in key technological areas which are economically important. However, patent offices are not impartial bystanders in this process, but have a vested interest in the outcome as service providers in a competitive, market-oriented environment. This requires that patent offices meet the needs of their customers, a large proportion of which are companies. The USPTO tacitly recognized this fact when becoming a Performance Based Organization (PBO)[84] in April 2000. There is evidence that the Trilateral Offices have taken account of corporate needs in relation to biotechnology. Their decision to commence project 12, 'Harmonization of Patent Practices', which examined biotechnology and computer-related inventions, emerged in response to private interest in their activities.[85] Furthermore, the content of the first comparative biotechnology study drawn up by the USPTO was to incorporate 'pertinent industry views'.[86] This is a trend which seems set to continue, since the twentieth anniversary celebrations for trilateral co-operation will be directed to ascertaining the needs of European industry in relation to trilateral activities, including those involving biotechnology.[87]

---

83 Slaughter, op. cit. (2001), n 16.
84 The American Inventors Protection Act (1999) applied the term PBO to the USPTO. As such, the USPTO will be a results-driven organization which is committed to achieving '... specific measurable goals, customer service standards and targets for improved performance'. R. Maulsby, and M.V. Hernandez, press release 29 March 2000 <http://www.uspto.gov/web/offices/com/speeches/00–21.htm> last accessed 12 June 2001.
85 'The three offices, taking note of the interest shown by the private sector in the results of trilateral co-operation ... have agreed to investigate areas where harmonization of their respective practice appears to be feasible and to evaluate at agreed upon times results of studies to be conducted at the level of experts ... Such studies were to proceed on a step by step basis, starting with studies with the greatest practical potential for resulting in harmonization, which is of benefit to the Offices and the private sector.' *Proceedings of Second Annual Trilateral Conference* (1984) 10–11.
86 *Proceedings of Third Annual Trilateral Conference* (1984) 520.
87 Interview EPO 5 July 2001.

The Trilateral Offices' approach towards harmonizing certain procedural[88] aspects of the patent grant process and their discussions on substantive patentability also raise the question of legitimacy. Their activities have involved them in the development of trilateral standards, which they have then attempted to extend to other patent ofices and intellectual property institutions. Although the three offices process 84 per cent of patents globally and are each financially self-sufficient, the Trilateral Offices are clearly not *politically* autonomous.[89] Each is accountable to national government and international coordination formally requires inter-governmental agreement which, in this case, takes place through WIPO.

WIPO is a key node in the global patent networks which in turn is linked to nodes comprising other intellectual property institutions. The work of Dezalay and Garth[90] does much to explain 'grass-roots' activity within the global patent networks. Applying Bourdieu's concept of a legal field to explain the growth of a global market for legal expertise, Dezalay and Garth explain how international arbitrators were able to build 'symbolic capital' for themselves and thus to facilitate their movements between national and international fields. Within the global patent networks, certain individuals appear to have accrued sufficient 'symbolic capital'[91] from their various positions in national and international intellectual property institutions and committees to enable them to move between national and international nodes, and indeed, they may belong to multiple nodes simultaneously. The curriculum vitae of Shozo Uemura,[92] deputy director of WIPO, indicates how he has gradually expanded his experience in relation to international intellectual property. After joining the METI in 1969 as a patent examiner he

---

88 MOU of Tenth Trilateral Conference 1992 states their intention '... to develop common or harmonized policies for the dissemination of databases jointly developed.' The trilateral decision to commence project 20 for Electronic Filing ('EASY') in 1993 was based on the JPO's success in establishing a paperless filing system. The USPTO and EPO initially started this project and WIPO was to be invited to join (*Tenth Trilateral Conference Proceedings* (1992) 35). It was hoped that '... this will soon lead to an international standard' (*Proceedings of Eleventh Annual Trilateral Conference* (1993) 12).

89 The USPTO is accountable to the State Department for its international activities and the JPO to the Ministry of Economy Trade and Industry (METI) formerly the Ministry of International Trade and Industry (MITI). The EPO must seek approval for its activities and policy documents such as Trilateral Technical Reports, from its Administrative Council. At the outset, trilateral activities were initially coordinated through the 'Club of 15', Japan, the United States and the member states of the EPC (38 PCTJ, 465, 1989).

90 Y. Dezalay and B.G. Garth, *Dealing in Virtue: International Commercial Arbitration and the Construction of a Transnational Legal Order* (1996) 15–16.

91 id., p. 20.

92 See 'Curriculum Vitae of Shozo Uemura', WIPO document WO/CC/41/2. <http://www/wipo.org/eng/document/govbody/wo_gb_cc/cc41_2a2.htm> accessed 2 May 2000.

became assistant director of METI in 1978 and was assistant director at the Examination Standards Office between 1983–1986. His appointment as director of the Multilateral Negotiation Policy Office and International Cooperation Office in 1988 marked the beginning of his extensive involvement with international negotiations. Mr. Uemura was the chief negotiator for GATT and TRIPs for the JPO from 1988–1993 and participated in the Hague and Geneva revision conferences for the Paris Convention. He has also participated in the activities of the Trilateral Offices and in the WIPO Committee of Experts on Biotechnological Inventions and Industrial Property. The career of Christopher P. Mercer[93] is similar. As a member of the Federation International des Conseils en Propriété Industrielle (FICPI), Secretary of the European Patent Institute's (EPI's) Biotechnology Committee, Member of the Union of European Practitioners in Industrial Property, and a Council member of the Chartered Institute of Patent Agents, (CIPA), his trajectory must have facilitated an exchange of views and ideas between the various nodes in the global patent networks.

The Trilateral Offices portray their relationship with WIPO in terms of the latter being a 'bridge' to other participants in international meetings and negotiations.[94] However, this relationship also indicates that the views of an informal group of technical specialists are in reality the same as those of the formal institutions that they represent and may ultimately be translated into national law. This may help to explain why employees from the three Patent Offices may attend international negotiations as representatives of their respective patent offices, but not infrequently, the Trilateral Offices themselves may be allocated a specific task during those negotiations.[95]

The Trilateral Offices' relationship with WIPO could also be conceptualized as one which helps to dispell fears regarding the 'politics of imposition'[96] by institutionalizing trilateral actions. Formally, WIPO is an IGO and one of the sixteen specialized agencies of the UN which is accountable for its actions to the international community, perceived as representing the interests of the developed and developing countries alike. Yet, as indicated above, top-level participants in the trilateral, such as Shozo Uemura, are also key players in the WIPO. In practice therefore, the actions of WIPO are strongly influenced not only by technical specialists within the organization, and the wider networks surrounding it but, perhaps crucially, by the key input which can be made by participants who can move between

93 See <http://www/carpmaels.com/partners/mercer.html> accessed 2 June 2000.
94 Interview EPO 5 July 2001.
95 Representative from the USPTO and JPO attended the Second Session of WIPO's Standing Committee on Information Technology (SCIT) held from 8–12 February 1999 without the EPO yet, '... the SCIT Plenary welcomed the offer by the *Trilateral Offices* [my emphasis] that they would provide, as soon as possible, a first draft of the standard for review [of electronic filing] and finalisation by the task force.' WIPO document SCIT/2/8 12/2/1998, 9 accessed 12 December 2000.
96 See Slaughter, op. cit. (2000), n 16, p. 180.

WIPO and the Trilateral Offices. Thus, WIPO's relationship with the three offices raises the question as to whether the key policy-makers within the trilateral might be able to influence substantive as well as procedural patent issues. The next section will consider trilateral involvement in relation to the key area of biotechnology.

III. TRILATERAL COOPERATION AND BIOTECHNOLOGY

The Trilateral Offices' interest in harmonizing substantive patentability is intertwined with events occurring within the formal international framework during the mid 1990s and broader developments in biotechnology. Before 1995, their focus on biotechnological inventions was a response to private sector pressures for the coordination of patent procedures. Initially they were wary of any commitment to substantive harmonization and the objectives of project 12, 'Harmonization of Patent Practice', adopted in 1984 were limited to comparing examination practices.[97] The three offices subsequently agreed to carry out various comparative studies, including one on 'Patent Practice in the Field of Biotechnology Related mainly to Microbiological Inventions'.[98] However, in 1990 they deferred work on biotechnology pending the outcome of harmonization efforts being conducted within the formal international framework by WIPO and the WTO.[99]

The year 1995 appears to have marked a turning point, from which time the three offices resumed their comparative biotechnology studies and amended the objectives of the study carried out under project 24.1 (formerly 12.3) to include the harmonization of patent practices between their offices.[100] Their decision may have been influenced by a recent series of events. In December 1993, the TRIPs Agreement was concluded as part of the Uruguay Round, and as previously stated, it harmonized patentability at the level of general principle only. This was closely followed by the collapse of negotiations for WIPO's draft harmonization treaty in January 1994 and by the withdrawal of several contentious patent applications for expressed sequence tags (ESTs)[101] in February 1994 which had been submitted by Dr.

97 *Proceedings of the Second Annual Trilateral Conference* (1984) 10–11. This practice has been continued by the most recent Trilateral concurrent search pilot programme. See details on the Trilateral website <http://www.jpo.go.jp/saikine/tws/gen-4-1.htm> accessed 20 May 2000.
98 *Proceedings of Third Annual Trilateral Conference* (1985) 10.
99 See Eighth MOU, dated 25 October 1990, 5 signed at Eighth Annual Trilateral Conference.
100 *Proceedings of Thirteenth Annual Trilateral Conference* (1995) 39.
101 ESTs are short pieces of cDNA which have been isolated at random from tissue samples or cDNA libraries. They are primarily useful as intermediates in research and diagnostics, for example, to locate specific coding regions of their gene of origin, or as probes to isolate full-length genes (M.A. Holman and S.R. Munzer, 'Intellectual Property Rights in Genes and Gene Fragments: A Registration Solution

156

Craig Venter, at that time with the US National Institutes of Health (NIH), which will be discussed briefly below. Furthermore, the bilateral United States-Japan Patent Agreement, signed on 16 August 1994, was essentially procedural and did not address substantive patentability.[102]

The Trilateral Offices' interest in the patentability of gene fragments should also be considered within the context of the Human Genome Project (HGP), an internationally-coordinated effort initially launched by the US Department of Energy and National Institutes of Health in 1990, to sequence and map the human genome. The HGP held the promise of locating the genetic origin of certain diseases and the potential development of downstream products to diagnose and treat such diseases.[103] Gene patents quickly became the focus of multi-faceted socio-economic moral and cultural policy debates in which one of the issues raised was whether the patenting of raw 'upstream' sequence data, which it is claimed, is necessary to ensure investment in the commercialization of this technology, may prevent the development of 'downstream' products.[104] This issue was brought to the fore by the technical problems associated with patenting ESTs following three unsuccessful and well-documented patent applications filed between 1991–1993 by the NIH in the names of J. Craig Venter and others, for assignment to the NIH. The first application was timed to precede the publication of an article by Venter and his fellow scientists detailing the potential of the revolutionary use of ESTs to sequence the human genome[105] and each of the applications was disputed for lack of substantive patentability. The reasons cited by the USPTO for a preliminary rejection of the applications included novelty, non-obviousness, failure to provide an adequate written description and enabling disclosure, and lack of utility. Although the latter criterion was therefore cited as a key factor in their rejection, it has also been suggested that public attention focused on this issue. The NIH's applications were withdrawn in February 1994 and the USPTO

for Expressed Sequence Tags' (2000) 85 *Iowa Law Rev.* 735–845). See, for example. G.J.V. Nossall and R.L. Coppall, *Re-Shaping Life* (1989) 16, for a scientific description of EST production.

102 Text in (1995) 34 *International Legal Materials* 123. This agreement built upon the 'Mutual Understanding on Patents' signed on 20 January 1994, text in (1994) 33 *International Legal Materials* 313. S. Lesavich, 'The New Japan-US Patent Agreements: Will they really Protect US Patent interests in Japan?' (1995) *Wisconsin International Law J.* 155–82 discusses these agreements.

103 T. Wilkie, *Perilous Knowledge: The Human Genome Project and its Implications* (1993) 5; K. Davies, *The Sequence* (2001) 61–4. See, also, A.K. Haas, 'The Wellcome Trust's Diclosures of Gene Sequence Data into the Public Domain and the Potential for Proprietary Rights in the Human Genome' (2001) 16 *Berkeley Technology Law J.* 145–64.

104 Holman and Munzer, op. cit., n. 101, and Haas, id.

105 See article by M.D. Adams, J.M. Kelley, J.D. Gocayne, M.H. Dubnick, H.X. Polymeropoulos, C.R. Merril, A. Wu, B. Olde, R.F. Moreno, A.R. Kerlavage, W.R. McCombie, J.C. Venter, 'Complementary DNA Sequencing: Expressed Sequence Tags and the Human Genome Project' (1991) 252 *Science* 1651–6.

subsequently announced that it would draw up utility guidelines because of the concerns raised by members of the biotechnology industry regarding the application of this criterion at the USPTO's hearing on intellectual property issues in biotechnology in October 1994.[106] The USPTO eventually granted the first EST patent in 1998 for 'human kinase homologs'.[107] This controversy serves as a reminder to those attempting to produce greater convergence of interpretation of the criteria for patentability that classifying an issue as 'technical' does not make it easy to decide, even by experts.

Convergent interpretations – project B3b[108]

An important step towards convergent interpretations seems to have resulted from the Trilateral Offices' comparative study on the patentability of DNA fragments. At the time of the comparative study, each Patent Office was attempting to clarify its examination practice in relation to ESTs, the utility/industrial application criterion being one of the key issues. The focus of their discussions appeared to be whether a specific utility, as applied by the USPTO, or a more general industrial applicability requirement, as applied by the EPO and JPO,[109] should be disclosed. The conclusion of the study published in June 1999 therefore stated

106 R.S. Eisenberg and R.P. Merges, 'Opinion Letter as to the Patentability of Certain Inventions Associated with the Identification of cDNA Sequences' (1995) 23 *AIPLA Q. J.* 1–51,at 15 summarized the USPTO's decision on utility following rejection of one of the applications in 1992: '... the recited utilities were inadequate because a skilled person reading the specification would have to engage in further undue experimentation in order to put the claimed inventions to the suggested uses'. Under United States patent law, utility has two strands, operability and the need to establish a practical utility The operability aspect requires only that that the invention can fulfil its claimed use. (K.J. Burchfiel, *Biotechnology and the Federal Circuit* (1997) 47–52. The prevailing standard of practical utility was that of *Brenner* v. *Manson* [1966] (383 US 519,148 USPQ (BNA) at 695) in which the Supreme Court held that claims that the tumour-inhibiting steroids could be used for further research purposes did not constitute a practical utility. C. Roberts, 'The Prospects of Success of the National Institute of Health's Human Genome Application' (1994) 16 *European Intellectual Property Rev.* 30–6 also discusses these issues.

107 J. Pieroni, 'The Patentability of Expressed Sequence Tags' (2000) *Federal Circuit Bar J.* 401–16. However, although a large number of EST patent applications have been submitted, the number of patents issued is significantly lower. Pieroni (fn. 3) states that Human Genome Sciences (HGS) had applied for 200,000 as at 1999. The HGS website indicates that as at 12 November 2001 the USPTO had issued 189 patents to HGS for 'gene based inventions' <http://www.hgsi.com/patents/index.html>, accessed 13 November 2001.

108 Project B3b deals with 'Mutual Understanding in Search and Examination'. Comparative Study on DNA Fragments <http://www.european-patent-office.org/tws/sr-3-b3b-ad.htm>, last accessed 3 April 2001.

109 The JPO released Implementing Guidelines for Inventions in Specific Fields, ch. 2 of which dealt with Biological Inventions in 1997 <http://www.jpo.go.jp/infoe/txt/bio-e-m.txt>, last accessed 23 May 2001. Section 1.1.2.1.1(2) states '... in order to show

158

2. A DNA fragment of which specific utility, e.g. use as a probe to diagnose a specific disease, is disclosed, is a patentable invention as long as there is no other reason for rejection.

However, the more detailed explanation of the EPO's position on industrial application/utility in this study indicates some ambivalence, since the criterion of industrial application in Article 57 EPC is in more general terms, stating that an invention fulfils this requirement if it can be '... made or used in any kind of industry, including agriculture'. Nevertheless, the EPO commented that this could be reinterpreted in favour of a 'specific usefulness'.

Table 1 indicates that work on the comparative study was carried out in parallel with actions being taken at the national level by the USPTO and EPC to revise their Guidelines for Examination. The USPTO issued Revised Utility Guidelines in December 1999[110] which introduced the requirement that examiners should review the claims and written description to ensure that applicant had 'B (2) ... asserted ... any specific and substantial utility that is credible'. Subsequently, the Trilateral Offices added an additional conclusion to their study on 23 June 2000 which dealt with more specific biotechnological inventions, and for the first time spelled out the requirement of 'specific, substantial and credible utility'.

Additional Conclusion
1. All nucleic acid molecule-related inventions, including full-length cDNAs and SNPs, without indication of function or specific, substantial and credible utility, do not satisfy industrial applicability or written description requirements.
2. Isolated and purified nucleic acid molecule-related inventions, including full-length cDNAs and SNPs,[111] of which function or specific, substantial and credible utility is disclosed, which satisfy industrial applicability, enablement, definiteness and written description requirements would be patentable as long as there is no prior art (novelty and inventive step) or other reasons for rejection (such as, where appropriate, best mode (US) or ethical grounds (EPC/JPO).

The USPTO eventually issued its Utility Guidelines in January 2001 following completion of the public comment period, adopting the standard of

the industrial applicability of the invention described in the detailed description of the invention that the gene has the specific function (in case of a structural gene, the protein encoded by the said gene has the specific function).'
110 These were issued following an extension of public comments in relation to their Interim Written Description Guidelines. S.G. Kunin, 'Written Description Guidelines and Utility Guidelines' (2000) 82 *J. of the Patent and Trademark Society* 77–100. 64 Federal Register 71440 (21 December 1999).
111 SNPs, single nucleotide polymorphisms are not ESTs, but 'DNA sequence variations that occur when a single nucleotide (A,T,C,G) in the genome sequence is altered'. <http://www.ornl.gov/TechResources/Human_Genome/glossary/glossary_s.html>, last accessed 30 September 2001.

a 'specific, substantial and credible utility'.[112] At the same time, the EPO was also in the process of amending the Implementing Regulations to the EPC to ensure conformity of interpretation with the EU Biotechnology Directive.[113] Although there was no explicit reference to a 'specific, substantial and credible' use, recitals 23 and 24 of that Directive[114] significantly narrow the differences in interpretation of the industrial application and utility requirement.

Table 1: Chronology of events occurring contemporaneously with trilateral study on patentability of DNA fragments

Date	Event
November 1998	Trilateral initiates study on patentability of DNA fragments
4 June 1999	Publication of trilateral study
16 June 1999	EPO incorporates new chapter on patentability of biotechnological inventions into Implementing Regulations of EPC.[115]
21 December 1999	Revised US Interim Utility Guidelines issued
23 June 2000	Additional conclusion added to the comparative study
November 2000	Revision of EPC
5 January 2001	USPTO issues new Utility Guidelines
February 2001	EPO publishes new Guidleines for Examination

There seems to be clear evidence of a serious attempt to establish a convergence in the standard of utility, which has proven key to the patentability of biotechnological innovations. Some support for this claim comes from the bold statement made by JPO Commissioner Isayama[116] in May 1999, just prior to publication of this comparative study, that the Trilateral Offices had

112 A 'specific' utility is one which establishes a clear link between the utility claimed and the subject matter. A 'substantial' utility is one that defines a 'real-world' use. The credibility of the utility requires that claimed utilities are not based on factually misleading or inaccurate data. (2001) 66 *Federal Register* 1092
113 Directive 98/44/EC OJ 30 July 1998 L213 13–21.
114 '(23) Whereas a DNA sequence without indication of a function does not contain any technical information and is therefore not a patentable invention' and '(24) ... in order to comply with the industrial application criterion it is necessary in cases where a sequence or partial sequence of a gene is used to produce a protein or part of a protein, to specify which protein or part of a protein is produced or what function it performs.'
115 See OJ EPO 8 September 1999, 545–87. Part III, ch. IV, rule 23e(2) of the new EPO Guidelines for Examination affirms the patentability of partial gene sequences. Rule 23e(3) requires that, 'The industrial application of a sequence or a partial sequence of a gene must be disclosed in the patent application.'
116 Isayama, op. cit., n. 81, p. 686.

160

... reached agreement on common rules governing the patentability of biotechnological inventions, particularly expressed sequence tags (ESTs). The rules set out that ESTs are patentable where they fulfil a given set of conditions such as the clarity of their function, but that for the foreseeable future they will be rejected in all patent cases.

However, there is as yet no authoritative statement of the actual application of the standard in practice by the USPTO[117] and EPO and it will be interesting to see whether there is any convergence of interpretation in relation to the actual practice of examination of biotechnology patents.[118]

CONCLUSION

This paper has argued that trilateral cooperation is an informal transgovernmental regulatory network of bureaucratic, technical specialists which evolved from the common interests of the Trilateral Offices initially in harmonizing procedural patent issues. Since the offices perform a public function, their activities should reflect a broad spectrum of opinion rather than favouring specific private interests. Furthermore, it can certainly be said that the Trilateral Offices' technical expertise and resources enhance both WIPO's status and the influence of the Trilateral Offices within that institution, without necessarily usurping WIPO's role in the sphere of intellectual property as suggested by Cheek. However by institutionalizing the Trilateral Offices' views within WIPO as well as other international intellectual property institutions, this relationship also raises questions of legitimacy.

Admittedly, attempts to coordinate patentability informally are not easily achieved. In trilateral discussions, each office enters the forum with its own perspective and endeavours to harmonize at the technical, procedural and legal level. The interrelationship between the technical and political/policy aspects of patent law means that the greater the degree of harmonization required, particularly in relation to substantive patent law, the more difficult it is to achieve. This may not be because a common approach is lacking, but

---

117 In testimony given at the US Sub-Committee on Courts and Intellectual Property on Gene Patents and Genomic Inventions (13 July 2000) by the Head of the USPTO at that time, Q. Todd Dickinson, indicated that a biotechnology test case was due to be referred to the Board of Appeals later that year before being transferred to the Court of Appeals for the Federal Circuit (CAFC). <http://www.house.gov/judiciary/dick0713.htm> accessed 25 May 2001.

118 Roger Walker, Deputy Director, UK Patent Office has recently commented upon the USPTO Utility Guidelines, stating that although they , '... have no direct effect in the UK, the USPTO requirement that there must be disclosed a 'specific, substantial and credible' utility, is just the sort of disclosure we would expect to see in a UK patent application in the context of *industrial application* [author's emphasis]'. Speech on Patentability Options within Proteomics and Genomics. <http://www.patent.gov.uk/about/notices/genomics.htm> accessed 22 October 2001.

161

simply because the officials working through the Trilateral Offices are only able to harmonize within the scope of their respective patent and case law. They acknowledge that their colleagues' perspectives on interpreting the criteria for patentability may influence them, but they also emphasize that any decisions, which are made in relation to substantive patentability, would not be binding in either national or international law.[119] For these reasons, their contribution to the harmonization of substantive patentability has been stated to be fairly limited[120] in comparison with their achievements in relation to administrative and procedural issues.[121]

Informal networking by the Trilateral Offices does provide the opportunity to generate an informal consensus which can be put forward in formal international negotiations as well as informing national examination regulations and practices. A fresh, or indeed a complementary, approach to negotiating within the formal international framework is certainly required if the SPLT is ever to become a reality. However, this still raises the question as to whether sensitive issues such as gene patents should be dealt with in closed communities of regulators characterized as having a technical role. Certainly, Slaughter's suggestion[122] for greater public participation in these networks would be welcomed.

---

119 Interview at the EPO 5 July 2001.
120 Bardehle, op. cit., n. 21.
121 Differing claims have been made regarding the extent of trilateral influence. T. Takenaka, 'Harmonizing the Japanese Patent System with its US Counterpart through Judge-made Law: Interaction between Japanese and US Case Law Developments'(1998) 7 *Pacific Rim Law and Policy J.* 249–77 merely states that attempts are being made informally to harmonize patent practice between the Trilateral offices whereas S. Okuyama, *Biotechnology Patent Practice in Japan: Harmonizing Japanese Practice with the US and Europe* (1997) <http://www/okuyama.com/resources.html>, accessed 28 March 2001 argues more forcefully that Japan has altered its examination practice not only as a result of direct changes in patent law, but also as a result of 'concerted efforts' between the trilateral offices '... to harmonize day-to-day examination practice'.
122 See Slaughter, op. cit. (2001), n 16, p. 363.

162

JOURNAL OF LAW AND SOCIETY
VOLUME 29, NUMBER 1, MARCH 2002
ISSN: 0263-323X, pp. 163–96

Regulatory Conversations

JULIA BLACK*

The article proposes a new site of analysis for the study of regulation: regulatory conversations, and a new theoretical approach: discourse analysis. Regulatory conversations, the communicative interactions that occur between all involved in the regulatory 'space', are an important part of most regulatory systems. Discourse analysis, the study of the use of language and communication, suggests that such interactions are constitutive of the regulatory process, that they serve important functions, that they can be the basis of co-ordinated action, and that they are important sites of conflict and contestation. The article explores five key contentions of discourse analysis, considering how each may shed light on aspects of regulatory processes. These are, first as to the meaning of language and co-ordination of social practices; second, as to the construction of identities; third, the relationship of language, thought, and knowledge; fourth, the relationship of language and power, and finally, that meaning, thought, knowledge, and power are open to contestation and change.

The study of regulation is characterized by a kaleidoscope of lenses, notably economics,[1] cultural/anthropological theory,[2] institutionalism,[3] and systems

* Law Department and Centre for the Analysis of Risk and Regulation, London School of Economics and Political Science, Houghton Street, London WC2A 2AE, England

This paper was completed whilst I held a British Academy/Leverhulme Trust Senior Research Fellowship and I gratefully acknowledge the scheme's support. I thank Rob Baldwin and Christine Parker for comments on an earlier version; views, errors, and omissions remain my own.

1 G. Stigler, 'The Economic Theory of Regulation' 1971 2 *Bell J. of Economics* 1; R. Posner, 'Theories of Economic Regulation' (1974) 5 *Bell J. of Economics and Management Science* 335; S. Peltzman, 'Towards a More General Theory of Regulation' (1976) 19 *J. of Law and Economics* 211.
2 Particularly Hood, who has used the hierarchy/community/competition/fate matrix of world views developed in anthropological cultural theory as the base for describing types of techniques of governmental control: C. Hood, *Art of the State* (1998), adapted

163

theory,[4] through which regulation is viewed, though little work has been done on how they might be integrated, or whether they are instead 'incommensurable paradigms'.[5] Nevertheless, this article proposes another perspective, of discourse analysis. It is argued that examining regulation through this perspective may draw attention to aspects of the regulatory process that are as yet relatively unexplored, and provide a theoretical frame in which to place observations that have already been noted in empirical research, but which are under-theorized. In other words, it may help us to see what we have not already seen, and understand better what it is we have.

Why discourse analysis? Because, it is contended, regulation is in large part a communicative process. Communications between all those involved in the regulatory process concerning that regulatory system are an important part of their operation. Understanding such regulatory conversations is thus central to understanding the 'inner life' of that process.[6] Why then not look to discourse analysis, that loosely defined body of theory that ranges across the social sciences and humanities which is concerned with the analysis of language and communication?

Discourse analysis would go one step further in its own justification, for it contends that social action can be comprehended only by comprehending discourse, that discourse is the basis of social action in that it is constitutive, functional, and coordinative.[7] It is constitutive in that it builds objects, worlds, minds, identities, and social relations, not just reflects them. It is functional in that it is designed to achieve certain ends, for example, to persuade (its rhetorical and argumentative aspect). It is coordinating in that

in C. Hood, C. Scott, O. James, G. Jones, and T. Travers, *Regulation Inside Government* (1999) and C. Hood, H. Rothstein, and R. Baldwin, *The Government of Risk* (2001); C. Hall, C. Scott and C. Hood, *Telecommunications Regulation: Culture, Chaos and Interdependence Inside the Regulatory Process* (2000).
3 See, for example, M. Thatcher, *The Politics of Telecommunications: National Institutions, Convergence and Change in Britain and France* (1999).
4 G. Teubner, 'Substantive and Reflexive Elements in Modern Law' (1983) 17 *Law and Society Rev.* 239; 'Juridification – Concepts, Aspects, Limits, Solutions' in *Juridification of the Social Spheres*, ed. G. Teubner (1987); 'After Legal Instrumentalism? Strategic Models of Post-Regulatory Law' in *Dilemmas of Law in the Welfare State*, ed. G. Teubner (1986); R. Veld et al., *Autopoiesis and Configuration Theory: New Approaches to Societal Steering* (1991).
5 In contrast to organizational theory, see, for example, G. Weaver and G. Gioia, 'Paradigms Lost: Incommensurability vs Structurationist Inquiry' (1994) 15 *Organization Studies* 565.
6 E. Meidinger, 'Regulatory Culture: A Theoretical Outline' (1987) 9 *Law and Policy* 355; J. March and J. Olsen, *Rediscovering Institutions* (1989); P. DiMaggio and W. Powell, 'Introduction' in W. Powell and P. DiMaggio, *The New Institutionalism in Organizational Analysis* (1991): 'inner life' is used here to refer to the interactions of all engaged in the process, not just bureaucrats engaged in its administration. Contrast C. Hood, H. Rothstein, and R. Baldwin, *The Government of Risk* (2001) 141.
7 M. Wetherell, 'Themes in Discourse Research: The Case of Diana' in *Discourse Theory and Practice: A Reader*, eds. M. Wetherell, S. Taylor, and S. Yates (2001) 16.

in the activity of producing meaning and shared senses it requires and produces coordination, and the possibility of coordination is at the basis of social life.

If we were to transpose those claims to the context of regulation, the contention would be that discourse forms the basis of regulation. It constitutes regulation in that it builds understandings and definitions of problems (for example, 'market failure', 'risk') and acceptable and appropriate solutions (criminalization, 'meta-regulation', 'precautionary principle'), it builds operational categories (for example, 'compliance'), and produces the identities of and relations between those involved in the process. It is functional in that it is designed to achieve certain ends (for example, the strategic use of rule design; the deployment of skills of argumentation and rhetoric by all involved at every stage). It is coordinating in that it produces shared meanings as to regulatory norms and social practices which then form the basis for action (for example, the formation of regulatory interpretive communities).

These are very broad claims, and discourse analysis is a very broad church. How could we take the analysis further both theoretically and empirically? At the theoretical level, this article will focus on five principal contentions as to the relationship of discourse and social practices which stem from the above-mentioned constitutive, functional, and coordinative claims, and consider how we might think about them in a regulatory context. In doing so it will draw on writers that are considered to be within the mainstreams of discourse theory, on some others within related paradigms that have been relevant in legal and socio-legal theory,[8] as well as on discourse analysis as employed in organizational theory to illustrate some of the general claims.[9]

The five contentions that will be explored are first, as to meaning and coordination: that the meaning of language is in its use, that use and therefore meaning will vary with context and with genre, and that the development of shared linguistic practices entails coordination and forms the basis of social action. Secondly, as to the construction of identities: that communicative interaction is representative and in particular produces identities, which in turn affect social action. Thirdly, as to the relationship of language, thought, and knowledge: that language frames thought, and produces and reproduces knowledge. The fourth, closely related, contention is that language is intimately related to power: that it is marked by the values

---

8 It is not intended, however, to survey the field of law and communication as well: for an overview see, for example, D. Nelken, 'Law as Communication: Constituting the Field' in *Law as Communication*, ed. D. Nelken (1996).

9 For introductions to discourse analysis in organizational theory, see L. Putnam, N. Phillips, and P. Chapman, 'Metaphors of Communication and Organization' in *Handbook of Organization Studies* , eds. S. Clegg, C. Hardy, and W. Nord (1996); Clegg, Hardy, and Nord, id.; D. Grant, T. Keenoy, and C. Oswick, *Discourse and Organization* (1998).

165

of social groups, that it encodes perspectives and judgements, and can instantiate certain perspectives or orthodoxies. The final contention considered is that meaning, thought, knowledge, and power are contestable and contested; meaning, and thus thought, knowledge, and power, is never fixed and so is open to contestation and change. The paper will give a basic outline of each contention, including some of the principal fractures around each that exist within discourse theory, and will suggest how that contention could be explored in a regulatory context, and where discourse theory could provide an alternative frame for interpreting familiar regulatory phenomenon.

First, however, some initial clarificatory and positioning work needs to be done, relating both to discourse theory and to conceptions of regulation and regulatory conversations. So the first part gives a brief outline of discourse theory, its fractures, and its levels and domains of analysis. The second part sets out what is meant here by regulation and the aspect of regulatory processes that it is suggested should be explored, regulatory conversations. The third part considers the five contentions outlined above to suggest how they might be further explored in the regulatory context, and what they might add to current understandings and observations. The final part draws together principal threads and suggests directions for further research, noting in particular that in analysing regulatory conversations from a discourse perspective we need always to consider where conversations occur in the process, whom they are between, and whether or how they 'work'.

CENTRAL THEMES IN DISCOURSE ANALYSIS

Discourse analysis in essence is concerned with developing a theory of language in use,[10] and for some with taking a critical and reflexive stance, asking why was it that this was said and not that.[11] It is a relatively young discipline, and one in which central concepts are contested and its boundaries only loosely defined. Broadly speaking, it could be seen as the site in which the 'linguistic turn' in social science meets the 'social turn' in linguistic theory. The 'linguistic turn' in social science, as is well known, is the shift from the philosophy of consciousness to the philosophy of language.[12] In methodological terms it is represented by the 'interpretivist' turn, the view that social sciences can only interpret social behaviour by

10 M. Wetherell, 'Introduction' in Wetherell et al., op. cit., n. 7, p. 4.
11 I. Parker, *Discourse Dynamics: Critical Analysis for Social and Individual Psychology* (1992) 3–4.
12 See, for example, with H.-G. Gadamer, *Truth and Method* (1960); P. Ricouer, *From Text to Action* (1991); J. Habermas, *The Theory of Communicative Action* (1984); *The Philosophical Discourse of Modernity* (1987).

exploring the meaning that infuses and gives rise to complexes of social action. Strongly associated with it is the contention that the meaning of social reality is not 'out there' to be discovered but is always constructed through modes of representation, including language, and interpretation. Thus we can have no access to 'the truth' about, for example, justice, or morality, or the self. Rather our notions of these 'truths' are instead conditioned by various social structures: our history, culture, ideology.

The 'social turn' in linguistics is the shift away from the conception of language as an autonomous resource available for use,[13] but remaining unaffected by that use, to the conception of language as social, the meaning and structure of which lies in its use. For language users, language is not an abstract system of normative forms, and meaning is never fixed. Reference is always various and open ended. Meaning and use of language will vary with the context in which it is used, with different genres (for example, formal parliamentary debate, or gossip between friends), and with different speech communities. Moreover, meaning is dialogically constructed through communicative interactions, even if that dialogue is with a text, or with an unseen audience (for example, I am here engaging in dialogue with potential readers, and with other writers who have written before me). Further, language is a public resource: in one's own use of language one cannot escape the usages that have been made by it by others. All words bear the 'taste' of the other contexts in which they have been used: as the playwright Dennis Potter put it, 'the trouble with words is that you don't know whose mouth they've been in.'[14]

That discourse theory is a site of confluence of linguistics and social science, and has been adopted and developed in disciplines as diverse as psychology, sociology, anthropology, education, literary theory, politics, and organizational theory, is one reason for the multiplicity of conceptions of discourse, of methodologies, and of levels and domains of analysis that exist within in it.[15] As regards conceptions of discourse, one widely accepted definition, particularly for those coming from a linguistic base (though not confined to them), is that discourse is 'all forms of spoken interaction, formal and informal, and written texts of all kinds'.[16] Discourse in this sense means passages of connected writing or speech: text and talk.[17] Others however argue that the definition of 'text' has to be extended from linguistics to

13 F. Saussure, *Course in General Linguistics* (1974, first published 1916).
14 Quoted in J. Maybin, 'Language, Struggle, Voice: The Bakhtin/Volosinov Writings' in Wetherell, op. cit., n. 7, at p. 68.
15 See, for example, N. Fairclough, *Critical Discourse Analysis: Papers in the Critical Study of Language* (1995) 5; J. Potter and M. Wetherell, *Discourse and Social Psychology* (1987) 6; T.A. van Dijk, 'The Study of Discourse' in *Discourse as Structure and Process*, ed. T.A. van Dijk (1997); Parker, op. cit., n. 11, ch. 1.
16 Potter and Wetherell, id., p. 7.
17 See, for example, van Dijk, op. cit., n. 15; N. Fairclough, *Discourse and Social Change* (1992).

include semiotics,[18] and some extend it ultimately to Derrida's contention that 'there is nothing outside the text'.[19] The conception of discourse used in social science writing tends to be much broader than spoken or written language, including within 'discourse' not only language but all social practices. Foucault, for example, whose influence is strong, conceptualized discourse as a group of statements that provided the rules for representing the knowledge about a particular topic at a particular historical moment. Discourse is about the production of knowledge, and itself produces the objects of our knowledge. It governs the way that a topic can and cannot be meaningfully talked and reasoned about, and influences how ideas are put into practice and used to regulate the conduct of others.[20] Similarly Laclau and Mouffe's conception of discourse includes all the practices and meanings shaping a particular community of social actors. Discourses constitute symbolic systems and social orders, and for them, as for Foucault, the task of discourse analysis is to examine their historical and political construction and functioning.[21] Neither contends that nothing *exists* outside of discourse, that things do not have a real, material existence in the world, but rather that nothing has any *meaning* outside of discourse.[22]

There are different research traditions within discourse analysis, and analysts explore different domains of social life, notably micro-level social interaction and order, the mind, concepts of selves and how people make sense of the world, and macro-level issues of culture and social relations.[23] There are also central fissures and points of friction.[24] For some, discourse analysis is about analysing 'talk and text in context'.[25] The debate is then as to the 'context' that should be considered when analysing discourse: conversational analysis, socio-linguistics and critical discourse analysis all have different views on what the relevant context is. For others, such as post-Marxists and Foucauldians, the formulation 'talk and text in context' makes

---

18 See, for example, G.R. Kress and T. van Leeuwen, *Reading Images: A Grammar of Visual Design* (1996); G.R. Kress and T. van Leeuwen, *The Multi-Modal Text* (1997); and G.R. Kress, R. Leite-Garcia, and T. van Leeuwen, 'Discourse Semiotics' in van Dijk, op. cit., n. 15.

19 For example, Parker, op. cit., n. 11, at p. 7, citing J. Derrida, *Of Grammatology* (1976) 158.

20 M. Foucault, *The Archaeology of Knowledge* (1972); *Discipline and Punish* (1977); 'Politics and the Study of Discourse' in *The Foucault Effect: Studies in Governmentality*, eds. G. Burchell, C. Gordon, and P. Miller (1991); M. Cousins and C. Hussain, *Michel Foucault* (1984).

21 E. Laclau and C. Mouffe, *Hegemony and Socialist Strategy* (1985).

22 E. Laclau and C. Mouffe, 'Post-Marxism without Apologies' in *New Reflections on the Revolutions of Our Time*, ed. E. Laclau (1990) 100; Foucault, op. cit. (1972), n. 20.

23 M. Wetherell, 'Debates in Discourse Research' in Wetherell et al., op. cit., n. 7, at p. 381.

24 For a clear exposition see id.

25 van Dijk, op. cit., n. 15.

no sense, for there is no distinction between linguistic practices and social context. The aims of the various traditions are also different, and so are the questions they ask. Conversational analysis is concerned with the micro-level production of social order; Foucauldian analysis with the historical analysis of the production of knowledge and circulation of power; critical discourse analysis with the expression in language of relations of power and hegemony with a view to challenging and changing those relations, a challenge which for Foucault fails to accept the logic of its own argument. Very different positions are taken on the role of agency. Foucauldian analysis has little or no role for agency; critical discourse analysis adopts Giddens's theory of structuration to explain the relationship between agency and discourse, namely, that actions and interactions may be shaped by structures, but that those structures are expressed and transformed through actions and interactions.[26] Different understandings of meaning are also used: for example, whether meaning is created through difference from another term in a discursive system or whether it is created in use.[27] Different approaches to the relationship between micro and macro are taken: conversational analysis resides at the micro level; post-Marxists at the macro, and critical discourse analysis implicitly adopts versions of both an 'aggregation thesis': that macro-social structures are the aggregate product of micro-social interactions, including their unintended consequences, and a 'representation' thesis, in which macro-social structures are represented in micro-level, quotidian, communicative interactions.[28] Finally, there are deep fissures on the question of whether or not the analyst can or should be politically engaged.[29]

Whether and how different traditions may be integrated is not a debate to be entered into here. Rather, the aim is to consider how some of the contentions that emerge in different ways in discourse analysis may be explored in the context of regulation. Consideration of how each different strand of discourse analysis might have bearing is too big a question to consider here, however. Instead, a site of analysis is suggested: regulatory conversations, and only those strands of discourse analysis that appear, at least on an initial glance, to be most fruitful in a regulatory context are

26 A. Giddens, *Central Problems in Social Theory* (1979); *The Constitution of Society* (1984); *New Rules of Sociological Method* (1993).
27 See, for example, the discussion on aesthetics in A. Giddens, 'Risk, Trust and Reflexivity' in *Reflexive Modernization*, eds. U. Beck, A. Giddens, S. Lash (1994) 197.
28 On which, see K. Knorr-Cetina, 'Introduction: The Micro-Sociological Challenge of Macro-Sociology: Towards a Reconstruction of Social Theory and Methodology' in *Advances in Social Theory and Methodology: Toward an Integration of Micro- and Macro-Sociologies*, eds. K. Knorr-Cetina and A.V. Cicorel (1981).
29 N. Fairclough and R. Wodak, 'Critical Discourse Analysis' in T.A. van Dijk (ed.), *Discourse as Social Interaction* (1992); van Dijk, op. cit., n. 15, Wetherell, op. cit., n. 23, pp. 383–6.

drawn on. Nonetheless, there are strands which may have relevance but which are not considered, principally the 'argumentative turn' and the role of rhetoric,[30] and the 'emotive turn', the role of emotions in discourse use.[31]

REGULATION AND REGULATORY CONVERSATIONS

The conception of regulation adopted here is that of a process involving the sustained and focused attempt to alter the behaviour of others according to identified purposes with the intention of producing a broadly identified outcome or outcomes which may involve mechanisms of standard-setting, information-gathering and behaviour-modification. Regulation is thus not seen as an activity performed only by state actors, or as necessarily involving legal mechanisms, but the definition is not as wide as some sociologists might adopt. In this view, 'culture' or the 'market' do not regulate, though their influence may be significant in affecting the regulatory process.[32] Regulation is thus understood here to be the intentional, goal-directed, problem-solving attempts at ordering undertaken by both state and non-state actors. No particular institutional or organizational arrangement is assumed in the definition, neither are particular techniques, nor is success; there may also be unintended and unforeseen consequences. Regulators may operate at a transnational, supranational, national or sub-national level, and be governments, associations, or firms. The regulated may include governments, associations, firms, and/or individuals. The others involved may include professional associations, professional advisors, both legal and non-legal, accreditors, auditors, non-governmental organizations, consumer and other special-issue groups. Boundaries between regulator and regulated might shift, certainly in a transnational context, and they might be one and the same organizations.

By regulatory conversations I mean the communications that occur between regulators, regulated and others involved in the regulatory process

---

30 See, for example, M. Billig, 'Discursive, Rhetorical and Ideological Messages' in Wetherell, op. cit., n. 7; in regulation, see M. Hajer, *The Politics of Environmental Discourse* (1995); in organizational theory, see T.J. Watson, 'Rhetoric, Discourse and Argument in Organizational Sense Making: A Reflexive Tale' (1995) 16 *Organizational Studies* 805; in public administration, see Hood, op. cit., n. 2, pp. 173–89.

31 D. Edwards, 'Emotion' in Wetherell, op. cit., n. 7; for a discussion in the context of organizational theory see, for example, C. Hardy, T. Lawrence, and N. Phillips, 'Talk and Action: Conversations and Narrative in Interorganizational Collaboration' in Grant et al., op. cit., n. 9.

32 See, further, J. Black, 'Decentring Regulation: The Role of Regulation and Self Regulation in a "Post-Regulatory" World' in *Current Legal Problems*, ed. M. Freedman (forthcoming, 2001); 'Critical Reflections on Regulation' (2002) *Australian J. of Legal Phil.* (forthcoming).

170

concerning the operation of that regulatory system.[33] The term includes all forms of interpersonal communications, extending beyond standards, policy documents, and guidance notes to include all micro-level conversations that may occur in formal or informal settings, including policy briefings, seminars, and conferences, in the course of the regulatory process between individuals both within and across organizations or particular cohesive communities. In understanding the role played by regulatory conversations it is important to disaggregate the regulatory process and to identify at which points regulatory conversations occur, between whom, and about what. It may be that little role is played by conversations at certain stages: speed cameras which gather information about behaviour, for example, are not discursive in their operation. Enforcement techniques which adopt a sanctioning approach may be deliberately less dialogic than those emphasizing negotiation or education. Indeed some techniques of control based in cybernetics, for example, collibration, are described by their authors as being 'discourse-less',[34] a claim which in itself presumes a particular definition of discourse.[35] However, studies which have been done of the day-to-day development and operation of regulatory systems suggest that in practice regulation is far from discourse-less, in the sense of lacking in communicative interaction. As Braithwaite and Drahos discovered of global business regulation, regulation is 'surprisingly deliberative'.[36] Even Bentham's panopticon would have involved conversations in its design, adoption, and construction and, more particularly, in fashioning the rationality that made such a design seem appropriate and acceptable. So whilst certain aspects of the regulatory process may not be marked by communicative interactions, others will be.

That said, regulatory conversations are likely to be a particularly significant feature of regulation in a number of situations, including the following. First, where the regulatory process is characterized both by a reliance on written norms, and where discretion pervades (and it is difficult to think of a regulatory system that is not so characterized). Written norms

---

33 Note that this is a broader definition of regulatory conversations than that adopted in my original use of the term, where the focus was confined to conversations between regulators and the regulated on the meaning and operation of rules: J. Black, *Rules and Regulators* (1997) and 'Talking about Regulation' [1998] *Public Law* 77. No conceptual or other substantive change to my earlier argument is intended, it is simply that the purpose of this paper is to expand on those discussions. Note also that the term 'conversations' is used to denote a broader field of study than the naturally occurring conversations focused on by conversational analysis.

34 A. Dunsire, 'Tipping the Balance: Autopoiesis and Governance' (1996) 28 *Administration and Society* 299, 322.

35 Foucauldian analysis would see cybernetics and collibration itself as a discourse: knowledge systems that inform social and governmental 'technologies' which constitute power in modern society, for example, op. cit., n. 20 (1977).

36 J. Braithwaite and P. Drahos, *Global Business Regulation* (2000) 32, also 552, 553.

include rules, standards, and principles, and no clear distinction between rules and discretion can be assumed; rather, discretion is seen as the space both within and between rules in which decision makers exercise choice.[37] Written norms are central to a wide range of regulatory techniques: they form a core part of regulatory techniques or combinations of techniques including the various forms of self-regulation, meta-regulation, competition, associational or procedural regulation, and are the basis of many 'economic' tools of regulation such as taxes, subsidies and instruments such as tradeable permit systems, as well as franchising, licensing, and audit regimes. Written norms have two central features which make them particularly problematic regulatory instruments: their temporal aspect – they speak from the past or present but purport to govern the future – and their linguistic aspect: they are linguistic structures which require interpretation. How they will 'work' depends on the interpretation they receive. Regulatory conversations about the prescriptions for the conduct necessary to resolve particular problems and the meaning and application of those prescriptions in particular circumstances are likely to be a central feature of those regulatory systems that employ them.

Secondly, regulatory conversations are likely to be a central characteristic of the regulatory process in situations of uncertainty: where the task of regulation is uncertain and ambiguous, and where agreement on the definitions of problems and solutions presupposes an extensive intersubjective sharing of ideas and negotiations of meaning. Regulation of risk provides an obvious example; but conversations will also be important in the more general situation in which regulators are given broadly defined and conflicting objectives to fulfil or principles to follow, where they operate in a dynamic context in which problem definitions are complex and shifting, and the consequences of regulatory action uncertain.

Thirdly, particular techniques of regulation are themselves based on conversations. The vogue for 'proceduralization', for example, in the form of structuring institutional processes so as to require and facilitate deliberation, is a conversational technique. Strategies of 'co-regulation', in which various stakeholders are meant to produce principles, rules or standards, or jointly monitor or enforce regulation under the auspices of the state, rely on conversations. 'Meta-regulation', the regulation of firms' own internal regulation, is also likely to have strong discursive aspects.

Fourthly, the context in which regulation occurs may affect the incidence and character of regulatory conversations, as well as who become participants. If there is a requirement or expectation, for example, that regulatory actions will be based on consensus between a number of different participants, then the conversation will have a particular orientation, and certain preconditions, such as those akin to those of the

37 For discussion see Black, op. cit. (1997), n. 33, p. 216.

172

ideal speech situation, may be imposed. Or, for example, if there is a requirement or expectation of transparency of the regulatory process, this may affect who participates in the conversation, and further regulatory conversations within and across organizations or groups that are, or are to be made, transparent may have a different nature and form than those which are less visible.[38]

The conception of regulation used and the notion of regulatory conversations deployed suggest that certain aspects of discourse analysis might have more immediate relevance than others in helping us to understand a regulatory process. Thus merely to adopt the techniques of conversational analysis, for example, will not tell us much about the operation of the regulatory process as a whole, given the very narrow definition of context that is used in that approach. It would have to be combined with an approach which pays close attention to language use in a broader social context, for example, socio-linguistics and ethnography. Further, because of the nature of regulation as an instrument of governmentality (whether or not exercised by governments), attention is also drawn to Foucauldian perspectives and to critical discourse analysis. Because it is contended that linguistic practices in themselves are an important aspect of regulatory processes, evident, for example, in the strategic use of rule design,[39] the definition of discourse adopted will be that discourse consists of 'text and talk', and is separate from other social practices. Despite the tensions between these different strands, such a combination of micro and macro, of linguistic base and social science concerns has precedence in discourse analysis: Mehan, for example, combines ethnomethodological and conversational analysis of micro-level interactions with Foucauldian concerns to develop a discursive history about the emergence of concepts or objects, the forms of expertise that manage them, and the power relations afforded by them.[40] It is such a combination of micro-level analysis with macro-level concerns that may fruitfully be adopted and developed by regulatory theory. But that is to jump an important stage in the analysis – we turn therefore to consider five central contentions in discourse theory as to the role of language and linguistic interaction to suggest what implications they may have for regulatory theory and practice.

38 On organizational responses to transparency more generally see Hood, Rothstein, and Baldwin, op. cit, n. 2.
39 J. Black, '"Which Arrow?": Rule Type and Regulatory Policy' [1995] *Public Law* 94.
40 H. Mehan, 'The Construction of an LD Student: A Case Study in the Politics of Representation' in Wetherell, op. cit., n. 7.

173

FIVE CONTENTIONS OF DISCOURSE ANALYSIS AND THEIR RELEVANCE IN REGULATION

1. Communicative interactions produce meaning, coordination, and action

Two of the central tenets of the 'linguistic turn' in social science and the 'social turn' in linguistics are that communicative interactions produce meaning, and that understanding is situated. We understand meaning only in relation to our own situation and in the light of our own concerns. Understanding is anchored in the concerns of the interpreting subject, and so the meaning of any object is co-determined by one's own circumstances and expectations, or one's practical involvement.[41] Furthermore, as Gadamer argued, understanding always implies a pre-understanding which is a function of the prejudices (pre-judgements) of the interpreter.[42]

For Gadamer, variation arises because the pre-interpretive position of each differs and each interprets according to his or her own position and purposes.[43] For post-structuralists, such as Laclau and Mouffe, variation arises because it is impossible to fix meanings; representations are always various and open ended.[44] Nonetheless, a level of communicative order is produced, socio-linguists and ethnographers argue, because our interactions are located in a broader context which we all share. Meaning is thus inter-subjective, it comes from a shared language and social group. Both situated and abstract accounts of word order, sentence meaning, coherence or narrative assume that language users have knowledge; that they share a repertoire of socio-cultural knowledge and beliefs about the rules that govern such structures, and the strategies and contexts in which they apply.[45] The nature of the shared context and the source of that common repertoire varies between theorists. For Gadamer, for example, that context is our 'effective history'. Thus the issues that we bring to the process of interpretation are not ours alone but rather refer to issues and concerns that are part of the historical tradition to which we belong.[46] In contrast for Wittgenstein, whose influence in discourse analysis is far stronger, meaning is produced through the organization of the quotidian, the operative aspect of action establishes a grammar of language games and thus a pre-understanding that precedes any construction of possible meaning.[47] Based principally on Wittgenstein, interactional socio-linguistics has been extended and developed in

---

41 Gadamer, op. cit., n. 12; for discussion see G. Warnke, *Gadamer: Hermeneutics, Tradition and Reason* (1987) 75–82.
42 id.
43 id.
44 Laclau and Mouffe, op. cit., n. 21.
45 van Dijk, op. cit., n. 15, p. 17.
46 Warnke, op. cit., n. 41, p. 78.
47 L. Wittgenstein, *Philosophical Investigations* (1958); G. Baker and P. Hacking, *Wittgenstein: Rules, Grammar and Necessity* (1985).

174

anthropology and ethnography to demonstrate the social basis of communicative competence, and the links between cultural practices and language forms.[48]

As noted above, the relationship between the subjective and inter-subjective aspects of language use is a contested one in discourse theory. It suggests that an approach which recognizes an interactive relationship between language as a social structure and agency[49] is one which accords best with interpretive practices that tend to be found in regulation. In other words, how people interpret a text, or indeed a practice, is a function of their pre-interpretive positions, their knowledge of particular register of language and the tacit assumptions being invoked in its use, the interpretive conventions that they might adopt, and strategic behaviour on their part as to whether or not they choose to use the interpretive approach they know should be used in the particular context in which the interpretive activity is being performed (assuming in any particular case that they have the critical distance from the interpretive context to adopt such behaviour: that distance may vary in different situations).

Understanding and adopting the argument employed in discourse analysis as to the social and inter-subjective production of meaning, and as to the dialectical relationship between language and agency, has significant potential for understanding regulatory processes, in four respects. First, it provides a theoretical ground for opposing the formalist view of rules and interpretation. Second, it provides a basis for suggesting how and why inter-subjective, interpretive communities need to be created around regulatory language and regulatory practices. Third, it provides a basis for understanding how certainty as to language and practices might be produced. Fourth, and developing from the insights above, the coordination required for the production of inter-subjective meaning forms the basis for action by those involved in the regulatory process.

(a) Challenging formalism

The challenge to formalistic approaches of interpretation is not new to legal theory; but regulation can arguably learn more from socio-linguistics and the ethnography of discourse than from interpretivist debates in legal theory because the latter debates are so preoccupied with the issue of judicial reasoning and the autonomy of law that debates about interpretation in legal theory tend in practice to be debates about adjudication.[50] Thus, adopting a

---

48 K. Fitch, 'The Ethnography of Speaking: Sapir/Whorf, Hymes and Moerman' in Wetherell et al., op. cit., n. 7; D. Hymes, 'Models of the interaction of language and social life' in *Directions in Socio-linguistics: The Ethnography of Communication*, eds. J. Gumperz and D. Hymes (1972).
49 Giddens, op. cit. n. 26.
50 For discussion in the context of regulatory rules see Black, op. cit. (1997), n. 33, ch 1.

175

socio-linguistic approach to written norms would oppose the view that 'meaning resides "in" language as furniture resides "in" rooms'.[51] Written norms are not abstract, fixed and unchanging. Rather, their meaning is defined in their application, and they are open to continual reinterpretation, depending on the actor's preoccupations and goals, the context of action, and who else is involved in the encounter.[52] So regulatory norms will be interpreted in accordance with the strategies and pre-interpretive positions of those whose behaviour they seek to change.

(b) Creating interpretive communities and their role in regulation

Discourse analysis, and in particular socio-linguistics and ethnography, suggests how and why inter-subjective communities need to be created around regulatory language and regulatory practices. Those participating in the regulatory process (principally regulatees) may lack both understanding of the language used or practices adopted, and of the tacit understandings on which written norms or practices are based or which form part of the context in which they operate. Those involved may be completely ignorant (adopt a wrong interpretation in ignorance of its incorrectness), or honestly perplexed (they know they do not know the meaning of the norm or practice). Without such understanding, appropriate action is not possible. However, just as obviously, they may also deliberately misinterpret a norm or practice for strategic reasons.

These interpretive problems, and thus the need to create inter-subjective interpretive communities, are not unique to law, but they are exacerbated when law is being used. Legal use of language is distinct from ordinary use of language, such that it requires training to understand it. The extent of the difference is highlighted by formal linguistic analyses, which study the abstract rules that govern language use, though it is debated whether those differences make 'legalese' a different language, or a dialect or a separate register of an existing language.[53] Such analyses draw attention to the particular lexicality of law (its use of words which are unique to it), the greater instance of mononyms (using words with only one accepted meaning), a high incidence of 'restricted connotations' (the deprivation of words of their ordinary language connotations when transformed into legal discourse), and the particular syntactical structures of legal documents including statutes, all of which serve to distance 'legalese' from the ordinary language on which it otherwise draws.[54] Law tries to cope with the problem

51 G. Graff, '"Keep Off the Grass", "Drop Dead" and Other Indeterminacies: A Response to Stanford Levinson' (1982) 60 *Texas Law Rev.* 405, at 405.

52 B. Tamanaha, *Realistic Socio-Legal Theory* (1998) 144, following J. Wilson, *Social Theory* (1983), refers to this as the 'interpretivist' approach to rules; other labels are nihilism, or conventionalism.

53 B. Jackson, *Law, Fact and Narrative Coherence* (1988) 29–31.

54 B. Jackson, *Semiotics and Legal Theory* (1985) 41–3, 306–8; Y. Maley, 'The Language of the Law' and V. Bhatia, 'Cognitive Structuring in Legislative

176

of interpretation through what Goodrich terms the 'isolation of the code'.[55] Control over the interpretation of legal instruments lies in the preserve of lawyers and ultimately the courts and occurs in accordance with rules of interpretation. However regulatory practices, understandings, and reasoning may be very different from those of the legal interpretive community. Legal intervention may thus disrupt regulatory practices and understandings, an issue which in turn becomes significant in the battle for interpretive control, discussed below.

Thus the existence of a legal interpretive community will not resolve interpretive problems in a regulatory context, even where regulation is based in law, and furthermore may exacerbate them, for regulatory interpretive communities are likely to be distinct from legal interpretive communities. But what are the marks of an interpretive community? Exact characterizations vary with the writers' own preoccupations, and with their position on the issue of the relationship between structure and agency. Most familiar in legal theory is Fish's notion,[56] of which various criticisms have been made, notably that it has no room for a reflective and evaluative self,[57] that it is too monolithic,[58] and that it is too abstract.[59]

In response, a more fine-grained analysis of interpretive communities needs to be developed in the regulatory context which draws on aspects of discourse analysis. Such a conception should take the following form. First, it should place emphasis on the 'active' subject as well as the 'knowing' subject: that is, that individuals are shaped by but also shape the structures in which they

Provisions' in *Language and the Law*, ed. G. Gibbons (1994); P. Goodrich, *Reading the Law* (1986) 105–21.

55 Goodrich, id, pp. 123–4.
56 See S. Fish, *Doing What Comes Naturally* (1989) 141, and generally 141–60. See, further, *Is There a Text in this Class?* (1980); 'Fish v Fiss' and 'Don't Know Much About the Middle Ages: Posner on Law and Literature', both in *Doing What Comes Naturally* (1989). Jackson also uses the notion of 'semiotic groups' in legal semiotics to describe networks of people who communicate to each other using codes and other semiotic devices peculiar to that group: Jackson, op. cit., n. 53, p. 31, pp. 133–43. He uses the notion to distinguish the different types of discourse that exist in jurisprudential arguments between Hart and Dworkin.
57 This is the general thrust of the critique of ideology levelled against hermeneutics by Habermas, Apel, Althusser, and others, see discussion in Warnke, op. cit., n. 41; it is specifically directed against Fish by D. Cornell, 'The Problem of Normative Authority in Legal Interpretation' in R. Kevelson (ed.), *Law and Semiotics* vol. 1 (1987).
58 Tamanaha, op. cit., n. 52, pp. 170–2.
59 R. Benson, 'The Semiotic Web of the Law' in Kevelson, op. cit. n. 57, at p. 42 who cites Geertz: 'law is local knowledge not placeless principle' (C. Geertz, *Local Knowledge* (1983) 218). Dworkin also criticizes the notion for offering only rather nebulous and unstable constraints on interpretation, ultimately making interpretation subjective: R. Dworkin, 'Law as Interpretation' in *The Politics of Interpretation*, ed. W.T. Mitchell, (1983); see, further, R. Klinck, *The Word of the Law: Approaches to Legal Discourse* (1992) 115–23.

operate, including linguistic and interpretive structures.[60] Thus it is assumed, for example, that actors can deploy language and interpretations in a boundedly strategic manner. Secondly, it should recognize that regulatory communities will display a degree of internal heterogeneity.[61] This heterogeneity will stem from the strategic and creative uses of language that are implied in the assumption of structuration. In terms of the degree of mutuality that has to exist, there is no magic percentage figure at which such a degree of mutuality is arrived at, and battles within the same broad interpretive community may be hard fought. Rather, interpretive communities may be defined negatively by deploying a notion of difference, that is, that they are marked out from other communities in the sense that that those outside the community do not share the same validity claims, tacit understandings, or socio-linguistic register. Thirdly, it should recognize that regulatory communities may exist either at a 'surface' level only, or at a 'deep' level as well. At a surface level, an interpretive or regulatory community would consist only of a shared socio-linguistic register or understanding of practices, for example, enforcement strategies.[62] At a deep level, it would consist of shared validity claims and normative commitments. Developing an interpretive community at this deep level thus entails, among other things, developing shared understandings of, and commitments to, the goals and values of the regulatory system which may only be partly, and often inadequately, expressed in written regulatory norms, and shared senses of the ways in which the inevitable conflicts, inconsistencies, and trade offs that there will be between those goals may be addressed. Whether or not interpretive communities have to be formed at a deep level as well for regulation to be effective, or indeed whether or not the formation of such a deep normative consensus is desirable, is a moot point.[63] It may be that where regulation is relying on law for its implementation that interpretive communities need be formed at a surface level only, for regulation can rely broadly on the authority of law to make a 'practical difference' to people's conduct in that it will provide them with a reason for acting in the way required by law.[64] Where the authority of law is not respected, or where regulation is not using law, and in the absence of an analogous authority-bearing mediating

60 Giddens, op. cit., n. 26.
61 See, also, Tamanaha, op. cit., n. 52, pp. 170–2.
62 Thus Parker has used the notion of interpretive communities to suggest that conversations about, for example, the enforcement strategies that regulators will adopt, whether they will take the form of 'tit-for-tat' strategies, be risk-based, or based on some other criteria, will facilitate the regulatory process by creating 'enforcement communities': C. Parker, 'Compliance Professionalism and Regulatory Community: The Australian Trade Practices Regime' 26 *J. of Law and Society* 215.
63 It is of course the crux of theories of deliberative democracy, and of its opponents: See, for example, J. Habermas, *Facts and Norms* (1996); C. Taylor (ed.), *Multiculturalism: Examining the Politics of Recognition* (1994).
64 J. Raz, *Morality of Freedom* (1986); J. Coleman, 'Incorporationism, Conventionalism and the Practical Difference Thesis' (1998) 4 *Legal Theory* 381; C. Sunstein, *Legal Reasoning and Political Conflict* (1996) ch. 2.

institution, then it may be that a deeper normative commitment to the goals and values of the regulatory process is required for its effectiveness. If this does not take the form of consensus, which it may well not, then at least it will involve the translation by each involved in the process of the values of others into their own terms, such that they provide norms and standards for their own judgements and conduct.[65] Whether or not the creation of such interpretive communities at either a surface or a deep level is desirable in terms of the values that are expressed and pursued by those communities is of course a different matter, and depends on the conditions in which they were created, and the normative ends to which they are put.

Thus, to summarize, socio-linguistics and ethnography suggest how and why the creation of inter-subjective interpretive communities, at least at the surface level, for the interpretation of both written norms and practices will be critical to the regulatory process. Without that socio-linguistic competence, there will be little effective regulation, even where there is the will and capacity to comply. The development of shared understandings and tacit knowledge will help to address issues of certainty, rule entrepreneurship (though the location of interpretive control is critical here, see further below), of 'honest perplexity', and will also contribute to the development of 'instinctive' compliance: the inculcation of the habit of compliance on which successful regulation depends.[66] As a site of analysis regulatory 'conversations' are thus significant, for they are likely to be vehicles through which attempts may be made to build meaning and to change existing pre-interpretations by creating new interpretive communities with a view, ultimately, to changing behaviour.

(c) Producing certainty and repairing rules

As indicated, the analysis of interpretive communities and of the role of regulatory 'conversations' above has implications for the understanding and provision of certainty in regulation. Certainty is often a key demand of regulatory norms and practices: the assurance that my interpretation will accord with another's, in particular, with that of the body that has the power to determine interpretations and impose sanctions for breach. Certainty is thus mutuality of interpretation. Ensuring such mutuality is often addressed in legal regulation by a strategy of increasing the precision of rules.[67]

---

65 N. Rose and P. Miller, 'Political Power Beyond the State' (1992) 43 *Brit. J. of Sociology* 173, 184; J. Black, 'Proceduralising Regulation: Part II' (2001) 21 *Ox. J. of Legal Studies* 33.

66 A. Chayes and A.H. Chayes, *The New Sovereignty: Compliance with International Regulatory Agreements* (1995).

67 I. Ehrlich and R. Posner, 'An Economic Analysis of Legal Rulemaking' (1974) 3 *J. of Legal Studies* 257; C. Diver, 'The Optimal Precision of Administrative Rules' (1983) 95 *Harvard Law Rev.* 393.

179

However, increased precision will not on its own bring the certainty that is sought. Rather, as analyses of existing regulatory systems have demonstrated,[68] increasing the precision of rules results in rule overload (too many rules for the addressee to be able to absorb and remember, which means they are unlikely to comply with all of them), rule-system complexity, an increase in uncertainty as detailed provisions create internal inconsistencies and contradictions, the creation of loopholes, and the facilitation of legal entrepreneurship,[69] that is the creative and self-serving expansion of intepretations combined with compliance with the letter not the spirit of the rule: 'creative compliance'.[70] Thus the 'precision' of law is more a rhetorical device than a functional asset, as linguists have long argued.[71] Precision does not on its own produce certainty. Rather as socio-linguistics suggests, the certainty or uncertainty of norms has little to do with the way that they are expressed; it has everything to do with how they are understood and interpreted. Certainty, that is, mutuality of understanding and intepretation, is a product of socio-linguistic competence. Given that competence, apparently uncertain terms will be certain to that particular socio-linguistic community.

Further, conversation analysis suggests why regulatory 'conversations' will also be necessary to 'repair' rules in a similar manner to the 'conversational repairs' that have to be made to correct past mistakes in the use of language made in the course of conversation.[72] With respect to written norms, such 'repairs' are hard to make, and moreover adherence to the cooperative principle of communication is by no means guaranteed; indeed it is the deliberate refusal to adopt such a cooperative approach which is expressed in strategies of legal entrepreneurship. Analogizing from conversational 'repairs' in other interactions suggests that a conversational approach to rule use would involve the adoption, among other things, of strategies of rule amendment, the granting of exceptions or waivers, the individualized application of general rules, and a 'compliance' approach to enforcement, including the practice of negotiated settlements.[73]

---

68 See, for example, D. McBarnet and C. Whelan, *Creative Accounting and the Cross-Eyed Javelin Thrower* (1999); S. Long, 'Social Control and Civil Law: The Case of Income Tax Enforcement' in *Law and Deviance*, ed. H.L. Ross (1981); S. Surrey, 'Complexity and the Internal Revenue Code: The Problem of Management of Tax Detail' (1964) *Law and Contemporary Problems* 673; S. Breyer, *Regulation and its Reform* (1982) 78–9.
69 J. Braithwaite, 'A Theory of Legal Certainty', paper presented to the annual conference of the Australian Society of Legal Philosophers, Canberra, June 2001.
70 D. McBarnet and C. Whelan, 'The Elusive Spirit of the Law – Formalism and the Struggle for Legal Control' (1991) 54 *Modern Law Rev.* 848.
71 See, for example, Klinck, op. cit., n. 59, pp. 220–6.
72 van Dijk, op. cit., n. 29, p. 18.
73 See, further, Black, op. cit. (1998), n. 33.

180

(d) Producing coordination and action

The importance of the creation of intersubjective understandings as a basis
for action is again a central feature of discourse analysis. It is based on
Garfinkel's contention that coordination and meaningful actions, regardless
of whether they involve cooperation or conflict, are impossible without
shared understandings. Thus any conception of social action is incomplete
without an analysis of how social actors use shared common sense
knowledge and shared methods of practical reasoning in their joint affairs.[74]
This contention has also been developed in sociology by Collins, who
focuses specifically on the relationship between conversational interactions
and action.[75] In an argument that links the role of discourse in producing
meaning to the production of action, he contends that individual chains of
conversational experiences over time recreate people's cognitive beliefs
about social structures and in turn promote collective action based on these
tacit understandings and meanings. But if no such myth or shared meaning
arises, no collective action will ensue. Thus, through the activity of
conversation and through the content of that conversation, understandings
are produced on which action is then based.[76] His theory has been developed
and applied in a practical context in organizational theory.[77]

These contentions have significant theoretical and practical relevance for
regulation, not least for those regulatory strategies that inevitably, if not
deliberately, place conversations at their centre. In particular, the role of
conversations as providing a basis for action may be developed by exploring
the ways and the extent to which regulatory conversations and the formation
of regulatory communities may be central to the institutionalization of the
regulation, in both the 'old' and 'new' senses of institutionalism.[78] In the
'new' sense in that the development of interpretive communities involves the
development of new cognitive frames and forms of practical reasoning. In

74 H. Garfinkel, *Studies in Ethnomethodology* (1967).
75 R. Collins, 'On the Microfoundations of Macrosociology' (1981) 86 *Am. J. of Sociology* 984.
76 id.
77 Hardy et al., op. cit., n. 31; on the relationship between talk and action see, also, D. Boje, 'The Storytelling Organization: A Study of Performance in an Office Supply Firm' (1991) 36 *Administrative Science Q.* 106; J. Brown and P. Duguid, 'Organizational Learning and Communities-of-Practice: Toward a Unified View of Working, Learning and Innovation' (1991) 2 *Organization Science* 40; J. Woodilla, 'Workplace Conversations: The Text of Organizing' in Grant et al., op. cit., n. 9.
78 The 'old' and 'new' branches of institutionalism referred to are of sociological and organizational new institutionalism (Powell and DiMaggio, op. cit., n. 6); for a discussion of the other strands of old and new institutionalism and their relevance to socio-legal understandings see J. Black, 'New Institutionalism and Naturalism in Socio-Legal Analysis: Institutionalist Approaches to Regulatory Decision Making' (1997) 19 *Law and Policy* 51.

the 'old' sense because it involves, at a deep level, the formation of shared normative commitments. As many studies of firms' responses to regulation have pointed out, regulation is only fully effective if it becomes part of the internal morality of the organization: if it is institutionalized.[79] Formal systems of control are always supplemented by informal structures: practices, attitudes, experiences, personal codes of morality. The task for any system of regulation, be it of firms, bureaucrats, employees, and so on, is to ensure that those informal systems support the formal system by enhancing cohesion, initiative, and morale.[80] That regulatory conversations can perform this function is suggested in practice by Braithwaite and Drahos's work in global business regulation. They observe that 'webs of dialogue regularly deliver the goods in globalizing forms of regulation that are complied with moderately well'.[81] Discourse analysis provides the theoretical underpinning and explanation for such a claim.

However, as Collins also notes, some conversations simply do not work: '[n]ot all conversations, however, are equally successful rituals. Some bind individuals together more permanently and tightly than others; some conversations do not come off at all.'[82] Co-ordinated action may depend on the conversational development of shared meanings, but these of course may not arise. In the regulatory context, the issue of interpretive control then becomes central, discussed below. More generally, the task for further research into regulatory conversations is to ask which conversations 'work' to produce coordinated action, which do not, and why. Again, the normative desirability of the action thus produced is a separate issue.

2. Communicative interactions create identities

The second contention of discourse analysis to explore is that social communicative interactions position actors and constitute their identities. Individual identities are acquired interactively as people talk about a particular individual, creating his or her reputation.[83] Positions and identities may also be reflexive, in that one positions oneself, constructs one's own identity as a result of how one is positioned and addressed by others.[84] The identity constituted, however, is not a relatively fixed end product, but is always open and shifting depending upon the positions made available in

---

79 P. Selznick, *The Moral Commonwealth* (1992); W. Scott, *Institutions and Organizations* (1994).
80 Selznick, id., p. 235.
81 Braithwaite and Drahos, op. cit., n. 36, p. 556.
82 See Collins, op. cit., n. 75, p. 999.
83 id., and B. Davies and R. Harre, 'Positioning: The Discursive Production of Selves' (1990) 20 *J. of the Theory of Social Behaviour* 43.
84 Davies and Harre, id.; see, also, S. Hall, 'The Work of Representation' in *Representation: Cultural Representations and Signifying Practices*, ed. S. Hall (1997).

one's own and others' different discursive practices, and within those practices the stories through which sense is made of one's own and each other's lives.[85]

In relation to regulation, identity matters because it affects how individuals and organizations are viewed and thus responses to them, and because it affects action, for example, agenda setting or policy positioning.[86] The practical relevance of the role of conversations and in particular of narratives in producing identities is a central theme in organizational analysis,[87] and has been observed, for example, in the mediation context.[88] An institutional dimension can be usefully added. Identities are also acquired through institutional position: membership of committees, organizational responsibilities, or from being excluded from such positions.[89] Discourse analysis conducted in organizational contexts demonstrates how, through conversational interactions and institutional positioning, identities are in effect imposed on individuals, a fact which can be both enabling and constraining, but which limits the ability of an individual to deploy their identity strategically.[90] Further, that the identities constructed are rarely uniform, there is rarely one biography, or indeed autobiography, but a series which may contradict one another.[91]

The significance of the creation of identities and the positioning of different actors is illustrated by some of the work done on regulatory enforcement. Those studies demonstrate how enforcement officials construct identities of regulatees based on their willingness and ability to comply with the regulation, and suggests that those identities are discursively produced and communicated throughout the organization. Those identities then affect how the enforcement official interprets the actions of individual firms, and thus what enforcement response is considered appropriate.[92] The work in discourse analysis on the role of discourse in constituting identities provides a theoretical base for understanding these observations.

Analysis of the role of regulatory conversations might also be valuable in revealing how and what identities are constructed of other players in the regulatory process, not just regulatees. That such work would be fruitful is again suggested by Braithwaite and Drahos's study of global business

85 id.
86 Fairclough, op. cit., n. 17; Parker, op. cit., n. 11.
87 M. Alvesson, 'Talking in Organizations: Managing Identity and Impressions in an Advertising Agency' (1994) 15 *Organization Studies* 535; B. Czarniawska-Joerges, 'Autobiographical Acts and Organizational Identities' in S. Linstead et al., *Understanding Management* (1996).
88 S. Cobb and J. Rifkin, 'Neutrality as a Discursive Practice: The Construction and Transformation of Practices in Community Mediation' (1991) 11 *Studies in Law, Politics and Society* 69.
89 For example, P. Hall, *Governing the Economy* (1986).
90 Cobb and Rifkin, op. cit., n. 88; Czarniawska-Joerges, op. cit., n. 87.
91 Czarniawska-Joerges, id.
92 K. Hawkins, *Environment and Enforcement* (1984).

regulation, in which they emphasise the significance of 'webs of dialogue' in communicating informal praise or blame and in constituting an actor as legitimate or illegitimate, with subsequent implications for how problems are identified and agendas formed.[93] Attention could be given to the identities constructed of different regulatory organizations, non-governmental organizations, trade associations, technical committees, departments, legal advisors, consumer panels, or of particular individuals. Such a study could focus on the way in which these characterizations may be communicated, among other things, through myths and storytelling between actors. It could play a central role in understanding how these identities influence which issues or problem definitions raised by groups or individuals are noticed, considered legitimate and important, and so acted upon.[94]

In particular, the discursively produced identity of the regulator is likely to affect the de facto authority and legitimacy that is conferred on them by others in the regulatory process.[95] This will, amongst other things, affect the regulator's ability to set the policy agenda, and may also be significant in the battle for interpretive control, discussed below. Also worth examining could be the impact those discursively produced characterizations have on the regulated's response to regulation.[96] The effectiveness of enforcement strategies is sometimes said to depend not so much on the actual powers that the regulator possesses, but on the perception the regulated have of the regulator,[97] for example, the ability of the regulator to portray to the regulated that they are a 'benign big gun'.[98] Are regulatees less likely to contest regulatory practices if the regulator is generally respected as being knowledgeable, fair, and reasonable? Are they more likely to do so if the regulator is characterized as ignorant, out of touch, a 'pen-pusher', 'box-ticker', or 'petty'?

Both of the examples above refer to the interactive production of identities and positions, that is, the production of identities and positions for others. As noted above, conversations may also play an important role in constructing identities reflexively, that is, such that a person sees him or herself in accordance with how others see them.[99] This process of constructing an identity for another which is then adopted by that other may be open to manipulation, though given that the identity that is being imposed in one set of conversations is likely to be contradicted by another,

93 Braithwaite and Drahos, op. cit. n. 36, p. 555.
94 K.E. Weick, *Sensemaking in Organizations* (1995); Hardy et al., op. cit. n. 31.
95 Collins, for example, argues that conversations both enacted and circulated secondarily as reputations of other people, is what principally constitutes the social structure of authority: op. cit. n. 75, p. 1004.
96 On which see, generally, F. Haines, *Corporate Regulation: Beyond 'Punish or Persuade'* (1997).
97 Hawkins, op. cit., n. 92.
98 I. Ayres and J. Braithwaite, *Responsive Regulation* (1992).
99 Text accompanying nn. 83–85 above.

184

that scope should not be exaggerated.[100] What relevance does this have for regulation? Again, both a theoretical and practical one. The theme of how discourses (in the sense of languages producing and reproducing knowledge and power) can construct identities for individuals that then affect their actions and thus provide a fertile site for their governance is central to Foucauldian analyses, though again is absent from mainstream regulatory literature.[101] However, the role that the strategic manipulation of identities can play in regulation is again suggested implicitly in the enforcement literature. Braithwaite talks of the 'self' that regulators and firms choose to put forward in encounters, and argues that sophisticated regulators achieve their goals by manipulating 'vocabularies of motive'.[102] He draws on the work of psychologists to suggest that the way that the regulatee is treated by the regulator can affect how the regulatee sees themselves and their relationship to the regulation, and can in turn affect their attitude towards that regulation and ultimately their compliance (assuming they have the organizational capacity to back up the will to comply). For example, if a firm is treated as being responsible and law abiding, they are more likely to demonstrate that 'self' than if they are treated as amoral calculators. Bardach and Kagan's work shows a similar phenomenon. The conscious strategy of identifying certain firms as 'leaders', 'champions' or 'beacons' whose practices others might emulate has also been shown (when supported by other regulatory strategies) to be effective in improving internal compliance systems within firms.[103] Again discourse analysis may provide the theoretical underpinning for these observations.

Finally, interpersonal communicative interactions (conversations) may play a role in constructing a characterization of the regulatory process as a whole and enabling those involved to make sense of that process. An important theme in discourse analysis is the sense-making role of discourse: through communicative interactions people make sense of the world around them. Again work in organizational discourse analysis is suggestive.[104] Much of the focus in that literature is on how stories, particular narrative structures, provide a powerful means of constructing and understanding organizational identities, and how within an organization there may be

---

100 For discussion in the organizational context see Czarniawska-Joerges, op. cit., n. 87.
101 See, for example, N. Rose, 'Identity, Genealogy, History' in *Questions of Cultural Identity*, eds. S. Hall and P. Du Gay (1996).
102 Ayres and Braithwaite, op. cit. n. 98, at p. 32, citing C. Wright Mills, 'Situated Actions and Vocabularies of Motive' (1940) 5 *Am. Sociological Rev.* 904, at 908, 913.
103 C. Parker, *The Open Corporation: Self-Regulation and Corporate Citizenship* (forthcoming) at 327; manuscript on file with the author.
104 For example, Weick, op. cit., n. 94; Alvesson, op. cit., n. 87; Y. Gabriel, 'Same Old Story or Changing Stories' and A. Wallemacq and D. Sims, 'The Struggle with Sense' in Grant et al., op. cit., n. 9.

competing stories, and thus competing identities and patterns of sense-making which vie for dominance.[105] Most of that work focuses on a single organization. There are some studies that adopt a discourse perspective to understanding inter-organizational interactions,[106] which might be more pertinent in the regulatory context, as understanding both intra- and inter-organizational dynamics is a central part to understanding a regulatory process.

3. Language, thought, and knowledge

The third contention of discourse analysis to be explored concerns the relationship between language, thought and knowledge. This relationship takes a number of forms, three of which will be considered here. First is van Dijk's contention in critical discourse analysis that language and the world are mediated through cognition.[107] This is linked to the discussion of the constructive aspect of mental processes by which meaning is assigned. As van Dijk argues:

> the mental representations derived from reading a text are ... the result of strategic processes of construction or sense making which may use elements of the text, elements of what language users know about the context, and elements of beliefs they already had before they started to communicate.[108]

Knowledge thus refers to individual cognition, that is, the various mental processes and representations located in the memory of language users for comprehending both text and talk. It also refers to socio-cultural cognition. Socio-linguistics emphasizes, as hermeneutics did before it, that the knowledge on which interpretation relies and which conversations build is an extensive repertoire of socio-cultural knowledge of the rules that govern linguistic structures, the interpretive strategies to use, and the contexts in which they apply.[109] In this sense, the notion that regulatory conversations produce knowledge is simply a different way of stating that they build meaning and is thus linked to the discussion above.

The second relationship between conversations and knowledge is that conversations are a central vehicle for the dissemination of knowledge, and thus are critical in building the capacity to comply. In discourse analysis in the organizational context, the discursive production of knowledge and skills has been examined at a micro-level. That work illustrates how conversations are the medium through which knowledge and skills are both dissemi-

---

105 D.K. Mumby and R. Clair, 'Organizational Discourse' in van Dijk, op. cit., n. 29.
106 For a good example see Hardy et al., op. cit., n. 31.
107 van Dijk, op. cit., n 15 and 'Discourse as Interaction in Society' in van Dijk, op. cit., n. 29.
108 van Dijk, id. (1992), p. 18.
109 id.

186

nated[110] and acquired.[111] Conversations are also the sites where particular sets of knowledge and skills are invested with, or divested of, meaning and significance.[112] In the regulatory context, the importance of conversations in disseminating knowledge is emphasized indirectly, for example, in work on internal compliance systems in firms[113] and recent work in the United Kingdom public sector on dissemination of standards of best practice[114] (and also on the work that suggests how knowledge about how to resist regulation is disseminated[115]). That work considers how organizational capacity to comply with regulation can be built, and it is clear that communicative interactions play a key role, though for those interactions to 'work' the language used has to be one which participants understand. Both also point to the importance of the institutional settings in which conversations occur for the production and adoption of knowledge, and in the importance of content and expression. In particular, the successful acquisition and dissemination of knowledge and skills is dependent on the trust that conversants have in one another and the respect they have for the person giving the knowledge.[116]

There is a third, more fundamental sense in which language, thought, and knowledge are related, and that is that language frames thought, and reproduces and produces knowledge. The relationship between thought and language is one of the central debates in philosophy and linguistics, and again, there is a vast literature which can only be skated over for the purposes of this paper. For writers such as Locke, language expresses the thoughts that we have formed anterior to their expression,[117] whereas the Sapir/Whorf hypothesis is that the structure of language determines thought.[118] More generally, the shift towards a constructionist conception of language and representation displaced the individual from a privileged position in relation to knowledge and indeed thought: for Foucault, for example, thought or knowledge are not separate from language; rather each person is subjected to a discourse and must submit to its rules and conventions, to its dispositions of knowledge and power.[119] Others, for example in ethnography, have adopted an understanding of the relationships

110 Brown and Duguid, op. cit., n. 77.
111 K. Weick and F. Westley, 'Organizational Learning: Affirming an Oxymoron' in Clegg et al., op. cit., n. 9.
112 Hardy et al., op. cit., n. 31.
113 Parker, op. cit., n. 103.
114 Office for Public Management, *The Effectiveness of Different Mechanisms for Spreading Best Practice* (2000).
115 E. Bardach and R. Kagan, *Going By the Book: The Problem of Regulatory Unreasonableness* (1984).
116 Office for Public Management, op. cit., n. 114.
117 For discussion, see, for example, Klinck, op. cit., n. 59, pp. 8–24.
118 See Fitch, op. cit. n. 30.
119 For discussion, see, for example, Hall, op. cit., n. 89.

between agency and structure that allows for a reciprocal relationship between language, thought, and knowledge.[120] Language frames thought, it does not determine it.

The contentions as to the relationship between language, thought, and knowledge may be developed in the regulatory context in a number of ways. Most obviously, the study of regulation itself may be seen in Foucauldian terms as the study of the way in which knowledge is utilized through discursive practices in particular institutional settings to govern or control the conduct of others.[121] In the practice of regulation, discourse analysis suggests that it is through language and communicative interactions that issues are identified, problems and interests defined, and new sets of knowledge created. This in turn may lead to the creation of discursive spaces in which cooperation may be facilitated, or conflict hardened.

The discursive nature of the processes of problem definition, knowledge creation, and knowledge definition is noted in the regulatory context again by Braithwaite and Drahos in their analysis of global business regulation. They observe the ability of regulatory conversations to define problems and create new sets of knowledge, and to facilitate the modelling process through which that knowledge is disseminated and patterns of regulation adopted.[122] Meidinger also argues that it is through communicative interactions that issues are defined and redefined, identities constructed, interdependencies and inter-linkages recognized and formed.[123] The dialogic (and polylogic) formation of spaces in which concepts can be constructed, knowledge created, issues and problems defined, and cooperation facilitated is also well illustrated and well-theorized in Hajer's analysis of the role of 'storylines' in environmental regulation.[124] He notes that debates in environmental policy and regulation are characterized by a high degree of discursive complexity. Discussions of acid rain, for example, draw on the knowledges of a variety of disciplines: natural sciences, accounting, economics, engineering, and philosophy. Each discipline contributes its own knowledge; however that knowledge is not shared by others in other disciplines. The 'communicative miracle' of environmental politics, Hajer observes, is that despite the various modes of speech and sets of knowledge that are involved, conversants somehow seem to understand each other.

The means by which they do so, he argues, is the creation of 'storylines'. Storylines, such as 'acid rain', distil and simplify the complexity of their different components by creating narratives. They thus cluster knowledge and make the problem seem coherent and more accessible to those who do not

---

120 Fitch, op. cit., n. 48.
121 For example, P. Miller and N. Rose, 'The Tavistock Programme: The Government of Subjectivity and Social Life' (1988) 22 *Sociology* 171; M. Power, *The Audit Society* (1997).
122 Braithwaite and Drahos, op. cit., n. 36, pp. 578–601.
123 Meidinger, op. cit., n. 6.
124 Hajer, op. cit., n. 30.

188

share the complex of knowledge from which they are built. As storylines are accepted they acquire a ritual character, functioning as metaphors and becoming 'tropes' or figures of speech that seem to rationalize a specific approach to what seems to be a coherent problem. Finally, they allow different actors to expand their own understanding and discursive competence of the phenomenon beyond their own existing set of knowledge.[125] Storylines thus provide the narrative in which a specific actor can locate his or her own knowledge or social preference in the light of others, and can influence actors in their own production of knowledge. Storylines thus do not simply function to create the possiblity of coalition between different actors with different sets of knowledge, but they can create new discursive understandings, new sets of knowledge, which may in turn change practical reality.[126]

Hajer's account shows very well how discourse analysis may contribute to our understandings of regulation, particularly of the discursive production and reproduction of thought and knowledge in the regulatory context. It may also be related to Haas's analysis of epistemic communities in international relations.[127] Epistemic communities are networks of knowledge-based communities with an authoritative claim to policy-relevant knowledge within their domain of expertise. They are characterized by shared values or principled beliefs as to the normative rationales for social action, shared understandings of the nature of a problem and of causal linkages between possible policy actions and desired outcomes, intersubjective and internally defined criteria for validating knowledge; and a common policy enterprise.[128] We may link Haas's analysis of epistemic communities via discourse theory to Hajer's analysis of storylines in that storylines enable different epistemic communities to be formed, and once formed to communicate and to create a new knowledge.

Moreover, in highlighting the role of epistemic communities, Haas demonstrates how ideas may be a motivating source of interest, and how institutional learning mechanisms can influence the policy process. Combining Haas's work with discourse analysis, including the work on identities, above, and on the relationship of language, knowledge, and power discussed below, will enable us to better understand how and why different ideas, different sets

125 id, pp, 62–4.
126 id, p. 68.
127 P. Haas, 'Introduction: Epistemic Communities and International Policy Co-ordination' (1992) 46 *International Organization* 1; P. Haas, 'Obtaining International Environmental Protection through Epistemic Consensus' in *Global Environmental Change and International Relations*, eds. I. Rowlands and M. Greene (1992); P. Haas, 'Epistemic Communities and the Dynamics of International Co-operation' in *Regime Theory and International Relations*, eds. V. Rittberger and P. Mayer (1993).
128 Epistemic communities could be seen as a particular form of interpretive community: in addition to sharing linguistic practices and normative commitments, members of epistemic communities are professionals, and share a technical knowledge as to causes and effects and a common policy enterprise.

of knowledge, become relevant at different points and at different times. Discourse analysis, in other words, may rehabilitate the role of knowledge and ideas in regulation, and provide a theoretical base which is far richer than that provided by Derthick and Quirk,[129] with whose writing the 'theory of ideas' is usually equated, and as a result is just as usually dismissed.[130]

4. Language and power

The fourth contention is that language is intimately related to power: it is marked by the values of social groups, encodes perspectives and judgements, and can instantiate certain orthodoxies. Here the relevant streams of discourse analysis include Foucault, critical discourse analysis, and post-Marxism. The claim that discursive interactions express, perpetuate, and challenge existing relationships of power, ideology, and hegemony stems in part from the ideological critique levelled against philosophical hermeneutics by Habermas and others. Habermas argued that hermeneutics represented a 'linguistic idealism' – it assumes that traditions are self-contained, that nothing outside them affects their direction or influences the discussion that occurs inside them. Rather, he argued, hermenuetics had to consider that tradition is not only the locus of truth but of untruth and of continuing relations of domination.[131] Further, philosophical hermeneutics fails to provide any basis on which to adjudicate the validity of a tradition's self-understandings and therefore risks capitulation to them.[132] Critical, and post-structuralist, discourse analysis extends this critique. It draws on Althusser's conception of ideology, on Gramsci's notion of hegemony, and on Bakhtin and Volosinov's contention that language use is always motivated and therefore framed within the struggle between different social groups.[133] Thus the relationship between discourse, power, and hegemony is seen to be one in which discursive practices, events, and texts arise out of and are shaped by power and ideology and struggles over them, and in which the opacity of the relationship between discourse and society is a factor in securing power and hegemony.[134]

Critical discourse analysts such as Fairclough and Wodak, as well as post-Marxists such as Laclau and Mouffe, conceive of the relationships of power in

129 M. Derthick and P. Quirk, *The Politics of Deregulation* (1985).
130 For example, R. Baldwin and M. Cave, *Understanding Regulation* (1999) 26; Hood, Rothstein and Baldwin, op. cit., n. 2, p. 68.
131 J. Habermas, 'A Review of Gadamer's *Truth and Method*' in *Understanding and Social Inquiry*, eds. F. Dallmayr and T. McCarthy (1977); for discussion, see Warnke, op. cit., n. 41, ch. 4.
132 id. p. 140.
133 For discussion see, for example, Fairclough and Wodak, op. cit., n. 29; D. Howarth, *Discourse* (2000); D. Howarth and Y. Stavrakakis, 'Introducing Discourse Theory and Political Analysis' in D. Howarth, A. Norval, and Y. Stavrakakis, *Discourse Theory and Political Analysis: Identities, Hegemony and Social Change* (2000).
134 Fairclough, op. cit., n. 17; N. Fairclough, 'Critical Discourse Analysis and the Marketization of Public Discourse' (1993) *Discourse and Society* 133.

terms of a binary opposition of dominator and dominated, included and excluded, and focus on the destructive, dominating nature of power. Foucauldian analysis counters that power is productive, producing certain forms of knowledge, meanings, values, and practices rather than others. Moreover, power emerges from local arenas of action, and power is relational in that it cannot exist other than as a function of multiple points of resistance. The play of power relationships is therefore not binary (dominated against dominators), but strategic, complex, unstable, self-transforming, and never determinate in its effect.[135] Thus power is expressed not only in overt forms and in situations of conflict, but tacitly and implicitly in situations of apparent consent and consensus.[136] Finally power and knowledge are mutually constitutive, each constituting the other to produce the 'truths' of a particular historical period.

Conceptualizations of power and its role in regulation are under-explored in the mainstream regulatory literature. The debates in discourse analysis as to the relationship of language and power, and in Foucauldian analysis, of language, knowledge, and power, suggest some avenues to be explored, only a few of which may be mentioned here.

First, it would require regulationists to consider all dimensions of power. Attention has perhaps been given most in regulatory analysis to Lukes's first dimension, the overt expression of power in which A gets B to do something B would not otherwise do (a definition which bears striking similarity to many definitions of regulation).[137] Fuller consideration of the role of power requires, however, attention to how agendas are constructed, Lukes's second dimension of power, and to not just what is said but what is not said, not just to how issues are defined but how they are not defined, even where there seems to be little or no contention about that definition: his third, 'hegemonic', dimension of power.[138] Exercise of power in this form could be manifested in the conceptualizations of problems that dominate at different times, and attention given to how are they manipulated, and how to they shift over time and space. For example, how are new discursive structures, such as Hajer's 'storylines', created, and with what implications?[139]

Secondly, regulationists would have to consider whether power is binary or fragmented, and whether or how it is created through the enrolment and mobilization of persons, procedures, and technologies to pursue a particular end.[140] It is probably the fragmented understanding of the nature of power

---

135 See references at n. 20 above, Hall, op. cit., n. 89, Knorr-Cetina, op. cit., n. 28.
136 See, further, S. Lukes, *Power: A Radical View* (1974), though the assumptions he made as to the possibilities of identifying 'real' interests which his third form of power was identified as denying have been strongly contested by Foucauldian concepts of power, in which claims to know the real interests of any group cannot be separated from the techniques used to represent them.
137 id.
138 id.
139 Hajer, op. cit., n. 30.
140 B. Latour, 'The Power of Association' in *Power, Action, Belief*, ed. J. Law (1986).

191

which better fits the decentred nature of regulation observed by some.[141] Essentially, a decentred understanding of regulation recognizes a shift in the locus of the activity of 'regulating' from the state to other, multiple, locations, the changing nature of the limitations on the capacity of the state, and the adoption on the part of the state of particular strategies of regulation. 'Decentred regulation' thus involves a move away from an understanding of regulation which assumes that governments have a monopoly on the exercise of power and control, that they occupy a position from which they can oversee the actions of others, and that those actions will be altered pursuant to government's demand. In a decentred understanding of regulation, the regulatory process is characterized by several central features: complexity, the fragmentation and construction of knowledge, the fragmentation of the exercise of power and control, the recognition of the autonomy and interdependence of social actors, the recognition that regulation is the product of complex interactions between social and political actors in the regulatory process, the collapse of the public/private distinction in socio-political terms, and a set of normative proposals as to the type of techniques that should therefore be adopted.[142]

Third, attention should be given to the interpretations that are adopted and the rhetorical devices that are used in attempts to persuade others of the discursant's view. Again Hajer's study is instructive. How are certain conceptualizations or positions portrayed as acceptable or problematic? How do certain definitions open up issues such that they become seen as the preserve of many participants or potential participants, or how do they 'close down' issues, defining them as the preserve only of 'experts'?[143] A further example would be risk regulation, where contests over issue definition and language use are frequently observed.[144]

Fourth, the relationship between knowledge and power that forms a central part of Foucauldian analysis emphasizes that the possession of power may be unrelated to the possession of other more traditional resources of power, but may lie in the possession of knowledge, and more particularly in the ability of a body or group to render the uncertain certain. The ability to control uncertainty can thus be a source of power; this is a central issue in organizational literature.[145] Experts clearly are in an advantageous position

141 For discussion, see Black, op. cit., n. 32; C. Scott, 'Analysing Regulatory Space: Fragmented Resources and Institutional Design' [2001] *Public Law* 329.
142 See, further, id.
143 Hajer, op. cit., n. 30.
144 For a good overview, see Royal Society, *Risk: Analysis, Perception, Management* (1992); for discussion in the context of regulation of gene technology see J. Black, 'Regulation as Facilitation: Negotiating the Genetic Revolution' (1998) 61 *Modern Law Rev.* 621.
145 For a good overview, see C. Hardy and S. Clegg, 'Some Dare Call it Power' and M. Reed, 'Organizational Theorising: A Historically Contested Terrain', both in Clegg et al., op. cit., n. 9.

in this respect, and the role of expert discourses in patterning organizational structuring and control, and mediating between governmental policies and their localized implementation has been noted in the governance literature, by Miller and Rose, for example.[146] In the international relations context, Haas's work on the role of epistemic communities in international environmental regulation demonstrates a similar phenomenon. He shows how cooperation is achieved not through traditionally recognized mechanisms of state power, or the domination of particular interests, but through the transnationally organized networks of epistemic communities, which are knowledge rather than interest based.[147] Such communities are empowered through their claim to exercise authoritative knowledge. Their role is particularly significant in situations of uncertainty, and where state interests are undefined. Under such circumstances, information is at a premium, and leaders look to those with knowledge to address that uncertainty. Epistemic communities can thus be influential in defining the dimensions of a problem, in helping actors to define and recognize their interests, and be privileged in identifying solutions.

Fifthly, an institutional dimension could usefully be added. What role do decision-making structures play? Haas, for example, notes that the power of epistemic communties is reinforced if it they can also consolidate bureaucratic power in areas such as finances, staffing, and enforcement authority. We could ask further how, if at all, do institutional and decision-making structures 'mobilize bias'?[148] For example, do they allow the definition of issues to be located with particular participants and what implications does that have for the way the conversation is conducted between those participants and for the relative exercises of power within that conversation? To take a different example: do negotiations about individualized rule waivers or modifications where the regulated has been given no right of demand or veto, for example, take a different form than negotiations over a licence modification where the licence holder does have such a right? A more general consideration of the question brings us to the issue of the institutional preconditions which make conversations an acceptable mechanism of regulation, but as that would require a further excursus into discussions of conditions of deliberation, ideal speech situations, and so on, that topic cannot be pursued here.[149]

Finally, paying close attention to the exercise of power within and over regulatory conversations would facilitate a more fine-grained analysis of the hierarchical or heterarchical nature of the regulatory arrangements, and is

146 P. Miller and N. Rose, 'Governing Economic Life' (1990) 19 *Economy and Society* 1.
147 Haas, op. cit., n. 127.
148 Lukes's second dimension of power, op. cit., n. 136.
149 See, further, Black, op. cit., nn. 33 and 55, and J. Black, 'Proceduralising Regulation: Part I' (2000) 20 *Ox. J. of Legal Studies* 597.

likely to reveal that the relationship between participants does not in fact follow the formal pattern of organizational relationships assumed or defined in the regulatory system, or match particular techniques of regulation. Again this is a central theme in organizational analysis.[150] Thus attention to regulatory conversations may reveal that what 'on paper' looks to be a hierarchical system of command and control is in fact characterized by significant interdependencies, power dispersal, and fragmentation (as indeed the decentred analysis of regulation suggests). Or in contrast, that systems that 'on paper' are meant to be systems collective self-regulation based on mutuality (and thus 'heterarchical') are in fact characterized by the display of considerable discursive power by one firm or individual: their interpretations of rules are adopted, or their conceptualizations of issues or problems, or criteria of success or failure.

5. Discourse and contestation

Contestation of meaning, identities, knowledge, and power is the final central theme in discourse analysis that we will consider here. Contestation is the vehicle for change. Because meaning is never completely fixed, because identities and positions may be contested in different discourses, because knowledge and power will be contested, change will occur as new meanings develop, different identities are constructed, and different systems of knowledge and configurations of power come in to prominence. Understanding change is thus to understand this process of contestation. Within a regulatory context this might require attention to, for example, how problem definitions change (for example, the current shift in financial regulation to the definition of the regulatory problem in terms of risk rather than market failure), and what the implications are of such changes.

There is one particular area of contest in regulation which stands out, and which highlights the importance of the institutional context. That is the contestation of meanings in a system in which some person or body has the authority to fix meanings. The battle for interpretive control in regulation is a critical one. Contesting the interpretation of written norms can be a central feature of regulation. However, from a regulatory (and legal/ constitutional) standpoint, interpretations must be disciplined, otherwise they will multiply beyond limits that are deemed acceptable. This observation can be linked to the discussion of power, above, in that different interpretations may favour different participants, providing the potential for new powers and positions to be produced, and existing ones transformed.[151] Control over interpretation is thus control over a central power resource. There are further implications of the battle for interpretive control, for the formal, legal location of

---

150 Again, this is a central theme in organizational analysis: see Hardy and Clegg, op. cit., n. 145.
151 id., p. 634.

194

authority to issue binding interpretations and the way that authority is exercised are critical to the formation of interpretive communities, to the certainty of legal provisions, and to the effectiveness of different types of rules.[152]

Regulatory conversations as to the interpretation (meaning and application) of rules may vary both in linguistic practices and in participants depending on who is perceived as having the authority, de facto, to make the decision. For example, if in a legally based system of regulation the interpretation of the rule is seen in practice to lie with the regulator rather than a court (or where the regulated does not want for whatever reason to take the issue to court (for example, non-significant interpretations of a rule or licence)) then it might be that the conversation is not marked by legal language, legal values or legal participants. That is, even though the rules being used may have legal status there may be little 'juridification'.[153] In contrast, if the interpretation is seen in practice, as well as in law, to lie with a court (for example, significant interpretations of what constitutes 'abuse of dominant position', or an 'investment service'), the matter may quickly become one in which lawyers are involved, and participants in the conversation and its nature may change quite significantly. Focusing on regulatory conversations from a discourse perspective thus has a bearing on assessments as to the 'juridification' of the regulatory process, again requiring a more fine-grained analysis.

CONCLUSIONS

Discourse analysis has its critics, as does any theoretical paradigm, and those criticisms would have to be considered in any use of the analysis.[154] There is clearly more theoretical work that needs to be done. Nonetheless, it is suggested that drawing on discourse analysis would facilitate a better understanding of regulatory processes. It would require regulationists to look at whom conversations are between, where they occur within the regulatory process or regime, what they are about, and how they 'work' to co-ordinate

---

152 See, further, Black, op. cit., n. 33, and 'Using Rules Effectively' in *Regulation and Deregulation: Policy and Practice in the Utilities and Financial Services Industries*, ed. C. McCrudden (1999).

153 'Juridification' is usually used with negative connotations to deplore the introduction of excessive legality into non-legal realms. This is unfortunate for in its original conception it is only the final stages of juridification which are regrettable, the earlier stages are seen as beneficial: Teubner, op. cit., n. 4 (1987), and indeed many observers of regulation worry about the absence of juridical values such as the 'rule of law' in regulatory processes, for example, Braithwaite and Drahos, op. cit., n. 36.

154 For criticism of discourse analysis in the organizational context see, for example, M. Reed, 'Organizational Analyis as Discourse Analysis: A Critique' in Grant et al., op. cit., n. 9.

action and constitute regulation. It would look at the way that interpretations and conceptualizations are formed, at what understandings are shared and by whom, at which are contested and between whom, and at the strategies used in developing or contesting those understandings, including rhetorical devices.

The argument is not a reductionist one, however; it is not argued that discourse analysis should supplant the other theoretical perspectives through which regulation is observed. Which it could be combined with is another question. Indeed the incommensurability or otherwise of different theoretical paradigms applied to regulation is a debate which is beyond the scope of this paper, though it is one that is needed in regulatory theory. Nonetheless, it has been suggested above at various points that discourse analysis and institutionalism could be complementary perspectives. Institutionalism is itself an undisciplined discipline, with many conflicting strands. However, to the extent that it also draws attention to the significance of interpretive constructs, organizational discourse, and the interaction of micro-processes with mezzo and macro contexts, aspects of institutionalism have clear resonances with aspects of discourse analysis.[155] A creative synthesis of strands of both theories could facilitate analysis in particular of the historical, organizational, cognitive, and communicative aspects of regulation.

From an empirical point of view, how could research be carried forward? The issue of methodology is again a contested one in discourse analysis, and different strands of that analysis use different methodologies. In general the data on which discourse analysis is based are familiar: interviews, focus groups, documents and records, media representations, naturally occurring conversation, and policy statements, though different strands will prioritize different sources (conversational analysis, for example, does not look at documentary records; Foucauldian analysis does not consider naturally occurring conversations).[156] Methodologies and sites of study vary with the questions being asked. The question asked here is how can we better understand particular regulatory processes. Understanding such a process requires understanding the detailed level of its operation, the perceptions of its participants, and how those 'internal' processes interact with a broader context. Thus a combination of micro and macro, of linguistic base and social science concerns may be a fruitful course to follow.[157] It has to be said that neither the theoretical nor the empirical task will be easy, for the tensions that exist within both discourse analysis and institutionalism reflect some of the central fissures in social science. That does not mean it is not worth doing. Not a great sell, perhaps, but at least an honest one.

155 See, for example, March and Olsen, op. cit., n. 6, pp. 26–7.
156 M. Wetherell, S. Taylor, and S. Yates, *Discourse as Data: A Guide for Analysis* (2001).
157 Mehan, op. cit., n. 40.

196

JOURNAL OF LAW AND SOCIETY
VOLUME 29, NUMBER 1, MARCH 2002
ISSN: 0263-323X, pp. 197–225

The Emotional Dimension in Legal Regulation

BETTINA LANGE*

This article argues that the study of legal regulation can be further developed through an analysis of emotions because it can bring into sharper focus the social nature of regulation. The article illustrates this point by discussing the notion of regulatory law as an emotional process. It then suggests various ways in which an analysis of emotions can promote understanding of a key issue in legal regulation, the role of structure and agency. The article concludes with a brief discussion of how existing social science research methods can be adapted to the study of emotions.

INTRODUCTION

This article suggests that emotional processes are one aspect of legal regulation. Sociological analysis has made important contributions to the understanding of regulatory processes. It has shown the significance of a range of contextual factors, beyond formal law, in shaping the design and implementation of legal regulation. It has, however, been limited by focusing on cognitive aspects and by neglecting emotional dynamics of social action. Hence, this article aims to open up a sociological analysis by suggesting that regulating also involves the generation, expression, and management of emotions. In order to make a contribution to regulatory theory, however, an analysis of emotions has to be more than simply the addition of another dependent variable or the introduction of new terminology, such as relabelling attitudes or values of regulators and regulated as emotional dispositions.[1] An analysis of emotions should open up new analytical terrain. Hence the 'opening up' of the sociological analysis of legal regulation has to be accompanied by a 'narrowing down' which brings into sharper focus a

* Law Department, Keele University, Staffordshire ST5 5BG, England

1 A. Hochschild, 'Ideology and Emotion Management: A Perspective and Path for Future Research' in *Research Agendas in the Sociology of Emotions*, ed. T. Kemper (1990) 117.

197

key issue in legal regulation. These are law and society interrelationships and, in particular, the possibility of constructing close links between a social and a legal realm on the basis of an analysis of emotions. Section one of the article further strengthens the case for analysing emotions as part of legal regulatory processes by presenting a range of reasons for the relevance of emotions. Section two argues that an analysis of emotions and, in particular, the notion of regulatory law as an emotional process, enables us to perceive strong links between a social and a legal realm. Section three illustrates how an analysis of emotions might further develop a key area of debate, the role of structure and agency in legal regulation. Section four concludes the article with a discussion of methodological issues raised by integrating an analysis of emotions into research designs on legal regulation. First of all, however, the question what are emotions has to be addressed.

WHAT ARE EMOTIONS?[2]

1. Emotion as linked to body and cognition

How to define emotions has been a matter of debate. A range of social scientists, however, agree that emotions involve both cognitive and physiological processes. Hence feeling is inextricably linked with thinking and physical arousal. The definitions of emotions of two sociologists who work within different theoretical traditions illustrate this point. Arlie Hochschild, a social constructionist defines emotions as:

> an awareness of four elements that we usually experience at the same time: a) appraisals of a situation, b) changes in bodily sensations, c) the free or inhibited display of expressive gestures and d) a cultural label applied to specific constellations of the first three elements.[3]

2 Some sociologists use the terms emotion, feeling, sentiment, and affect interchangeably (see, for example, M.L. Lyon and J.M. Barbalet, 'Society's Body: Emotion and the ''Somatization'' of Social Theory' in *Embodiment and Experience: The Existential Ground of Culture and Self,* ed. T. Csordas (1994) 48. Others distinguish, for instance, between feeling and sentiment. According to Homan (referred to in T. Kemper, *A Social Interactional Theory of Emotions* (1978) 23), feelings are actual feelings, while sentiments are the 'activities that the members of a particular verbal or symbolic community say are the signs of the attitudes and feelings' that social actors develop in interaction. Kemper (id., p. 48) uses the terms affects or sentiments for the more enduring emotions, such as hostility or love. Levy distinguishes emotion and feeling because they involve different relationships between the self and the body (R. Levy, 'The Emotions in Comparative Perspective' in *Approaches to Emotion*, eds. K.R. Scherer and P. Ekman (1984) 401–3).

3 Hochschild, op. cit., n. 1, pp. 118–19.

198

Similarly Theodore Kemper who has a more positivist orientation describes emotions as:

> a relatively short–term evaluative response essentially positive or negative in nature involving distinct somatic (and often cognitive) components ... Cognitive components consist of verbal judgements or labels that identify the emotion.[4]

Sociologists and anthropologists disagree, however, on how exactly the body and the mind become involved in the production of emotions. More important for the discussion of legal regulation, however, is the fact that lawyers have often worked with a different concept of emotion. In fact, some facets of lawyers' definitions of emotions have implied a limited view on how they can be taken into account in an analysis of legal regulation.

2. Emotion as 'other'

Three ideas are central to lawyers' definition of emotions. First, lawyers have often perceived emotion and cognition as in tension with each other and have distanced emotion in particular from reason and rationality. Moreover, rationality and reason are frequently understood as being inherent in the law itself, for instance in the due process model of criminal law.[5] Consequently emotion is constructed as 'other' to law.

Second, emotions are considered as potentially anarchic, unbounded, and associated with a lack of control. Therefore when lawyers have discussed the role of emotions in legal processes they have emphasized the importance of containing them.[6] The 'messy individuality' of emotions is contrasted with hard and fast 'categorical rules'.[7] Thus, lawyers' construction of emotion as 'other' distances emotion not just from cognition but also from normative processes. This again is different from sociologists' understanding of emotions. In particular, social constructionists have emphasized that the generation, expression, and management of emotions is subject to normative practices. For example, according to Hochschild 'feeling rules' shape what emotions are felt.[8]

Third, lawyers have not considered emotions as a social fact but have discussed them from a normative angle. Hence, they have been less concerned with analytical links between emotional and legal processes. Instead they have debated the question whether emotions should play a role in legal proceedings.[9] The normative angle has been extended even to

---

4 Kemper, op. cit., n. 2, p. 47.
5 See, for example, T.M. Massaro, 'Show (Some) Emotions' in *The Passions of Law*, ed. S. Bandes (1999) 98–9.
6 See, for example, Massaro, id., p. 99; C. Solomon, 'Justice v. Vengeance: On Law and the Satisfaction of Emotion' in Bandes, id., pp. 138, 144.
7 S. Bandes, 'Introduction', id. p. 7.
8 Hochschild, op. cit., n. 1, p. 122.
9 For contrasting views on this see, for example, Massaro, op. cit., n. 5 and D.M. Kahan, 'The Progressive Appropriation of Disgust' in Bandes, op. cit., n. 5, pp. 63–79.

emotions themselves when lawyers have discussed what are 'bad' and 'good' emotions.[10]

To conclude, the term emotion describes those aspects of social life that involve feeling. For social scientists, however, emotions cannot be understood in isolation but are closely linked to cognition and the body. Different definitions can fulfill various analytical tasks. While lawyers have tended to construct emotion as 'other', sociologists' definitions provide firmer analytical ground for exploring emotional processes as an integral part of legal regulation. The next section will suggest various reasons why emotions should be taken into account in an analysis of legal regulation.

WHY DOES AN ANALYSIS OF EMOTIONS MATTER FOR UNDERSTANDING LEGAL REGULATION?

1. Emotionalized societies – emotionalized legal regulation

Academic analysis of legal regulation often reflects the broader social and intellectual contexts in which it is produced. As societies and intellectual fashions change, so do accounts of legal regulation. Systems theory has influenced academic analysis of legal regulation considerably also because it reflects and explains a widespread perception that – despite globalization – societies are increasingly differentiated, complex, and diverse.[11] More recently, however, societies are described as becoming increasingly 'emotionalized'.[12] This 'emotionalization' takes various forms. It can involve the expression of emotions as an accepted, routine part of public discourse. For example, criminal justice debates about the release of the two young British men who killed the toddler James Bulger were conducted in emotionalized terms. They referred to compassion and forgiveness on the one hand and vengeance, hatred, and disgust on the other hand.[13] 'Emotionalizing' societies, however, can also mean to problematize the generation, expression, and management of emotions and subject social actors to increasing social control through formal and informal practices of intervention in their emotional lives. For example, deviant emotions can be perceived as a cause for crime and hence the appropriate response becomes

---

10 Bandes, id., pp. 5, 13, 14.
11 N. Luhmann, *The Differentiation of Society* (1982); K. Dammann, D. Grunow, and P. Japp (eds.), *Die Verwaltung des Politischen Systems* (1994); J. Kooiman (ed.), *Modern Governance, New Government – Society Interactions* (1993) 3, and chapter by T.B. Jørgensen, 'Modes of Governance and Administrative Change' in Kooiman, id., p. 219.
12 S. Karstedt, 'Emotions, Law and Crime' in *Crime and Emotions*, eds. W. de Haan and J. Loader (2003), special issue of *Theoretical Criminology*, forthcoming.
13 L. Barton, 'The Problem With Children Who Kill' *Guardian*, 10 July 2001; S. Rushdie, 'Who Will Rehabilitate the British Tabloid Press?' *Guardian*, 7 July 2001.

the treatment and correction of the emotional make-up of the offender.[14] To conclude, if societies are becoming increasingly emotionalized, then it is difficult to argue that legal regulation is untainted by this and that the academic analysis of legal regulation does not require any reference to the role of emotions in regulatory processes. The next section will argue that emotions do not just become a topic in regulatory analysis because of the social changes that societies undergo but also because of innovations in intellectual trends.

2. Emotions as a topic in postmodernist perspectives of legal regulation

An analysis of emotions can help to take the postmodern turn fully on board in the analysis of legal regulation. A significant part of the literature has examined legal regulation within a modernist framework. This has involved a particular view of law and society relationships. It has been assumed that in principle regulated and regulators, can act in a goal-oriented, rational way pursuing their interests.[15] Regulatory law has been seen as a tool which can be employed in an instrumental manner to achieve through linear cause-effect relationships the ends that have been specified in legal regulation. Analysis of legal regulation from systems-theoretical or other postmodernist perspectives has departed from these ideas by questioning, for instance, the possibility of agency. In systems-theoretical accounts agency is not presupposed but is the outcome of communicative processes. Hence actions are simply elements of systems and agency is understood as a form of reduction of the complexity of systems.[16]

Some aspects of postmodernist, and in particular post-structuralist analysis, however, are not fully taken on board in these contributions.[17] Post-structuralist accounts have focused upon one particular aspect of social actors; their body.[18] The body replaces subjects and can be a key site for the exercise of social control.[19] Significant concepts, such as power[20] and governance, as well as structure and agency, are reconceptualized through an analysis of the body. For example, speech acts are a manifestation of power.[21] Emotions are one important aspect of the functioning of bodies.

14 K. Williams, *Textbook on Criminology* (1994) 181, 228.
15 E. Bardach and A. Kagan, *Going by the Book, the Problem of Regulatory Unreasonableness* (1982); A. Kagan, N. Gunningham, and D. Thornton, *Regulatory Regimes and Variations in Corporate Environmental Performance: Evidence from the Pulp and Paper Industry* (2001).
16 N. Luhmann, *Soziale Systeme* (1992) 192–3.
17 For a different perspective see G. Burchell, C. Gordon, and P. Miller, *The Foucault Effect, Studies in Governmentality* (1991).
18 See, for example, M. Foucault, *The History of Sexuality* (1981, tr. by R. Hurley).
19 T. Turner, 'Bodies and Anti-Bodies: Flesh and Fetish in Contemporary Social Theory' in Csordas, op. cit., n. 2, p. 30.
20 For example, Foucault's concept of biopower.
21 Turner, op. cit., n. 19, p. 35.

Analysing them as an aspect of regulatory processes means to develop further postmodernist perspectives of legal regulation. Moreover, an analysis of emotions can help to overcome some of the limitations of post-structuralist accounts. Foucault's notion of the body has been criticized as too abstract and too removed from the 'flesh' of real bodies.[22] Hence, an analysis of emotions, as part of the physical body, allows us to draw on a fuller and more material account of the body.

3. Correcting the 'cognitive bias' through taking emotions into account

Exploring emotions as an aspect of legal regulation does not mean to declare cognition as unimportant. Instead it means to correct the current bias in most accounts of legal regulation which focus exclusively on cognitive processes in legal regulation. Emotional processes might even constitute a larger part of social life than cognitive processes. According to Kemper we feel more than we know and one of the reasons for this is that we do not have the language to label all our feelings.[23]

Correcting the cognitive bias can take two forms. First, cognition and emotion might be perceived as two separate variables.[24] Being able to control for the influence of either cognition or emotion in legal regulatory processes allows us to draw firmer conclusions. Hence research on legal regulation that considers emotions as a possible factor in regulatory processes may show that in some regulatory processes emotions do not play a role and that these regulatory processes are driven by cognition. The value of such an analysis would be to confirm explicitly the importance of cognitive processes which currently are just assumed.

Second, correcting the cognitive bias could mean acknowledging that discussions about cognition in legal regulation inevitably need also to address emotions because cognition and emotion are closely related. According to Durkheim emotions are inextricably linked with thought and belief.[25] Emotions can come into play in various ways in cognitive processes.[26] Some commentators have even perceived emotions as cognitive

22 id., pp. 28, 36, 38.
23 Kemper, op. cit., n. 2, p. 86.
24 Accounts of relationships between emotion and cognition are subject to cultural variation. In Chinese culture, for example, thought and emotion are strictly differentiated: T. Ots; 'The Silenced Body – The Expressive *Leib*: On the Dialectic of Mind and Life in Chinese Cathartic Healing' in Csordas, op. cit., n. 2, p. 119.
25 E. Durkheim, *The Elementary Forms of the Religious Life* (2001, 1st edn. 1912, tr. C. Cosman) 312. The possibility of a close link between emotion and cognition is also reflected in the terminology that some commentators adopt. For example, Levy and Frijda distinguish between 'feelings' which are just a bodily sensation and 'emotions' which involve a cognized interpretation. R. Levy, 'Emotion, Knowing and Culture' in *Culture Theory: Essays on Mind, Self and Emotion*, eds. A. Shweder and A. LeVine (1984) 218–33. N. Frijda, *The Emotions* (1987).
26 Bandes, op. cit., n. 5, p. 14.

constructions. From this perspective situations can require the production of a certain emotion.[27] It is only through the thought processes that arise from this production of emotions that emotions become real. Thought processes can also be involved in the production of emotions because, according to Kemper, a large class of emotions result from 'real, imagined, or anticipated outcomes in social relationships'.[28]

For social constructionists, cultural cognitive constructs play an important role in shaping what emotions are felt and expressed,[29] for example, whether and when the emotion shame is triggered is informed by social actors' previous experiences. Cognition, in turn, is involved in the making of experiences. 'Our affect system is heavily modulated by our analytical capacities'.[30] Similarly, the emotion of disgust has been defined as: '... not an instinctive and unthinking aversion but rather a thoughtpervaded evaluative sentiment'.[31] Also, by referring to language in definitions of emotion, cognitive processes have been closely linked to emotions. Emotions are often expressed through language and hence they have been perceived as 'complex narrative struggles that give shape and meaning to somatic and affective experiences'.[32] Thus, emotions are 'types of self-involving stories which make it possible for us to tell about our feelings'. They are 'linguistic ploys' which can also fulfill social functions, such as attributing blame or reinforcing conduct through praise.[33]

For Collins a close link between cognition and emotion arises from the fact that both are generated through group processes and, in particular, the engagement of individuals in group rituals. For example, feelings of moral solidarity in a group can generate acts of altruism and love as well as anger, for example, in the persecution of individuals perceived as outcasts of the group. But cognitive constructs can also arise from high-solidarity rituals.[34] These then become invoked in thinking and communicating and in this process individuals feel again the emotions of group solidarity they felt when they first participated in the group.[35] Also Collins's concept of emotional energy points to close links between emotion and cognition. Emotional energy has a cognitive component because it is based on the expectation to be a member of a group or to be dominant in interaction.[36]

27 T. Kemper, 'Introduction' in Kemper, op. cit., n. 1, p. 11.
28 Kemper, op. cit., n. 2, p. 43.
29 Hochschild, op. cit., n. 1, p. 117; C. Lutz, *Unnatural Emotions: Everyday Sentiments on a Micronesian Atoll and their Challenge to Western Theory* (1988).
30 Massaro, op. cit., n. 5, p. 85.
31 Kahan, op. cit., n. 9, p. 64, referring to Miller.
32 Massaro, op. cit., n. 5, p. 86, referring to A. Shweder ' "You're not sick, you're just in love": Emotion as an Interpretive System' in *The Nature of Emotion: Fundamental Questions*, eds. P. Ekman and R. Davidson (1994).
33 Massaro, id., p. 86.
34 R. Collins, 'Stratification, Emotional Energy, and the Transient Emotions' in Kemper, op. cit., n. 1, p. 34.
35 Collins, id.
36 id., p. 40.

In whatever way emotions are taken into account in the analysis of legal regulation, as a separate variable or as closely linked to cognition, an analysis of emotions in legal regulation is important in order to avoid an uncritical reproduction of legal ideology in research on legal regulation. Legal ideology, and in particular the notion of the autonomy of law, is premised on the idea that legal processes are based on reason to the exclusion of emotion. It is clear, however, that emotions play a role in a range of legal processes. For example, victim impact statements are part of the United States capital sentencing process and these can influence the jury's emotional disposition towards the offender. Where the existence of emotion in legal processes has been recognized, emotions have been assigned to specific, narrowly defined places and only a limited list of law-related emotions has been acknowledged, such as anger, compassion, mercy, vengeance, and hatred.[37] Emotions have been recognized to exist in particular in the criminal courts. For example, defendants sometimes present particular emotional states to a jury in order to influence favourably the trial outcome.[38] Thus, the expression of emotions is in particular attributed to those without legal training, such as defendants, juries, and witnesses. Legal personnel are expected to be impartial, distant, and detached and empathy should not influence decision-making. The rule of law assumes that laws can be applied in a predictable and logical way.

Socio-legal research aspires to discover the social realities of law and to document how law lives. Correcting the cognitive bias in studies of legal regulation can contribute towards this aim. Moreover emotions should not be excluded from an analysis of legal regulation because according to some definitions of legal regulation they might be inextricably linked with the process of regulating.

4. Regulating as involving emotional processes

Emotions can not be excluded from an analysis of legal regulation because regulating draws on emotional processes. A growing body of literature in the context of both the United States and United Kingdom legal systems argues that emotions are important for understanding the operation of law generally.[39] Moreover, definitions of regulation suggest that emotions are an integral part of regulating. There is no agreement on how to define legal

---

37 S. Bandes, op. cit., n. 5, p. 2.
38 A. Posner, 'Emotion versus Emotionalism in Law' in id., p. 319.
39 See, for example, Bandes, id., in the United States context; in the United Kingdom context, see T. Murphy and N. Whitty, 'Crowning Glory: Public Law, Power and Monarchy' (2000) 9 *Social and Legal Studies* 7–27; L. Gies, 'Contesting the Rule of Emotions? The Press and Enforced Caesareans' (2000) 9 *Social and Legal Studies* 515–38.

regulation.[40] A number of commentators, however, have perceived behavioural control as a key aspect.[41] This occurs in two ways. First and more obviously, successful legal regulation either by the regulator or through self-regulation implies control over the behaviour of the regulated. Secondly, and increasingly discussed in the literature, legal regulation involves control of the behaviour of the regulators themselves. This implies not just traditional accountability mechanisms but also more diffuse processes such as culture within regulatory agencies.[42] Explanations for such behavioural control, however, are too narrow if they refer just to either thought processes or emotions. Both what social actors think and feel produces behaviour. Also, other definitions suggest that emotions cannot be excluded from an analysis of legal regulation. Selznick's definition of regulation, which is adopted by a number of contributors to debates about legal regulation,[43] suggests that regulation is: 'sustained and focused control exercised by a public agency over activities that are valued by a community'.[44] Hence, regulation is here defined as an activity in the public interest. For some sociologists, values, which can underpin notions of the public interest, are 'cognitions infused with emotion'.[45] For instance, environmentalist values which include emotional dispositions can underwrite environmental legal regulation. According to holistic, integrated environmental regulation, the natural environment is not to be exploited and dominated by human social actors. Instead human actors recognize their interdependence with ecological systems and therefore care for and sustain the natural environment.[46] Furthermore, some commentators use terms such as compassion or a 'passion' for equity, justice, and fairness when talking about values which can inform legal regulation.[47] The idea that emotions are involved in the process of regulating through law can be further developed through the notion of regulatory law as an emotional process.

40 J. Black, 'Decentring Regulation: Understanding the Role of Regulation and Self Regulation in a "Post-Regulatory" World' *Current Legal Problems* (forthcoming).
41 L. Hancher and M. Moran,'Organizing Regulatory Space' in *A Reader on Regulation*, eds. R. Baldwin, C. Scott, and C. Hood (1998) 148; Black, id.
42 C. Hall, C. Scott, and C. Hood, *Telecommunications Regulation, Culture, Chaos and Interdependence inside the Regulatory Process* (2000).
43 See, for example, A. Ogus, *Regulation: Legal Form and Economic Theory* (1994) 1; G. Majone, 'The Rise of the Regulatory State in Europe' in Baldwin, Scott, and Hood, op. cit., n. 41, p. 196.
44 P. Selznick, 'Focusing Organizational Research on Regulation' in *Regulatory Policy and the Social Sciences*, ed. R. Noll (1985) 363.
45 Collins, op. cit., n. 34, p. 27.
46 For a polemic account of environmentalist values which perceives emotions as part of these values, see J. Porritt, 'Seeing Green' in *Holistic Revolution*, ed. W. Bloom (2000).
47 Bandes, op. cit., n. 5, p. 2.

Law and society interrelationships have been a key issue in the analysis of legal regulation. Various different ideas on how legal and social realms can become linked have been discussed. Some have perceived regulated systems as 'normatively closed but cognitively open'.[48] A legal and social realm can become linked through 'structural coupling'.[49] Others have argued that legal regulation needs to draw on social dynamics through the concepts of 'co-regulation',[50] 'co-steering',[51] and 'socio-political'[52] regulation. This constructs closer relationships between state and society in regulation than traditional, instrumental, top-down, 'command-and-control' approaches.

This section argues that an analysis of emotions allows to identify close interrelationships between a legal and a social realm because emotions are a crucial 'link concept'.[53] On the one hand, emotions are clearly anchored in a private sphere of civil society, but, on the other hand, they are also involved in the creation of social structures, such as forms of governance and law. As Lock suggests: 'emotion is the mediatrix among the individual body, the social body and the body politic'.[54] This section illustrates such close links by describing regulatory law as an emotional process. Three points support this. First, legal regulation can be the source of emotions. Secondly, legal regulation can be the outcome of emotional processes. Thirdly, 'regulatory law in action' can be understood as the interaction between regulatory state law and the 'laws of emotions'.

1. Legal regulation as the outcome of emotional processes

In Western legal systems legal regulation is often considered as the outcome of cognitive processes. Rational discussion is usually focused upon in accounts of the production of legal regulation. For example, political lobbying, an important aspect of the creation of legal regulation, is often

---

48 G. Teubner, *Law as an Autopoietic System* (1993) 32–4.
49 N. Luhmann, *Das Recht der Gesellschaft* (1993) ch. 10.
50 Co-regulation is also advocated as an important technique of regulation in the European Union's Sixth Environmental Action Programme. Communication from the Commission to the Council, the European Parliament, the Economic and Social Committee and the Committee of the Regions, *'Environment 2010: Our Future, Our Choice'*, 24 January 2001, COM (2001) 31 final 61.
51 D. Osborne and E. Gaebler, *Reinventing Government* (1992).
52 J. Kooiman, 'Social-Political Governance: Introduction' in Kooiman, op. cit., n. 11, p. 4
53 M. Lyon, 'C. Wright Mills meets Prozac: the Relevance of "Social Emotion" to the Sociology of Health and Illness' in *Health and the Sociology of Emotions*, eds. V. James and J. Gabe (1996) 57.
54 M. Lock and P. Dunk, 'My Nerves are Broken' in *Health in Canadian Society: Sociological Perspectives* (1987), referred to in Csordas, op. cit., n. 2, p. 14.

described as a process in which various actors try to assert their self-interests and in that sense act rationally. Even where politicians act as advocates on behalf of other groups, this behaviour can still be described as rational. According to public-choice theories of regulation, politicians acting on behalf of interest groups act rationally because they can expect to maintain or be voted into positions of political power in return.[55]

Furthermore, institutions for the production of legal regulation, such as parliaments and their specific procedural rules for debate, are meant to ensure that legal regulation is produced on the basis of rational criteria. The idea that reason and rationality are driving forces in modern society and its legal regulation has, of course, been criticized and questioned,[56] but new forms of rationality have been considered as possible. According to Habermas, communicative rationality involves the conduct of social relations 'according to the principle that the validity of every norm of political consequence be made dependent on a consensus arrived at in communication free from domination'.[57] Stenvall even suggests that:

> When it comes to governability in the sense of creating order, a world which remains inaccessible to human intervention, can also not be affected by its argument or logic.[58]

Not just cognitive but also emotional processes are important in the formation of legal regulation. Both from a 'top-down' and a 'bottom-up' perspective, emotions are significant for explaining how legal regulation is produced. Interactionist studies of the day-to-day enforcement of legal regulation have shown that its meaning is constructed from 'the bottom up' through small-scale transactions between regulators, regulated, and sometimes third parties, such as non-governmental organizations.[59] Legal regulation 'in action' is composed of small-scale, social orders which are established during the practical implementation of state legal regulation.[60] So far, the literature on

---

55 Ogus, op. cit., n. 43, p. 59.
56 See, for example, M. Horkheimer and T. Adorno, *Dialectic of Enlightenment* (1972, tr. J. Cumming).
57 J. Habermas, *Knowledge and Human Interests* (1971, tr. J. Shapiro) 284.
58 K. Stenvall, 'Public Policy Planning and the Problem of Governance: the Question of Education in Finland' in Kooiman, op. cit., n. 11, p. Similiarly, Gunningham et al. argue: 'There are those who may be *irrational*, intransigent, or incompetent and who may lie beyond the reach not only of voluntary, but also of incentive-based mechanisms' (emphasis added): N. Gunningham, P. Grabosky, and D. Sinclair, *Smart Regulation, Designing Environmental Policy* (1998) 316.
59 Hall, Scott, and Hood, op. cit., n. 42, pp. 193–4; K. Hawkins, *Environment and Enforcement, Regulation and the Social Definition of Pollution* (1984); W.G. Carson, 'The Institutionalization of Ambiguity in the Early British Factory Acts' in *White Collar Crime: Theory and Research*, eds. G. Geis and E. Stotland (1980).
60 For example, Hawkins, id. documents that water pollution control officers developed a set of social norms which defined the 'just' and 'efficient' treatment of water pollution cases. These also influenced when prosecutions would be initiated and hence the form and content of the legal regulation in practice.

207

legal regulation has focused on the cognitive dimension of these small-scale social orders. For example, actors' interpretations of formal legal regulation feed into the establishment of these social orders. Mundane social orders, however, can also be an element of these small-scale social orders. Some sociologists have argued that emotional processes are key to understanding how such mundane social orders become established. Collins, in analysing Garfinkel's work,[61] suggests that the limits of human cognitive abilities are essential for an explanation of how the micro elements of mundane social order, such as rules governing conversations or encounters between family members, are established. Social actors employ a range of practices in order not to recognize that mundane social order is established in a rather arbitrary fashion.[62] Hence social actors keep up conventions because emotions buttress them, not because they have evaluated these conventions as valid and consciously support them.[63] This insight was generated through experiments conducted by Garfinkel. During these, participants showed strong negative emotions when the experiment revealed to the respondents that they were constructing their own social world in an arbitrary and conventional way, rather than responding to an exterior, objective reality. Hence, not to question the conventions that make up social order is accompanied by positive emotions. Collins concludes from this that 'social order cannot be based on rational, conscious agreement' and that 'reality construction is an emotional process'.[64]

Also, from a 'top down' perspective legal regulation can be perceived as the outcome of emotional processes. In this approach legal regulation is equated with formal, regulatory state law. On the most simple level the feelings that social actors have about the issues which are legally regulated can influence the form and content of legal regulation. For example, the expression of emotions, such as fear about health or aversion to interference with the 'laws of nature', are part of debates about the regulation of GMOs and can feed into its design.[65] Moreover, emotion can feed into the establishment of cognitive constructs on the basis of which a law-making debate is conducted. For example, notions of romantic love can help to explain the different legal regulation of same-sex and heterosexual relationships.[66] The point that emotions feed into law-making processes can be made even more strongly. Emotions also inhere in large-scale social structures, such as the state and systems of governance. Legal regulation, in turn, reflects the nature of these large-scale social structures.[67] For example,

61 H. Garfinkel, *Studies in Ethnomethodology* (1967).
62 Collins, op. cit., n. 34, p. 29.
63 id., pp. 29, 30.
64 id., p. 30.
65 J. Black, 'Regulation as Facilitation: Negotiating the Genetic Revolution' (1998) 61 *Modern Law Rev.* 622.
66 C. Calhoun, 'Making up Emotional People: The Case of Romantic Love' in Bandes, op. cit., n. 5, pp. 217–40.
67 M. Barbalet, 'A Macro Sociology of Emotion: Class Resentment' (1992) 10 *Sociological Theory* 150–63.

Barbalet suggests that resentment is a key ingredient of class structures. Economic structures, such as a differential distribution of resources, or cognitive constructs, such as class consciousness, are not sufficient to explain the social phenomenon of class.[68] Emotions, such as resentment, also construct class. Furthermore the control and management of emotions can be important for the maintenance of systems of governance. Barbalet, referring to Fantasia, argues that some capitalist systems require 'massive structures and resources', such as unions, for the control of collective impulses.[69] Similarly Scheff has explored how shame and anger sequences can inform collective behaviour and influence international relations between states.[70] Also, anthropologists have argued that states can become involved in the construction and strategic management of emotions and legal regulation bears the imprint of the 'emotional economy' of a state.[71] To conclude. this section has argued that legal regulation can be the outcome of emotional processes. The next section will suggest that legal regulation can also give rise to emotional processes.

2. Legal regulation as giving rise to emotional processes

The idea that legal regulation can give rise to emotional processes has been discussed in particular in the context of enforcement. Particular types of law may lead to specific emotions. Regulatory or coercive law may elicit fear.[72] For example, Hood suggests that the power of school inspectors to recommend school closures generated levels of fear among the regulated unknown in business regulation. Moreover, it has been argued that a gap between the behaviour of the regulated and the requirements of formal legal regulation, can be the basis for attempts to generate the emotion of shame in offenders.[73]

This section suggests, however, that any legal regulation can give rise to the full range of emotions, not just negative emotions, such as shame and fear. According to Kemper's social interactional theory, emotions are a response to environmental stimuli. These stimuli are produced in social relationships between individuals. Kemper considers power and status distributions as key aspects of these relationships. Changes in their distribution lead to the production of emotions.[74] The feelings produced vary depending if the self or the other person are seen as the source of one's excessive, sufficient or insufficient status or power. For example, if one actor perceives the status others grant to him or her as adequate then this actor will

---

68 id., p. 152.
69 id., p. 159, referring to R. Fantasia's work.
70 T. Scheff, *Microsociology: Discourse, Emotion, and Social Structure* (1990) 76–8.
71 H. Jenkins and M. Valiente, 'Bodily Transactions of the Passions: El Calor among Salvadorean Women Refugees' in Csordas, op. cit., n. 11, p. 164.
72 Miller, referred to in Bandes, op. cit., n. 5, p. 6.
73 J. Braithwaite, *Crime, Shame and Reintegration* (1989).
74 Kemper, op. cit., n. 2, p. 26.

feel secure.[75] When a person, however, thinks that too much status is allocated to them by another person then the emotion produced is shame. This, however, can be 'extrojected' in the form of hostility or anger towards the other.[76]

Legal regulation can impact directly on the distribution of power and status among social actors. For instance, command-and-control regulation, can enhance the power of regulators, or where devices of 'creative compliance' are successfully used it can enhance the power of the regulated.[77] Even where legal regulation is not enforced in practice, simply its existence can affect the distribution of power and status between social actors. For example, bargaining between regulators and regulated can occur in the shadow of the 'big stick' of sanctions.[78] According to Kemper, status exists when social actors possess positive attributes in response to which other social actors grant voluntary compliance with the demands of such actors.[79] For example, regulators are sometimes perceived as providers of expert consultancy advice by the regulated.[80] The regulated at times comply voluntarily with regulators' demands because regulators are attributed status on the basis of their knowledge and expertise. Legal regulation can affect the distribution of status between the regulated and regulators. For example, the invocation of criminal sanctions can lead to status loss.[81] According to Kemper, the perception of the distribution of status between social actors as adequate, insufficient or excessive, in turn, leads to the production of emotions.[82] Understanding how legal regulation generates emotions is important because emotions can help to explain social dynamics between the regulated and the regulators. For example, anger might lead to behaviour which is directed at change, while security might underpin behaviour which is aimed at the preservation of the status quo between regulated and regulators. The next section will argue that legal regulation involves emotional processes also because regulatory law in action is the outcome of interaction between formal state law and the 'laws of emotions'.

The literature on legal pluralism and the enforcement of legal regulation has documented that the meaning of the law in action results from interactions between formal state law and various types of small-scale social orders created in the field. According to some sociologists,

---

75 id., p. 50.
76 id., p. 62.
77 D. McBarnet and C. Whelan, 'The Elusive Spirit of the Law: Formalism and the Struggle for Legal Control' (1991) 54 *Modern Law Rev.* 848–73
78 Gunningham et al., op. cit., n. 56, p. 261; I. Ayres and J. Braithwaite, *Responsive Regulation: Transcending the Deregulation Debate* (1992) 161.
79 Kemper, op. cit., n. 2, p. 30.
80 Hawkins, op. cit. n. 59, p. 45.
81 See, for example, the publication of a list of named companies which are considered as 'bad environmental performers' by the UK Environment Agency: <www.environment-agency.gov.uk/business>.
82 Kemper, op. cit., n. 2, ch. 3, p. 5.

emotional processes can give rise to such small-scale social orders because social norms govern the generation, expression and management of emotions.[83] Hence there are specific 'laws of emotions', and regulatory law in action can be described as the outcome of interactions between formal state law and these 'laws of emotions'.

3. What are the 'laws of emotion'?

Some sociologists have argued that emotions do not just happen spontaneously but 'unarticulated ground rules of social interaction', such as expression and feeling rules, govern whether emotions are actively invoked or suppressed.[84] Feeling rules regulate how social actors ought to feel in a particular situation.[85] Their fluid nature makes their normativity different from state law. Feeling rules simply establish 'zones that mark off degrees of appropriateness'.[86] Expression rules, in turn, regulate what feelings are appropriate to display.[87] Organizations are one arena in which the 'laws of emotions' and formal state law can interact in order to produce 'regulatory law in action'. Feeling rules are central to the operation of organizations because they can be considered as the ' "underside" of an organization's occupational ideology'.[88] Law-making and enforcement organizations, as well as the organizations of the regulated, in turn, are crucial for constructing the meaning of regulatory law. Some aspects of regulating through law may more strongly than others involve interaction with the 'laws of emotions'. Rules for the guidance of behaviour, such as emotion rules, become particularly relevant when various, mutually exclusive opportunities for action exist, such as in the case of conflict. Conflicts of interests can arise between regulated and regulators. They can also arise between different parts of a regulated organization, such as health and safety, environmental management or compliance departments on the one hand, and commercial and operational sections on the other hand.[89]

Not just organizations, but also systems of social stratification can be another key site for interactions between formal legal regulation and the 'laws of emotions'. Emotions help social actors to define and construct relationships between themselves and the world around them.[90] They help

---

83 Hochschild, op. cit., n. 1, pp. 120, 122.
84 id.
85 id., p. 122.
86 id., p. 123.
87 id., p. 122.
88 id., p. 118.
89 B. Lange, 'National Environmental Regulation? A Case-Study of Waste Management in England and Germany' (1999) 11 *J. of Environmental Law* 76.
90 Hochschild, op. cit., n. 1, p. 119.

people to find their 'place' in social relationships.[91] 'Place', in turn, defines an individual's relationship to others with reference to power, status, and social distance. These relationships can vary among different social actors, and hence emotions contribute to the establishment of systems of social stratification.[92] Social stratification can also be expressed and reinforced through emotions. Emotions can be directed at confirming what constitutes the 'low' or 'high end' of a system of social stratification.[93] For example, disgust reflects particular social norms according to which some people or objects are judged as 'low' and shame can help to avoid status reducing behaviour.[94]

Furthermore, according to some commentators, feeling rules and emotional strategies help to explain how emotions become involved in the construction of systems of social stratification. Social actors have an 'intuitive grasp' of their location in systems of social stratification and in the light of this awareness particular feeling rules appeal.[95] Thought and feeling feed into 'strategies of action'.[96] Such emotional strategies can either confirm or change existing patterns of social stratification.[97]

Not just emotions, however, but also legal regulation feeds into the establishment of systems of social stratification. For example, social security and taxation law can influence social status through the allocation of resources. Furthermore criminal law or anti-discrimination legislation can affect status allocation by simply defining what is acceptable and unacceptable behaviour.[98] Different forms of legal regulation, such as command and control as well as self-regulation, influence the distribution of power and thus systems of social stratification.

Various forms of interaction between legal regulation and the 'laws of emotions' in systems of social stratification can be imagined. On the one hand, both the 'laws of emotion' and formal legal regulation can uphold the same, existing system of social stratification. For example, emotions such as disapproval and shame can support a system of social stratification where actors who damage the natural environment are considered as 'low'. Legal regulation might also confirm and support this social stratification system. On the other hand, the 'laws of emotions' and legal regulation might support different social stratification systems which are in conflict with each other. For example, the 'laws of emotion' might support a social stratification

91 C. Clark, 'Emotions and Micropolitics in Everyday Life: Some Patterns and Paradoxes of "Place"' in Kemper, op. cit., n. 1, p. 305.
92 Collins, op. cit., n. 34, p. 28.
93 Kahan, op. cit., n. 9, p. 64.
94 id., p. 85.
95 Hochschild, op. cit., n. 1, p. 137.
96 A. Swidler, 'Culture in Action: Symbols and Strategies' (1986) 51 *Am. Sociological Rev.* 273–86.
97 Hochschild, op. cit., n. 1, p. 139.
98 Massaro, op. cit., n. 5, p. 82.

system where the maximization of economic gains is considered as 'high'. Formal legal regulation, however, may support a social stratification system where maximization of economic gains ranks considerably lower than the protection of health and safety at work. The specific outcome of various possible interactions between the laws of emotions and formal legal regulation is regulatory law in action. So far this article has argued that pointing to the emotional aspects of legal regulation which originate both from private and public social orders, allows to see law as closely linked to a social sphere. The next section will illustrate in more detail how an analysis of emotions can further develop a key area of debate, the role of structure and agency in legal regulation.

EMOTIONS AND STRUCTURE AND AGENCY

1. Structure and agency as a key issue in debates about legal regulation

Issues relating to structure and agency have shaped key questions in regulatory analysis. Agency describes the undetermined and voluntary aspects of social action.[99] Structure refers to recurring patterns of social behaviour. Economic and political institutions, as well as norms, values, and social roles can be considered as structural aspects of a society.[100] Key questions are, for example: do regulators regulate and, if so, to what extent? Do regulators 'row' or do they just 'steer'?[101] If regulators only steer is this because of structural restraints within which they operate? How does the internal regulation of government activity through accountability systems associated with New Public Management restrain the delivery of legal regulation?[102] How does agency of the regulated, expressed for instance through co-regulation, 'creative compliance',[103] and 'capture'[104] curtail regulators? Limited notions of structure and agency, however, have informed these questions because structure and agency have been assumed to mainly involve cognitive processes.

99 G. Marshall, *Oxford Dictionary of Sociology* (1998) 10.
100 id., p. 648.
101 D. Osborne and T. Gaebler, *Reinventing Government* (1992) 25–48.
102 C. Hood, C. Scott, O. James, G. Jones, and T. Travers, *Regulation Inside Government: Waste Watchers, Quality Police, and Sleaze Busters* (1999); C. Hood and C. Scott, 'Bureaucratic Regulation and New Public Management in the United Kingdom: Mirror-Image Developments?' (1996) 23 *J. of Law and Society* 321.
103 D. McBarnet and C. Whelan, *Creative Accounting and the Cross-Eyed Javelin Thrower* (1999); D. McBarnet, 'Whiter than White Collar Crime: Tax, Fraud, Insurance and the Management of Stigma' (1991) 42 *Brit. J. of Sociology* 324–44.
104 M. Bernstein, *Regulating Business by Independent Commission* (1955); F. Pearce and S. Tombs, 'Ideology, Hegemony and Empiricism, The Compliance Theory of Regulation' (1990) 30 *Brit. J. of Criminology* 423–43; T. Makkai and J. Braithwaite, 'In and Out of the Revolving Door: Making Sense of Regulatory Capture' in Baldwin, Scott, and Hood, op. cit., n. 41.

213

Where the literature has departed from this narrow view it has usually only implied that emotions also play a role, without further developing an analysis of these emotional processes. The activities of the regulated and regulators, as well as restraints on them have been characterized mainly in terms of cognitive processes. This has occurred through a focus on the cognitive tasks that are involved in legal regulation which have been distanced from emotions, by portraying them as part of a 'rational' process. Cognitive tasks have also been perceived as a justification for regulation.

2. Regulation as involving cognitive tasks

Tasks such as generating, managing, and maximizing information have been considered as crucial to legal regulation both at the stage of design as well as at the stage of its practical implementation.[105] For example, a range of studies refer to information asymmetries between regulators and the regulated as a restraint on regulators' ability to regulate.[106] Hence, acquiring information has been perceived as a prerequisite for regulating and successful regulation also requires the appropriate management of information flows among different parts of regulator's and regulated's organizations.[107] Moreover, the involvement of NGOs in regulatory processes is often discussed in terms of their access to information, for example, through 'community right to know legislation'.[108]

Information has also been a criterion for classifying different enforcement styles. For example, the possibility of a match between regulators' information demand and the regulateds' information supply is one characteristic of the 'cartesian-bureaucratic' style of regulation of the United Kingdom telecommunications regulator OFTEL.[109] By considering cognitive tasks as central to legal regulation, the limits of social actors' cognitive abilities have often been equated with the limits of regulation. The collection and management of information, however, has not just been key to descriptions of what regulating involves. It has also been an important justification for regulatory tasks. Public interest theories of social regulation have seen legal regulation as a significant tool for reducing information deficits which impair the proper functioning of markets.[110] Furthermore the emergence of different forms of legal regulation[111]

105 Gunningham, Grabosky, and Sinclair, op. cit., n. 58, p. 44. ; P. Kleindorfer and E. Orts, *Informational Regulation of Environmental Risks*, Working Paper, University of Pennsylvania (1996); S. Breyer, 'Typical Justifications for Regulation' in Baldwin, Scott, and Hood, id., p. 72.
106 Hawkins, op. cit., n. 59; Osborne and Gaebler, op. cit., n. 101, p. 285.
107 Hall, Scott, and Hood op. cit., n. 42, p. 13.
108 Gunningham et al., op. cit., n. 105, pp. 63–5, 202–5.
109 Hall, Scott, and Hood, op. cit., n. 42, p. 9.
110 Ogus, op. cit., n. 43, p. 4, ch. 7.
111 R. Baldwin and M. Cave, *Understanding Regulation: Theory, Strategy and Practice* (1999) 182.

214

has been explained as a result of competition between different regulatory regimes and information is also key to the efficient operation of these markets in legal regulation. Another way in which the literature has emphasized cognition is by distancing legal regulation from emotional processes.

3. Characterizing legal regulation as a rational process

A number of commentators have characterized legal regulation as a rational process.[112] For example, a study of OFTEL, the United Kingdom telecommunications regulator, suggests that rationality was an empirical fact, documented in one of the three regulatory decision styles, and a normative expectation for the regulator's behaviour in general.[113] There are a number of sources from which rationality in legal regulation can be said to originate. First, legal regulation might be considered as a rational process because it is implemented by bureaucracies. According to Weber, bureaucracies provide legitimacy to the exercise of power because power is wielded in a rational and legal manner. Bureaucratic organizations are characterized by a separation of official activities from private affairs, as well as calculability of routinized decisions because they are taken on the basis of legal rules which reduce uncertainty for those subject to bureaucratic oversight, such as private economic actors.[114]

Secondly, legal ideology has been another source for characterizing legal regulation as rational. Modern Western state law is based on the idea of the rule of law, not the rule of man. Governing according to clear, formal, predictable rules is differentiated from decision-making that also takes emotions into account.[115] Even in critical accounts of the role of law in modern Western societies, rationality, which is open to and depends on communicative reason, has been considered as also inherent in law. Hence formal legal rules which are the outcome of processes of communicative rationality can legitimate themselves.[116]

Moreover, by recognizing that often there are various different rationalities at play in legal regulation, the literature has qualified and further strengthened the idea that regulating is a rational process. For example, Gunningham et al. discuss possible conflicts between the 'logic' of private enforcement of environmental regulation through granting pressure

112 See, for example, Gunningham, Grabosky and Sinclair, op. cit., n. 58, p. 36.
113 Hall, Scott, and Hood, op. cit., n. 42, p. 205. The strength of this normative expectation is also illustrated by the fact that the subjects of the study did not agree with the finding that other decision-making styles, which conformed less to the rationality paradigm, such as an 'adhocratic-chaotic' style, also characterized their work.
114 M. Albrow, *Bureaucracy* (1970).
115 Bandes, op. cit., n. 5, p. 6.
116 K. Baynes, 'Democracy and the Rechtsstaat: Habermas's *Faktizität und Geltung*' in *The Cambridge Companion to Habermas*, ed. K. White (1995) 206–7.

groups access to the courts, and the 'logic' of informal enforcement relationships just between regulated and public regulatory agencies.[117] Moreover, regulated organizations have been perceived as subject to different rationalities, such as the pursuit of short-term profits, 'bounded rationality',[118] and long-term sustainable business goals.[119] While a significant part of the literature on legal regulation has discussed agency and structure in cognitive terms, some accounts have gone further and have implicitly acknowledged that regulating involves more than cognitive processes.

4. Recognizing the limits of cognition in regulatory processes

Some contributions to the literature on legal regulation have implied that legal regulation involves more than thinking and doing based on this thinking. This has occurred in particular where concepts, such as culture, ideology, attitudes, beliefs, and personality traits of regulators and regulated, motivation, values, and behaviour are employed. For example, the personality traits of the directors of United Kingdom utility regulatory agencies,[120] the chief inspector of prisons,[121] and project leaders in the civil service[122] have been discussed.[123] Personality traits have even been considered as key to explanations of regulation within government.[124] For example, Heclo and Wildavsky found that power was allocated in the 1970s inside the British civil service on the basis of reputations which were constructed in the process of peer review. Reputations were defined by reference to personality traits such as brightness, dullness, strength, and weakness as well as trustworthiness.[125] What can an explicit analysis of emotions add to such accounts?

5. Fuller accounts of agency and structure

On the most simple level, an analysis of emotions can provide for a fuller and more rounded account of agency. Human actors clearly do more in social life, including regulating through law, than to think and to act on those thoughts. Regulating is often described as involving the active construction

117 Gunningham, Grabosky and Sinclair, op. cit., n. 58, p. 105.
118 H. Simon, *Economics, Bounded Rationality and the Cognitive Revolution* (1992).
119 Gunningham, Grabosky and Sinclair, op. cit., n. 58, p. 415.
120 Hall, Scott, and Hood, op. cit., n. 42, pp. 74, 75, 78.
121 Hood, Scott, James, Jones, and Travers, op. cit., n. 102, p. 135.
122 Hall, Scott, and Hood, op. cit., n. 42, p. 46.
123 For a general discussion of individual traits of expert regulators see Baldwin and Cave, op. cit., n. 111, p. 199.
124 See, for example, Hall, Scott, and Hood, op. cit., n. 42, p. 5.
125 H. Heclo and A. Wildavsky, *The Private Government of Public Money: Community and Policy Inside British Politics* (1974) 14–15.

of an image of regulator.[126] This task, however, cannot be just understood in cognitive terms but has to be analysed with reference to the emotional strategies that regulators employs.[127] For example, the building up of trust between regulated and regulators in order to promote the enforcement of legal regulation; the invocation of shame in the regulated in order to promote compliance; and the use of emotional strategies, such as display of anger or calm in bargaining between regulated and regulators are important.[128] What some sociologists have called dramatic or 'hot' emotions, which interrupt the flow of activity, are especially relevant for an analysis of agency.[129] Emotions have been perceived as enabling agency to various degrees. In particular those commentators who have emphasized the physiological basis of emotions have perceived them as an important source of agency. The body is perceived as enabling social agency because it prepares for behaviour:

> One of the major functions of emotion consists of the constant evaluation of external and internal stimuli in terms of their relevance for the organism and the preparation of behavioural reactions which may be required as a response to those stimuli. [130]

Specific emotions enable particular types of behaviour. For example, the essence of anger can be seen as the mobilization of energy in order to overcome an obstacle.[131]

Emotions, however, have not been considered just as a source of agency. Emotions can also help to establish social structure and they can inhere in it. In particular long-term or 'cool' emotions have been linked to the building up of social structure.[132] For instance, underlying moods can stabilize social action. They have been called by some sociologists 'emotional energy'.[133] An example of a long-lasting emotion which has been discussed in the sociological literature is solidarity, which involves feelings about identity and membership.[134] Similarly, Kemper distinguishes structural, anticipatory, and consequent emotions. Structural emotions arise from the structural aspects of a social relationship such as the perception of the distribution of status and power in that relationship as adequate, excessive or

---

126 Hood, Scott, James, Jones, and Travers, op. cit., n. 102, p. 131.
127 Hochschild, op. cit., n. 1.
128 See, for example, Posner who discusses the impact of emotions on bargaining in contractual relationships and how the expression of emotions can influence the search for appropriate remedies for breach of contract. A. Posner, 'Law and the Emotions' (1977) 89 *Georgetown Law J.* 2006–10.
129 Collins, op. cit., n. 34, p. 41.
130 K. Scherer, 'On the Nature and Function of Emotion' in *Approaches to Emotion*, eds. K. Scherer and P. Ekman (1984) 296.
131 Collins, op. cit., n. 34, p. 34.
132 Massaro, op. cit., n. 5, p. 98.
133 Collins, op. cit., n. 34, p. 32.
134 id., p. 31.

217

insufficient.[135] Anticipatory emotions are linked to how actors view the future state of the social relationship. What is being anticipated, in turn, is based on interactional outcomes of past relationships and the specific distribution of power and status that they involved.[136] Consequent emotions are the emotions which result from the next interaction episode. Hence, these three types of emotions illustrate how emotions can be part of ongoing social relationships and how emotions become involved in the building up of social structure. While some commentators have analysed how emotions become involved in the establishment of social structure, others have emphasized that emotions can also become subject to social structural forces. For example, the social constructionists have emphasized that emotions are culturally constructed, such as through vocabularies of emotions.[137] According to Gordon, anger exists as a raw emotional arousal but it is through social processes that sentiments, such as rage, bitterness and jealousy are created.[138] For others the body and emotions are just another site of social control. In Foucault's work the body is a 'text upon which the power of society is inscribed'.[139] For Elias emotions, especially shame and embarassment, play a central role in making bodies, and their natural functions, conform to the particular behavioural norms of specific societies.[140]

HOW CAN FULLER ACCOUNTS OF STRUCTURE AND AGENCY ADVANCE DEBATES ON LEGAL REGULATION?

1. Questioning structure and agency as differentiated concepts

An analysis of emotions challenges the idea that structure and agency are two separate concepts. In the literature on legal regulation, structure and agency are often considered as differentiated in two ways. First, structure and agency are perceived as the opposite ends of a horizontal continuum because they are in tension with each other. Structural restraints, such as economic or political dynamics are often referred to in order to explain why regulators or regulated have limited agency.[141] Secondly, structure and

---

135 Kemper, op. cit., n. 2, p. 50.
136 id., p. 74.
137 Lyon and Barbalet, op. cit., n. 2, p. 58; A. Hochschild, 'Emotion Work, Feeling Rules, and Social Structure' (1979) 85 *Am. J. of Sociology* 551–75; A. Thoits, 'The Sociology of Emotions' (1989) 15 *Annual Rev. of Sociology* 320; L. Gordon, 'Social Structural Effects on Emotions' in Kemper, op. cit., n. 1, pp. 145–79
138 Gordon, id., p. 150.
139 Lyon and Barbalet, op. cit., n. 2, p. 49.
140 N. Elias, *The Civilizing Process, The History of Manners* (1978) ch. 2.
141 G. Winter, *Das Vollzugsdefizit im Wasserrecht* (1975); W. Carson, *The Other Price of Britain's Oil: Safety and Control in the North Sea* (1981).

218

agency are often perceived as located on the opposite ends of a vertical continuum. Agency is placed on a micro level while structures are situated at the macro level of social dynamics.[142]

These differentiations are justified if behavioural consequences which flow from structure and agency are the reference point. Structures imply that there are limits to what actors can do and agency suggests that actors can engage creatively in voluntary social action. However, if structure and agency are described with reference to their source it becomes more difficult to differentiate them. Emotions are a common source for both structure and agency. Emotions can prepare for social action. They are also a source for structure because the 'bottom-up' emotions that actors feel on a micro level in everyday interactions feed into the development of social structures, such as institutions and norms. 'Top-down' emotions which are crystallized into social structures, such as the feeling rules of occupational ideologies in private companies or enforcement bureaucracies, shape emotions and actions in everyday regulatory situations.

Perceiving agency and structure as less differentiated concepts can enable us to ask different questions about legal regulation. For example, instead of asking how and what structures can restrain the agency of both regulated and regulators, social actors' role in creating social structures can be explored.[143] In particular the role that the generation, expression, and management of emotions plays in constituting both agency and structure can be addressed. For instance, emotions can inhere in political structures. Collectivist political structures may be associated with emotional cultures which involve co-operation and empathy among social actors. Individualist political structures which rely on a free play of market forces may be more closely allied to emotional cultures based on self-reliance and competition. Such different political structures have been perceived as giving rise to various forms of legal regulation.[144] Hence, the scope of agency that regulators and regulated have under these various forms of legal regulation is not the result of separate, independent social structures but can be linked to collective emotion management work that both regulated and regulators participate in. An analysis of emotions, however, can also help to deepen an understanding of concepts which already implicitly acknowledge emotions.

2. Developing the concepts of culture, values, and ideology

Some sociologists have argued that culture does not just comprise knowledge, symbols, and meanings but also emotions and their bodily

---

142 For a critical perspective on this, see R. Collins, 'The Romanticism of Agency/ Structure vs the Analysis of Micro/Macro (1992) 40 *Current Sociology* 77, 82.

143 A. Giddens, *The Constitution of Society: Outline of the Theory of Structuration* (1986).

144 Ogus, op. cit., n. 43, pp. 1–2.

219

dimension.[145] Emotions are not 'anarchic' or 'unbounded' but their production and management is subject to feeling rules.[146] This allows us to explore how culture does not just set 'social' and 'cognitive boundaries'[147] but also behavioural boundaries according to what is appropriate to feel. Such a broader concept of culture may, in turn, change how some key concepts in the analysis of legal regulation are used. For example, different styles of legal regulation are often distinguished according to their degree of formality.[148] Where the form or implementation of legal regulation is described as informal, culture is often considered as an important resource in regulating. For example, professional cultures[149] and conventional 'ways of doing business'[150] and regulation can be such cultural resources. Hence, informality is sometimes used as a criterion for describing regulatory processes, as distinct from the normative processes of the formal law. An analysis of emotions, however, highlights that culture is not necessarily a resource for regulating informally. The norms relating to the production and management of emotions, can introduce a highly formal dimension to the concept of culture. Hence, adding an analysis of emotions can require us to rethink how concepts, such as formality and informality, are used in the description and explanation of regulatory processes.

Furthermore an analysis of the variation in the norms which govern the production and management of emotions might further promote understanding of legal regulation in a comparative dimension. National cultures have been perceived as giving rise to specific emotional responses.[151] Hence, an important issue for the literature on comparative regulation might be how national cultures give rise to different emotional cultures and how this in turn affects legal regulation.

An analysis of emotions can also further develop an understanding of the concept of values. Different relationships between legal values and emotions can be traced. First, in particular, lawyers have discussed legal values and emotions as two separate concepts. From this perspective it is possible to explore how emotions may affect the operation of legal values in regulatory processes. For example, Massaro points to the dangers of using disgust in the enforcement of legal regulation because this can jeopardize the realization of legal values, such as fairness, expressed, for instance, in the legal principle of proportionality.[152] Secondly, some sociologists have perceived emotions and

---

145 C. Geertz, *The Interpretation of Cultures* (1973); J. Csordas, 'Introduction: The Body as Representation and Being-in-the-World' in Csordas, op. cit., n. 2, pp. 1–14.
146 Hochschild, op. cit., n. 1, p. 122.
147 Hall, Scott, and Hood, op. cit., n. 42, p. 5.
148 id., p. 201.
149 Hawkins, op. cit., n. 59, chs. 3, 4.
150 Gunningham et al., op. cit., n. 105, pp. 157, 163.
151 M. Barbalet, 'A Macro Sociology of Emotion: Class Resentment' (1992) 10 *Sociological Theory* 158–9.
152 Massaro, op. cit., n. 5, pp. 98–9.

legal values as closely intertwined by suggesting that emotions are the basis of moral commitments.[153] For example, legitimate expectation, a value protected through English administrative law, which is to guide the enforcement activities of regulators, contains the emotional aspects of safety and trust. Similarly, the legal value of unbiased administrative action involves emotional distance from those who are affected by regulators' decisions. An analysis of emotions, however, can also help to develop further the concept of ideology in legal regulation.

Ideologies are belief systems about how particular aspects of social life should affect social action. Some sociologists have argued that feeling rules are an important aspect of ideologies.[154] In particular the role that emotions play in the establishment of small-scale ideologies has been analysed. Hochschild, for example, has explored gender ideologies, that is, belief systems about how gender should impact on social life. Since social actors' ideological frameworks are sometimes at odds with real life situations, emotions and active attempts to change them play an important role in managing tensions between belief systems and reality.[155] It is the successful management of these tensions which produces social action: 'we try to change "how we feel" to fit "how we must feel" in order to pursue a given course of action'.[156]

These general insights about the role of emotions in ideologies may be transferred to the context of legal regulation. Here, for instance, belief systems about what power is and how it should operate in relationships between the regulated and the regulators are important.[157] Similarly, legal and economic ideologies, such as notions of the 'rule of law' and 'the efficient operation of markets', matter in the context of legal regulation. Hence, an analysis of emotions may develop further an understanding of ideological processes in legal regulation which have so far focused on macro aspects, such as grand-scale political ideologies about state-market relationships. Finally, however, the question how we can actually study emotions needs to be addressed.

153 Collins, op. cit., n. 34, p. 27.
154 Hochschild, op. cit., n. 1, p. 125.
155 id., p. 129.
156 id.
157 See, for example, Reichman's concept of 'cultural authority' in N. Reichman, 'Moving Backstage: Uncovering the Role of Compliance Practices in Shaping Regulatory Policy' in Baldwin, Scott, and Hood, op. cit., n. 41, p. 326.

INTEGRATING AN ANALYSIS OF EMOTIONS INTO RESEARCH DESIGNS

1. Introduction

Is it more difficult to know what other people feel than what they think? Emotions might be considered a less visible part of social life.[158] Their particular nature, for example, that they can be spontaneously and quickly expressed, might make them more difficult to study through the tools of social science analysis.[159] This section argues that the study of emotions poses some specific challenges but these can be overcome through creative adaptation of existing social science research methods.

Arguments that either emotional or cognitive aspects of social life are intrinsically visible or invisible are questionable because perceptions of the visibility of aspects of social order to its participants or researchers are influenced by prior theoretical assumptions about social actors' role in the construction of social orders. On the one hand, social actors can be perceived as knowledgeable agents who actively shape social order and hence know and can report about its cognitive and emotional aspects.[160] On the other hand, social actors might be perceived as objects of social forces about which they know little. Hence there might be no intrinsic aspects which make emotions more difficult to study than cognitive elements of social life. Moreover, a range of sociological studies using quantitative and qualitative approaches provide evidence that emotions can be studied through empirical research methods. The range of usual techniques of data collection, such as observation of emotions in natural or laboratory settings, surveys, interviews, and self-reported data, such as journals kept by research participants, have been employed.[161] In applying these familiar tools to the study of emotions researchers have identified specific methodological problems which have varied according to the definition of emotions that researchers have worked with. Some have studied emotions from a positivist perspective and have perceived them as a separate, self-contained phenomenon which exists objectively in social reality and which is in turn shaped by social structural and interactional conditions.[162] For these researchers a key problem has been to access pure, primary emotions, for example, in a laboratory setting, because primary emotions often interact directly with secondary emotions and cognitions. For example, the first emotion in an anxiety situation may be

158 Bandes, op. cit., n. 5, p. 2.
159 Jenkins and Valiente, op. cit., n. 71, p. 167.
160 A. Giddens, *Central Problems in Social Theory* (1979) 71.
161 Jenkins and Valiente, op. cit., n. 71, p. 165. See, also, S. Farrall on how to conceptualize 'fear of crime' in large crime surveys: S. Farrall, J. Bannister, J. Ditton, and E. Gilchrist, 'Social Psychology and the Fear of Crime' (2000) 40 *Brit. J. of Criminology* 399–413.
162 Kemper, op. cit., n. 1, p. 11.

fear, but fear may lead quickly to distress, shame or anger.[163] Furthermore, only a specific range of emotions may be expressed and hence accessible for study. Particularly embarassing or shameful emotions, such as shame itself, might be less freely and openly expressed than other emotions.[164] Emotions can also be contrived, such as the expression of remorse by defendants in criminal trials in order to impress juries favourably.[165] Moreover, there might be little agreement among social actors on what counts as a particular emotion. Experiments have revealed that people who were shown pictures of various emotional states used a range of different labels to describe the emotions.[166] Hence within and between different language communities there might be considerable variation in labelling emotions.[167]

For social constructionists, however, these points are not methodological problems but simply reflect one of their prior assumptions about social life. Emotions are socially constructed and hence understanding the process through which only some emotions become expressed, or how they interact with other emotions and cognition, constitutes valid knowledge about emotions. Also the idea that emotions can be pretended and contrived is not necessarily a problem for social constructionists but an opportunity to study the particular feeling and expression rules which influence what emotions are felt and expressed. Furthermore, research into cognitive aspects of social life has to deal with the possibility that social actors provide 'false' accounts of events or engage in impression management. This can be addressed, for instance, by accessing other sources of information about the events under study. Moreover, understanding the reasons for the provision of 'false' accounts can provide interesting insights.

Methodological problems identified have also varied according to which emotions are studied. For example, it has been considered more difficult to study long-term emotions, or 'emotional energy' because information about changes in people's long term emotions requires data about a whole chain of interactions.[168] This can be achieved, for example, through long periods of continuous observations or through periodic sampling and it has been suggested that the long emotional effects of interactions may last only 'a few days'.[169] Furthermore, methodological problems have been addressed through the application of quantitative and qualitative approaches to the study of emotions.

163 Kemper, op. cit., n. 2, p. 185.
164 Massaro, op. cit., n. 5, p. 114, fn. 87.
165 For a discussion of remorse in the context of capital sentencing see A. Sarat, 'Remorse, Responsibility, and Criminal Punishment: An Analysis of Popular Culture' in Bandes, op. cit., n. 5, pp. 168–90.
166 Kemper, op. cit., n. 2, p. 85.
167 id., p. 86.
168 Collins, op. cit., n. 34, p. 50.
169 id.

223

2. Applying quantitative and qualitative approaches to the study of emotions

One of the advantages of quantitative methods is that they can help to predict what emotions will arise in a particular situation.[170] Quantitative research designs require to specify dependent and independent variables. Some commentators have perceived status and power as independent variables which can correlate with the dependent variable emotion. The key issue then has been how to operationalize these variables. It has been suggested that the operation of power in small-scale settings can be measured, for example, through providing numerical values for order-giving and order-taking.[171] How to operationalize emotions has been a more difficult question. Various different indicators have been suggested. A range of them are based on the idea that emotions have a physical basis. Hence, voice, eyes, body posture, and movements can express emotions, such as confidence, initiative or apathy.[172] Furthermore, aspects of the voice, such as its loudness and false starts, can provide further information about emotional states.[173] Other bodily experiences can also be indicators of emotions. For example, Jenkins and Valiente's analysis of links between political structures, culture, and emotion is based on narratives about 'el calor', anxiety-related experiences of women refugees from El Salvador.[174] Furthermore, mental representations of emotions, such as language and ethnopsychological knowledge, may be used as sources of information about emotions.

Problems of finding valid operationalizations of the concept of emotion in quantitative research designs can also be overcome through combining both quantitative and qualitative approaches. For example, out of qualitative data on emotions more abstract and rigorously defined concepts, such as emotion management have been developed which then can be measured.[175] Qualitative approaches, however, can raise ethical concerns about the protection of privacy of research participants.[176] For example, Hochschild carried out observation of domestic life which sometimes involved arguments in order to study the particular distribution of household and childcare work between women and men in married couples.[177] Such issues, however, can be addressed through careful access and consent procedures as

170 See, for example, the work of L. Smith-Lovin, 'Emotion as the Confirmation and Disconfirmation of Identity: An Affect Control Model' and R. Heise, 'Affect Control Model Technical Appendix' in Kemper, op. cit., n. 1, pp. 238–70 and pp. 271–80 respectively.
171 Collins, op. cit., n. 34, p. 49.
172 id., p. 50; P. Ekman and V. Friesen, *Unmasking the Face. A Guide to Recognizing Emotions from Facial Clues* (1975–1984).
173 K. Scherer, 'Methods of Research on Vocal Communication' in *Handbook of Methods in Nonverbal Behavior Research*, eds. K. Scherer and P. Ekman (1982).
174 Jenkins and Valiente, op. cit., n. 71, p. 165.
175 A. Thoits, 'Emotional Deviance: Research Agendas' in Kemper, op. cit., n. 1.
176 Collins, op. cit., n. 34, p. 50.
177 Hochschild, op. cit., n. 1, p. 125.

well as confidentiality agreements. To conclude, sociological and legal literature on emotions bears testimony to the possibilities of overcoming methodological problems. What specific problems are raised depends on the definition of emotion adopted. Where researchers proceed on the basis that emotion and cognition are closely linked current practices of data collection in empirical research about legal regulation might not even have to be radically changed. Instead, collection of data about cognitive processes, for example, through interviews, would just need to provide fuller accounts of interview data and include, for instance, information about emotions through indicators, such as facial expressions, use of voice, bodily postures, and so on. Often this additional information in interviews is edited out and only cognitive elements of the interview process are recorded and defined as research data on which the analysis is based. Noting and analysing this additional information as data in their own right and not just as interpretive aids to the ideas expressed in interviews could be the first simple step towards integrating an analysis of emotions into research designs on legal regulation.

CONCLUSION

This article has argued that an analysis of the generation, expression, and management of emotions can open up an important new aspect in the sociological analysis of legal regulation. This should enable new analytical insights to be gained about law and society relationships in regulatory processes. In particular, the analysis of emotions presented here allows us to trace close links between a legal and a social realm. Further and more detailed analysis is needed in order to address a number of issues that this article has raised. These concern relationships between emotion and cognition[178] and between law and emotions. Under what conditions does legal regulation work as an emotional process and when do regulatory law and emotions have to be understood as two separate concepts?

178 On this see, also, M. Nussbaum, *Upheavals of Thought: The Intelligence of the Emotions* (2001).